S0-ARW-172

Cabin
Porn

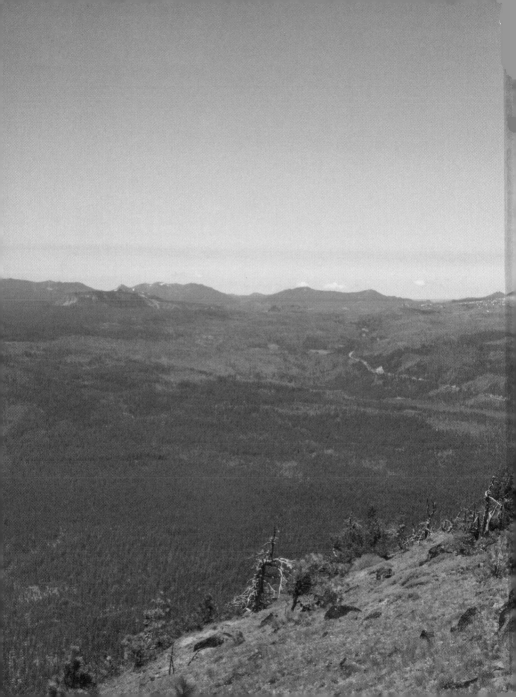

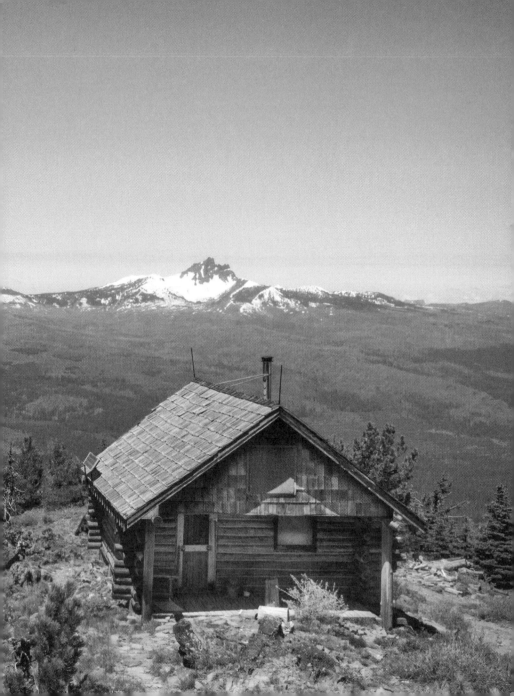

PENGUIN BOOKS

UK | USA | Canada | Ireland | Australia
India | New Zealand | South Africa

Penguin Books is part of the Penguin Random House group of companies
whose addresses can be found at global.penguinrandomhouse.com.

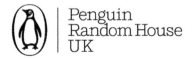

First published in the United States of America by Little, Brown and Company 2015
First published in Great Britain by Particular Books 2015
Published in Penguin Books 2016
010

Text copyright © Zachary Klein, 2015

The moral right of the author has been asserted

Unless otherwise noted, all photographs by Noah Kalina

Printed and bound in Italy by L.E.G.O. S.p.A.

A CIP catalogue record for this book is available from the British Library

ISBN: 978-0-141-98214-4

www.greenpenguin.co.uk

MIX
Paper from
responsible sources
FSC
www.fsc.org **FSC® C018179**

Penguin Random House is committed to a
sustainable future for our business, our readers
and our planet. This book is made from Forest
Stewardship Council® certified paper.

PREVIOUS Summit of Black Butte at
6,500 feet near Sisters, Oregon. Built
in 1934, the structure overlooks Three
Fingered Jack Mountain.
CONTRIBUTED BY Connor Charles

FRONT COVER Scott's Cabin, a
300-square-foot structure at
Beaver Brook in Barryville, New York.

BACK COVER Beaver Brook, a
tributary to the Delaware River.

Cabin Porn

Inspiration for Your Quiet Place Somewhere

COLLECTED BY
Beaver Brook

PENGUIN BOOKS

EDITED BY
Zach Klein

FEATURE STORIES BY
Steven Leckart

FEATURE PHOTOGRAPHY BY
Noah Kalina

Inside each of us is a home ready to be built. It takes a supply of ambition and materials to construct a cabin, but the reward is handsome: a shelter for yourself somewhere quiet, and a place to offer warm hospitality to friends.

Over the past six years, we've collected photos and stories of more than 12,000 cabins handmade by people using whatever they could find near places that mean something special to them. This book contains more than 200 cabins handpicked from our archives for your inspiration, as well as ten special stories and photo collections.

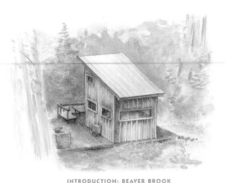

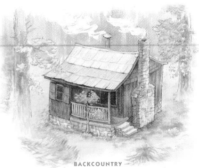

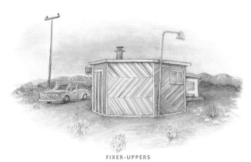

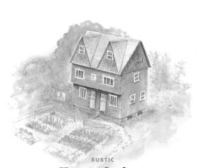

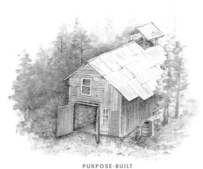
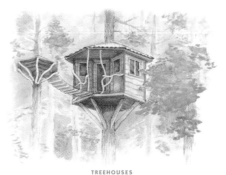
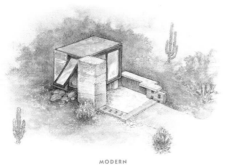
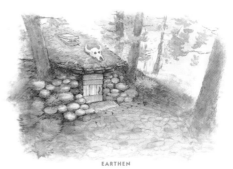
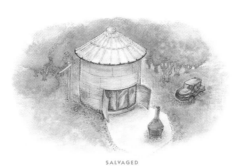
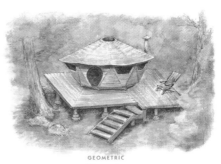

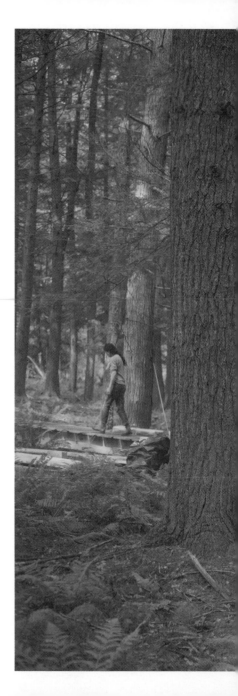

"There is one timeless way of building. It is a thousand years old, and the same today as it has ever been. The great traditional buildings of the past, the villages and tents and temples in which man feels at home, have always been made by people who were very close to the center of this way."

— *Christopher Alexander*

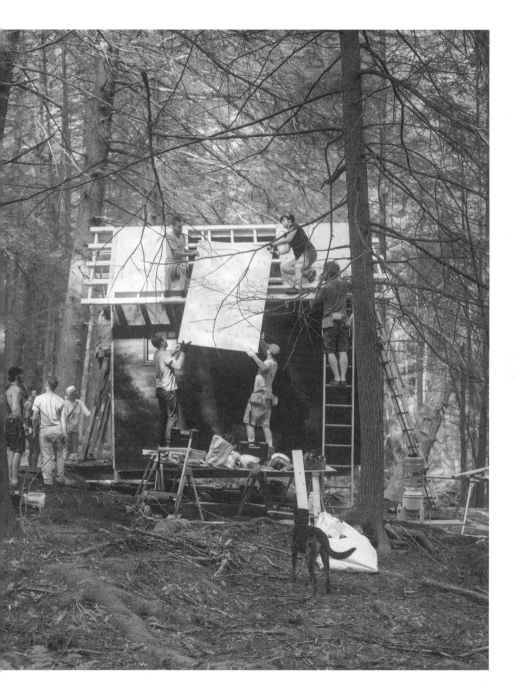

INTRODUCTION

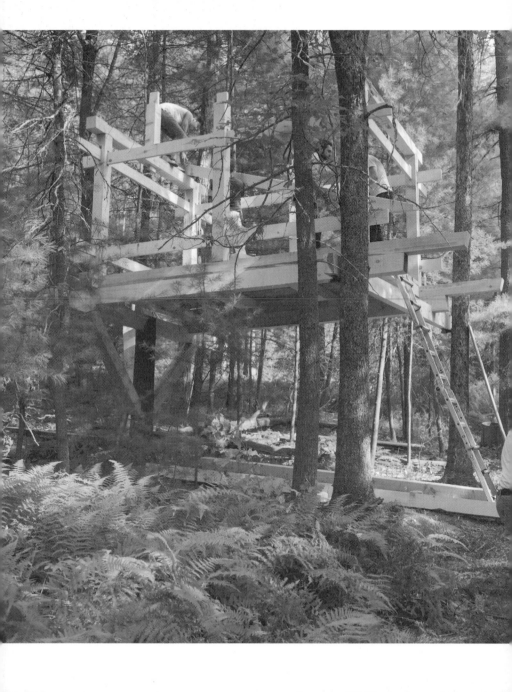

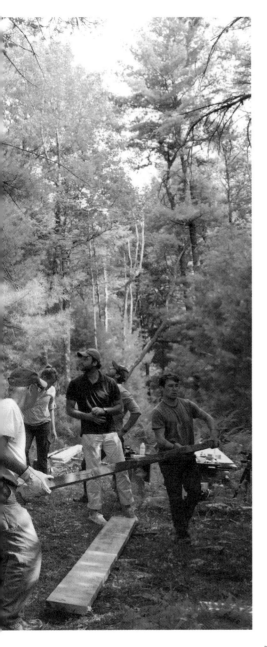

A beginner creates a shared retreat
in the woods for learning and doing.

How to Build a Community

Barryville,
New York

I needed a remote piece of land where anything was possible. I'd spent six years in the city building online communities and now I wanted to build one offline. Specifically, a place for a bunch of friends to be outdoors, somewhere we could be less preoccupied by our professions and more reliant on each other as we practice new skills together. I imagined a landscape nested with shelters we would make ourselves without any previous experience. My search began in upstate New York. I was looking for a place where the locals wouldn't mind our experiments with architecture, assembling what would surely look like a commune.

Like most people who go upstate, I had previously stayed close to the Hudson, a vital river in the Northeast, which runs down past the leeward side of the Catskill Mountains through a wide valley that reflects New England with its u-pick orchards and colonial towns. It's pretty, but I couldn't find land that felt sufficiently wild. I had decided to explore elsewhere. After a year driving wider and wider circles around

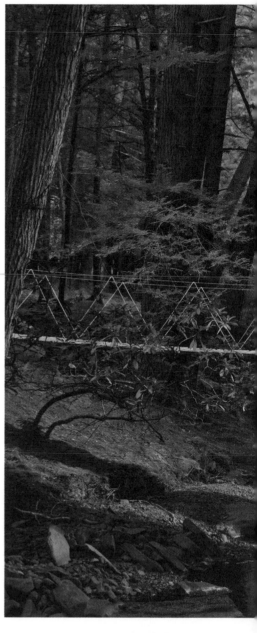

New York City, I got a tip on a barn and some property for rent in the hills above the majestic Upper Delaware Valley, a part of the state I had never visited before.

A friend and I made the trip in late April, and I knew as soon as we left the highway at Port Jervis that there would not be any gentlemen's farms here. The hills hemming the Delaware River are densely forested and slope steeply down to the banks, leaving just enough room for a sinuous county road to be carved out, with dilapidated houses serving as milestones. Alongside us, a thick band of fog hovered above the water, and streams trickled down muddy banks into shoulders of ferns. So much had grown back since the late 1700s, when these forests were nearly all clear-cut so that logs could be floated down to Philadelphia to be milled for lumber, or sometimes as masts for British ships (the King of England once laid claim to all large trees within ten miles of a navigable river). Nowadays the trees are cut for firewood, and out-of-towners float down the Delaware with rafts and coolers of beer.

The barn didn't work out; too many rooms lacked floorboards for the price. But I fell for the area. We stopped for BLTs at a motel restaurant, and I took out my phone to swipe through real estate listings. When I saw the thumbnails on the realtor's page, I just knew it. Two and a half miles upriver, 50 acres of forest were for sale. The property had a dirt road cutting through a stand of shagbark hickories, leading to a simple shed-style cabin with no electricity or plumbing that sat high above a brook feeding back down to the Delaware. Along the banks of this brook, century-old eastern white pines, known as the sequoias of the East, tilted at gravity-defying angles, their root systems exposed and clinging to the mossy, wet piles of stone left behind by erosion.

Beaver Brook's residents built a suspension bridge in 2011 using pressure-treated Douglas fir and zip line supplies.

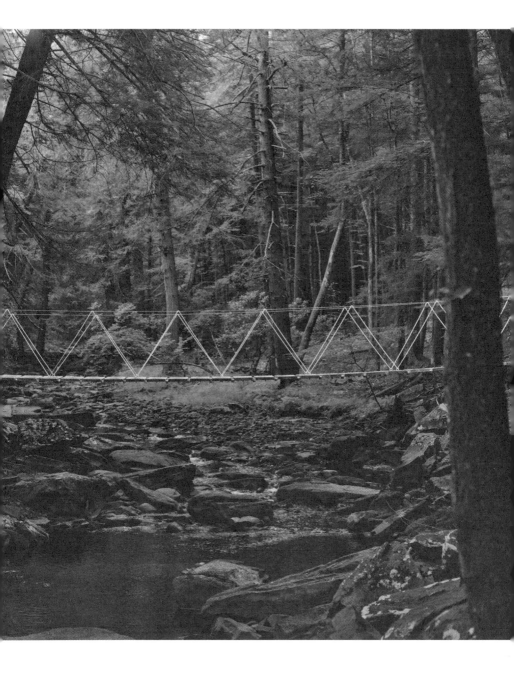

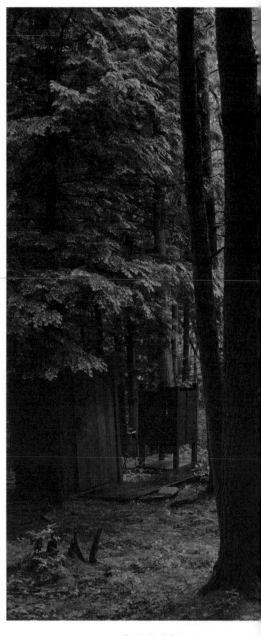

A few months later, in August, I headed up with my wife, Court, and two dozen friends to camp on our new land. At the market in town, river rafters spotted us and followed us for three miles back, believing we would lead them to a party. We invited them to stay, and all of us spent the day cleaning the outhouses and assembling a wood-fired hot tub, which we filled with fresh water from the brook. Chain saws whined as we thinned some birches and built our first supply of firewood. We wrenched field stones from the hillside to make a path for hauling water from the brook to the cabin. That evening, we braised lamb shoulders in Dutch ovens smothered with coals. The cooking took longer than expected, and we ate by headlamp after sunset. Later, we piled into the one-room cabin and lay beneath wool blankets while listening to our friend Jace Cooke read aloud. I was pleasantly warm from the long soak in the tub and looked around the cabin at all my friends. That weekend touched off what have become the happiest years of my life.

A bunch of us still share Beaver Brook, which is now named after the tributary running through it. It's our camp, where we experience splendid nature; make architecture, art, and food; practice community-building; learn new skills; and maintain a place where we—a diaspora of friends and family—can enjoy each other's company. It's a place of remarkable haves and have-nots: trout just big enough to eat; an international convention of fireflies every summer; in the winter, countless tracks of squirrels and snowshoes over the frozen brook. There's also no plumbing or electricity or insulation in most of the buildings. A total lack of cell service (a few of us will admit to seeking out the one spot on the top of the hill with some reception). Deafening quiet on some days, on others it's howling. And always plenty of mouse poop

Scott's cabin, the first structure on the property, was built using a salvaged timber frame barn.

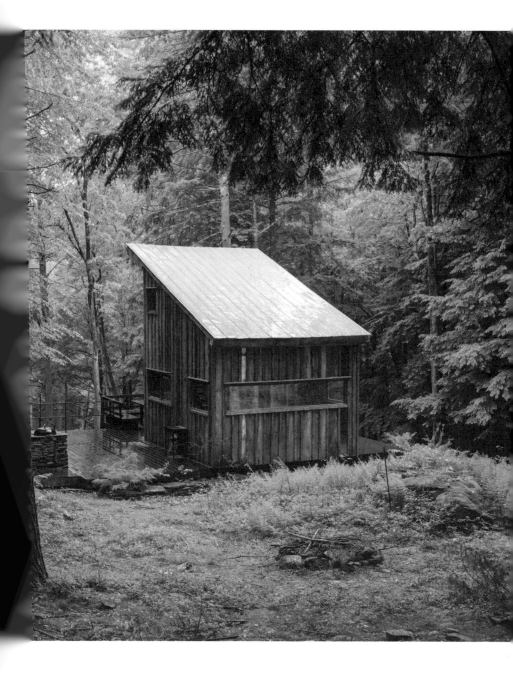

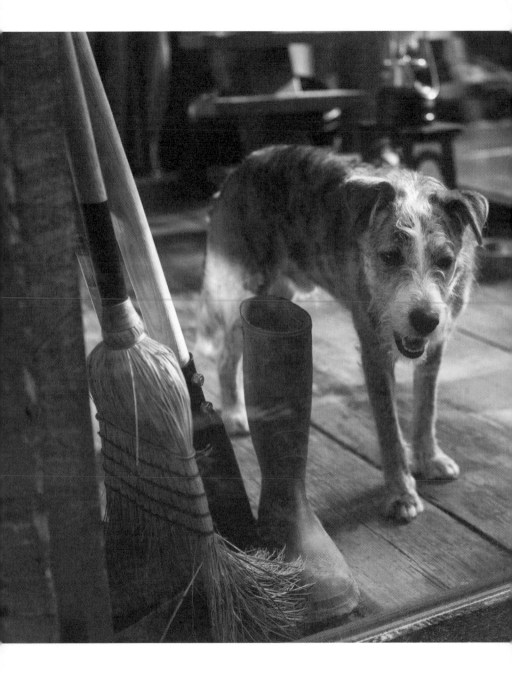

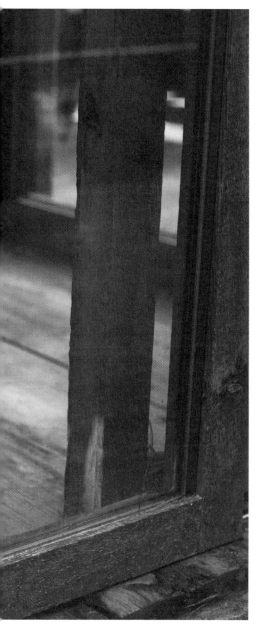

on anything you leave out overnight. We wouldn't have it any other way.

In the early 1800s, our land had been cleared and converted to farmland, then abandoned because of poor soil and growing conditions. Many old stone walls throughout the woods mark the boundaries of the ghost farm. Again in the early 1900s, the trees on the property were cut down to supply local factories that manufactured acid, charcoal, and wood alcohol. The property has since been allowed to regenerate naturally into a native hardwood and pine forest with ground that smells magnificently of resin when warmed by the sun.

The brook flows quietly most of the year but moves ferociously after a summer storm, further deepening the valley, revealing boulders and bluestone slabs in its bed, where we swim and bathe. Often during these storms, a lurching tree falls to a gust of wind or a lightning strike. The next day we busy ourselves with bucking it up for firewood. Once, one fell perfectly in place to make a bridge from one side of the brook to the other. For a summer, it was our only means of crossing besides wading, though it was dangerously slick. After a friend fell, we replaced the trunk with a suspension bridge made with zip line supplies. Since then, we've had no injuries to report.

Today, five years into our stay at Beaver Brook, we have an official process for residency, with dues and a few rules. The gist is that you come and do a lot of hard labor in exchange for good food and, once we're certain you have a good heart and a strong work ethic, an invitation to join. There are months when we visit only on weekends; then we take advantage with long summertime binges. Usually at least one person lives here year-round. We've collaborated to design and build various amenities. There are five shelters, a bunkhouse for large gatherings, a wood-fired sauna, all sorts of toolsheds, several outhouses, and a paddock for dumping our humanure, though we never really get around to it and mostly store firewood there.

One ambitious cabin conceived by my friends Brian Jacobs and Grace Kapin has been in progress for more than three years. It extends 20 feet over a hillside and is held by tree-mounted hardware designed to allow for the anchor trees to move in the wind. The couple has done all the work themselves, working on weekends, only getting help from the rest of us to transport heavy construction materials during summer sprints. The wood siding is coated with pine tar and linseed oil, a technique originally developed by Nordic shipbuilders to protect wood from moisture and harsh climates; it performs especially well in Beaver Brook's damp climate. One of the cabin's most striking features is the three pivoting windows, which permit seemingly aerial views of the brook. Nearly eight feet square, each window pivots open to let in the air and sounds of the brook in warm weather, and seals shut to keep in the warmth of the wood stove in winter.

More recently, we founded the Beaver Brook School, an annual invitation for a dozen applicants to come stay on the land and learn building techniques. Since 2013, students ranging in age from seventeen to seventy have traveled to Beaver Brook from all over the world, including Halifax and Helsinki. In 2014, participants with little experience felled a few trees and built a cabin on top of the remaining tree stumps using Japanese timber framing techniques. We plan to run the school year-round and hope it will help further our goal to make Beaver Brook a model for similar attempts at preservation and community. Taking the leap from fantasy to reality isn't difficult; it begins by looking around for inspiration.

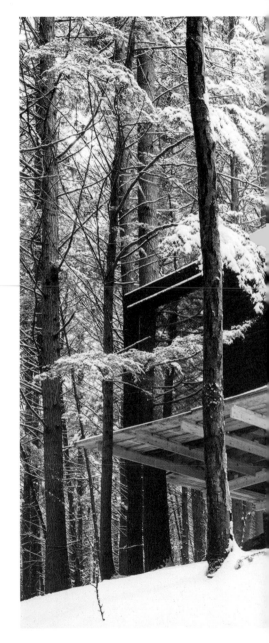

The hand-built, cantilevered studio in progress.

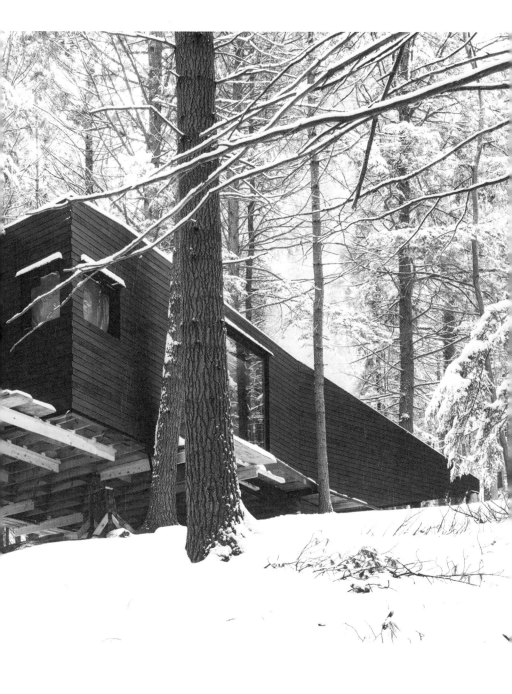

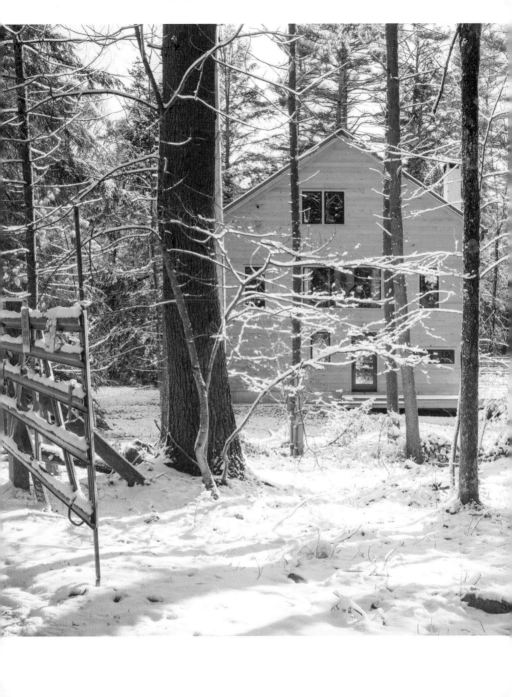

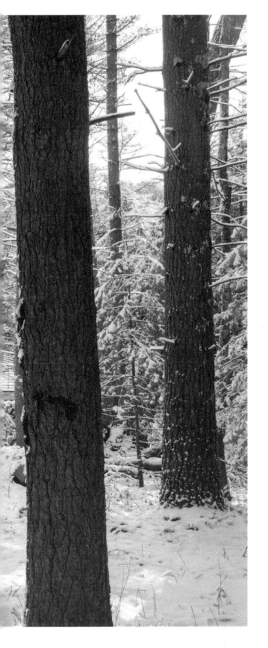

Not long after I founded Beaver Brook, I made a Web page called Cabin Porn. A few of my friends and I collected photos of buildings that had shaped our ideas of what homes could be: the kind of buildings that are made by hand, fashioned with imagination and easy-to-find materials made interesting by ingenuity and craftsmanship. The kind of buildings built by bold people who learned as they went along and never wavered in their determination. Nearly ten million people have visited the site since 2010, and twelve thousand people have shared their cabins with us.

It doesn't surprise me that Cabin Porn appeals to such a large audience. The more we migrate to a technical world, the more sublime nature is to behold. Pictures of cabins, for their part, often have an effect of recasting wilderness as move-in ready. While that's rarely ever true, what these photos do consistently— the part that interests me most—is remind each of us that we have a home inside us ready to be built if we try. It's a wonderful kind of confidence to discover that you can provide yourself shelter and offer warm hospitality with such simple construction. I hope more and more people realize the joy of the challenge and take it. The tools have never been cheaper, the know-how never more free. And online and offline communities are helping to connect us with mentors and models that show us what we are capable of making for ourselves.

—Zach Klein

The bunkhouse was constructed using a barn salvaged from Pennsylvania.

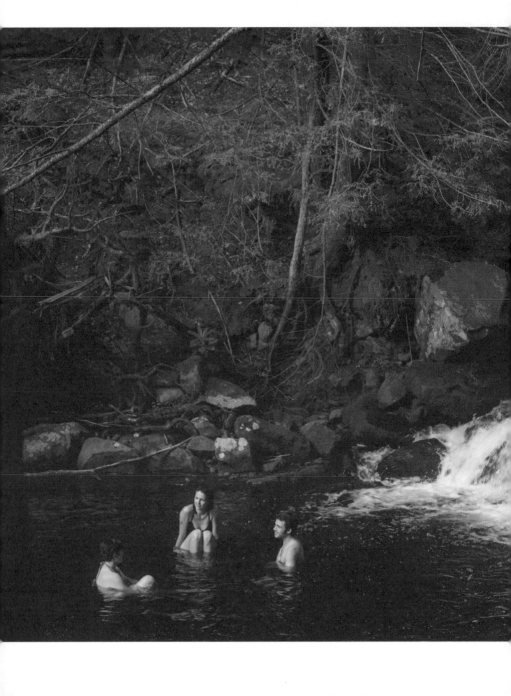

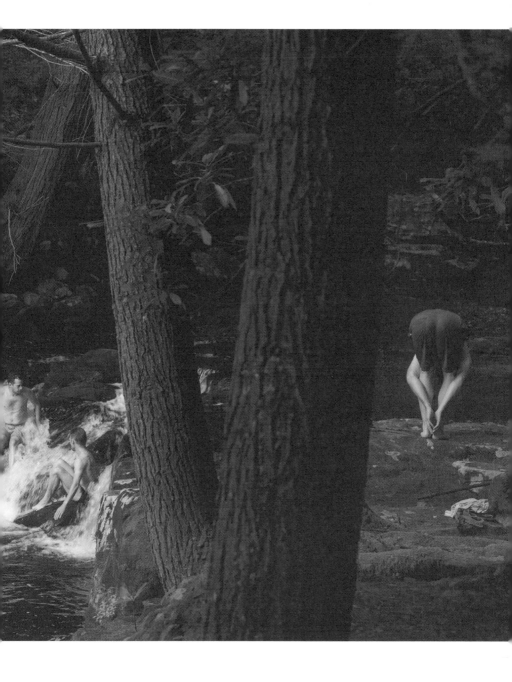

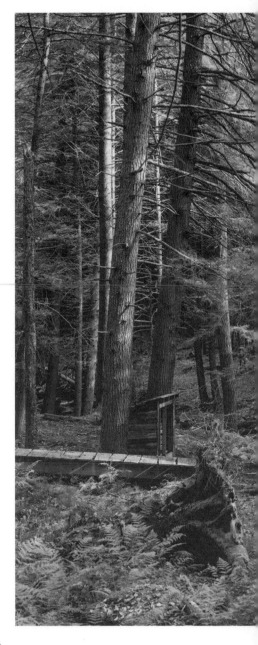

Most of the wood-fired sauna was
constructed by novices in ten days.

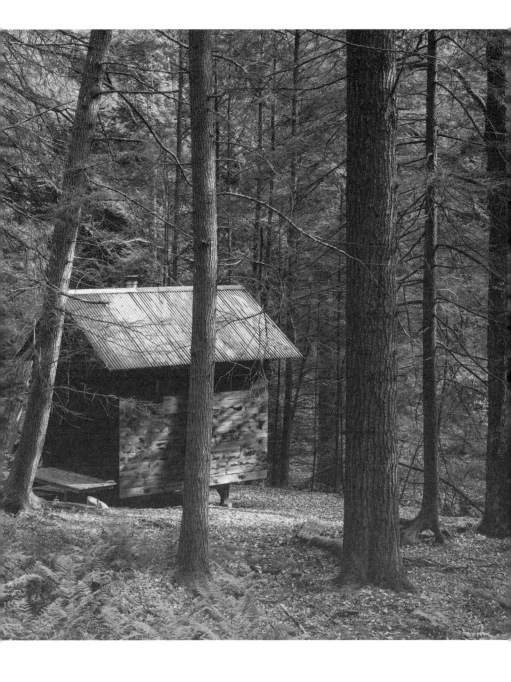

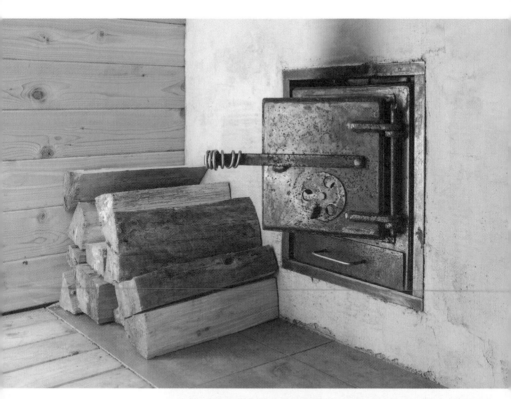

The stove is loaded from the entryway to keep the sauna free from debris.

R The exterior is clad in shiplap stained with pine tar.

OPPOSITE Beaver Brook's residents chose Knotty cedar, an affordable rot-resistant material. The benches are removable to make sweeping easy.

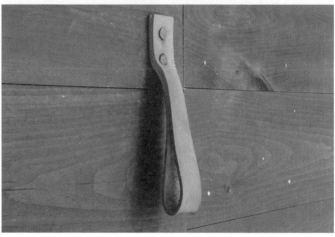

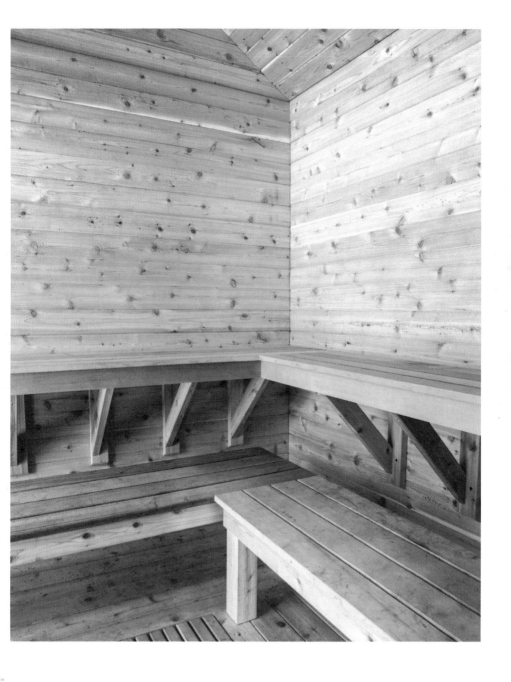

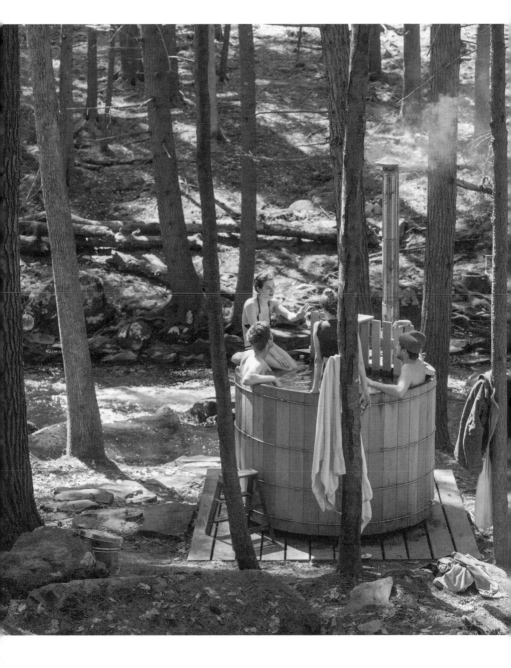

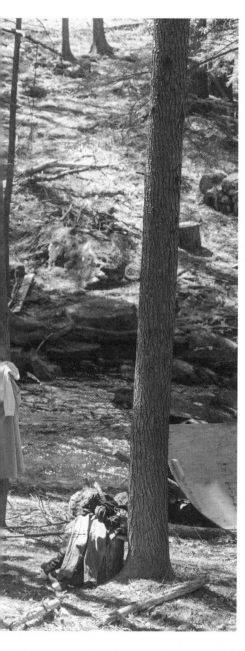

The wood-fired hot tub is filled with water from
the brook. In the summer months it takes about
two hours to heat the water to 105°F.

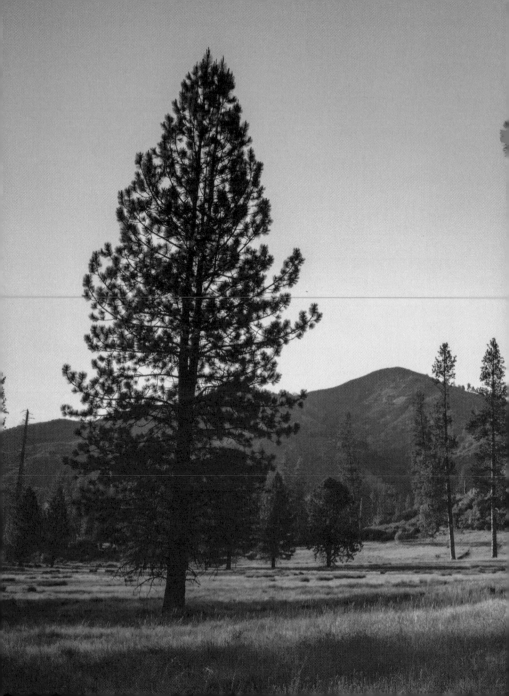

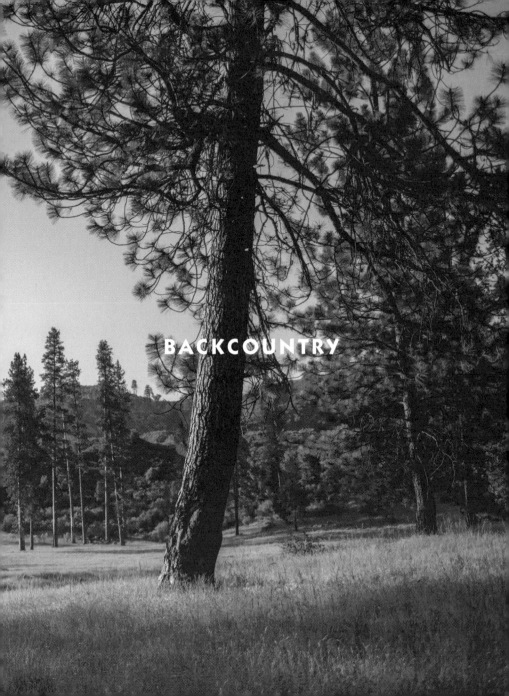

BACKCOUNTRY

1
BACKCOUNTRY

A father and son assemble a
rustic getaway miles from
where cars can travel.

How to Make
a Homestead in
the Wilderness

Pine Valley,
California

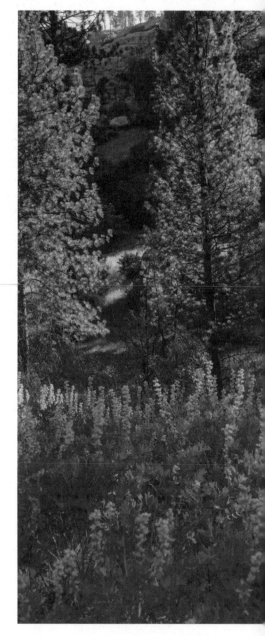

In September 1976, Jack and Mary English were hunting with their fourteen-year-old son, Dennis, in the
woods east of Big Sur, California. A 260-square-mile
section of national forest with rugged peaks, hidden
valleys, and hot springs, the Ventana Wilderness
is located in a region known for having California's
largest density of mountain lion, and abundant wild
hogs, turkeys, and deer. While Jack and Dennis were
off tracking deer, Mary encountered a small group of
twenty-something hikers who were looking around
curiously. They said they'd read a classified ad in the
local newspaper: someone was auctioning off a 5-acre
plot somewhere in the middle of this national forest
in a place called Pine Valley. The hikers had found the
right spot. Later, after they'd left and Jack and Dennis
returned, Mary relayed the news. "Somebody is gonna
get this land," she said. "It's gonna be us."

Since 1930, when Jack was eleven, he had been
frequenting Pine Valley to hike, camp, hunt, and fish
for rainbow trout. His family lived on a farm about

Located on a 5-acre plot of private land in
the middle of a national forest, this cabin is
only accessible by hiking a 6-mile footpath.

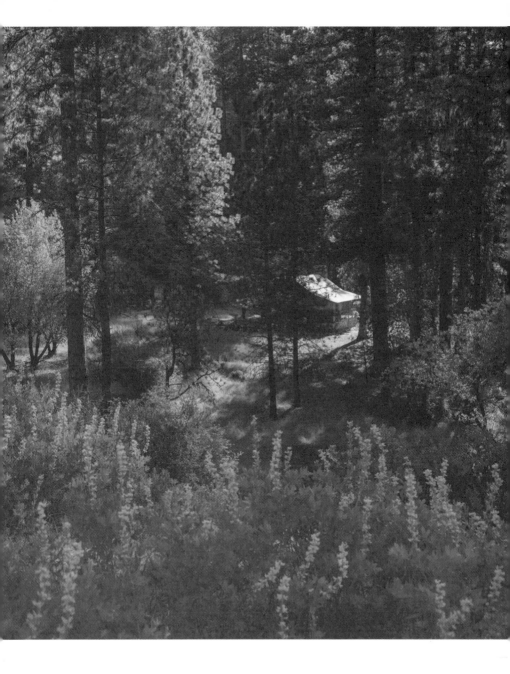

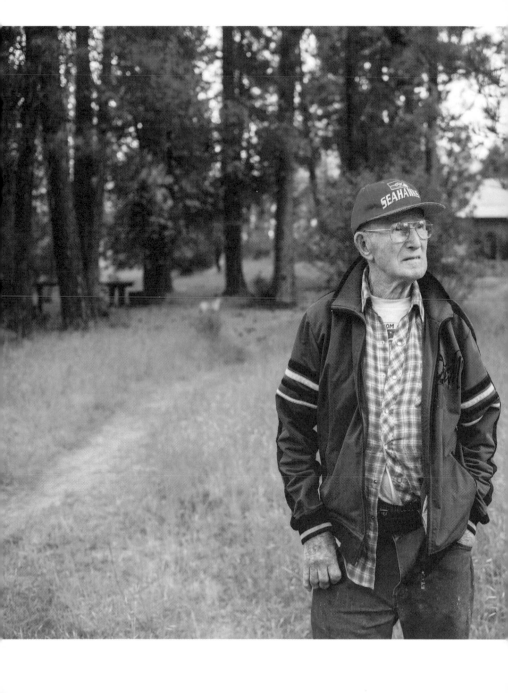

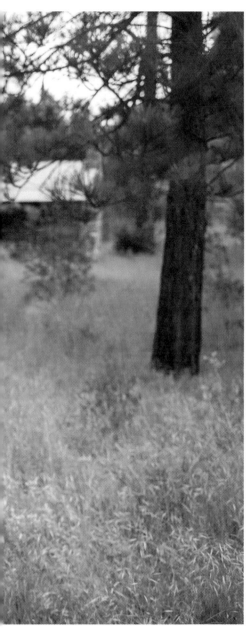

50 miles north, as the crow flies. Surrounded by a forest of ponderosa pine, Pine Valley is accessible only on foot or on horseback via a pair of dusty trails that descend and meander over 6 miles through the rocky Santa Lucia Mountains. Around 1880, after the passage of the Homestead Act, settlers began staking claims on 160 acres in and around Pine Valley. Over the years, families continued trading back their undeveloped parcels to the Forest Service. Jack had come to know one 15-acre plot well. It was situated right along a stream, near a sunny pasture, below a massive sandstone formation that glows in the moonlight. There were dilapidated remains of an old cabin, but no one had lived there in years. So in 1936, when Jack was seventeen, he contacted the owner. She wouldn't take less than $1,000 per acre. (For all 15 acres, that translates to roughly $257,000 today.) Oh, well, Jack figured.

After serving in World War II, Jack returned home and found work as a carpenter. By then, he'd met and married Mary, a feisty pig farmer's daughter who was a descendant of Abraham Lincoln. "She was a cute one," Jack recalls. "Five foot two, a hundred and five pounds, and never varied much." He nicknamed her Scrumptious. Together, the couple traveled to the backwoods of Alaska and Canada on hunting trips. Jack built them a house in Soquel, a two-hour drive from Pine Valley. Jack and Mary made the trek frequently. When Dennis was six months old, they brought along their son. By the time he was a teenager, the family had spent countless days on the trails and nights camping. So in 1976, when the opportunity presented itself for Jack and Mary to claim a small piece of Pine Valley, they didn't hesitate.

After dressing and packing up the deer Jack had shot, the family hiked 6 miles back to their

Jack English began building his off-grid cabin in the Ventana Wilderness in 1976.

forest-green 1966 Volkswagen Beetle and drove back into town. They picked up the local paper and found the ad. Sometime after 1936, when Jack had tried to buy that 15-acre plot, the land had been whittled down to 5 acres. The owner had recently died, and the family was liquidating assets. At the auction, there were four bidders. Jack and his brother, Phil, offered $11,000—more than three times the next closest bid.

A month later, Jack set out to build his family a proper cabin on his new acreage. Phil couldn't understand why his brother wouldn't settle for a campsite with tents. The land was 6 miles from anywhere you could park a truck. All the lumber would need to be gathered and milled on-site, which meant hauling in all the tools, equipment, and other materials by horseback and backpack. Jack picked out a site right below the sandstone formation. Phil warned him their cabin would eventually be pummeled with boulders. The brothers argued. Jack couldn't be dissuaded. He sat down and drafted a standard house plan for a rustic Colonial-style cabin with one big room and a tiny bathroom.

In Fall 1976, Jack and Dennis began transporting supplies into Pine Valley. They set up a big World War I–era canvas tent with sleeping bags, pads, lanterns, and flashlights, and not much else. The water source was a natural spring by a creek 300 yards away. Food was packed in and cooked by campfire. They'd catch fish and occasionally hunt deer.

On Fridays after work, Jack would load up his pickup and drive with Dennis to the nearest campground parking lot, arriving by 8:30 p.m. They would start hiking and would get to Pine Valley around 10:30 p.m. Each trip was meticulously planned out so they could avoid hiking back and forth more than once. With a handmade sifter he'd fashioned out of a

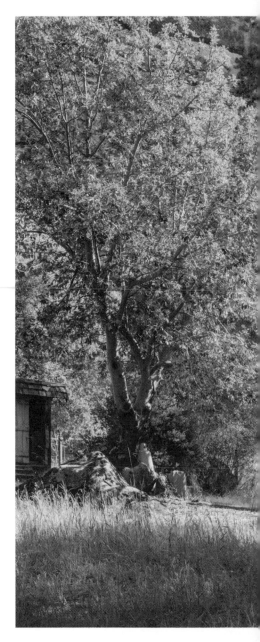

Lumber was cut and milled on site. All of the tools were packed in, hand carried, or carted by wheelbarrow.

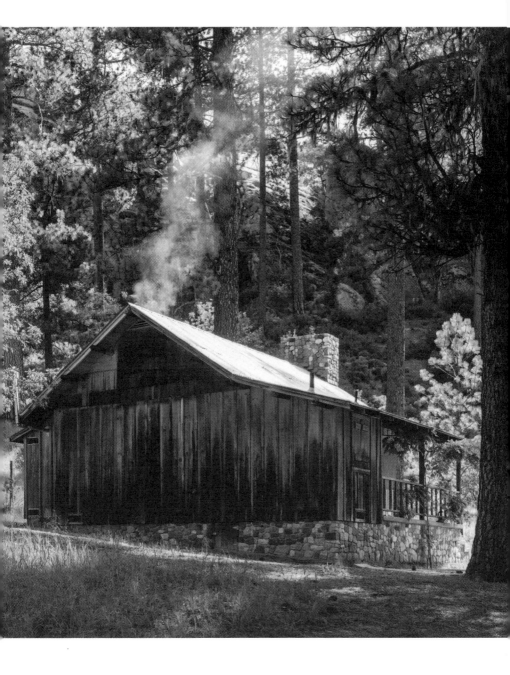

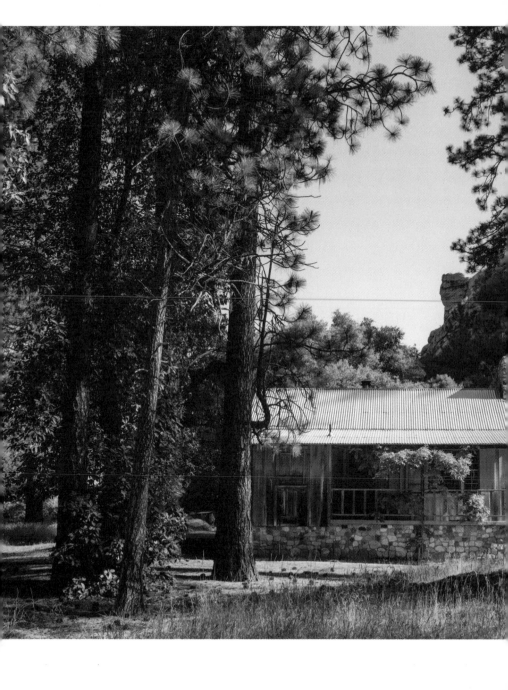

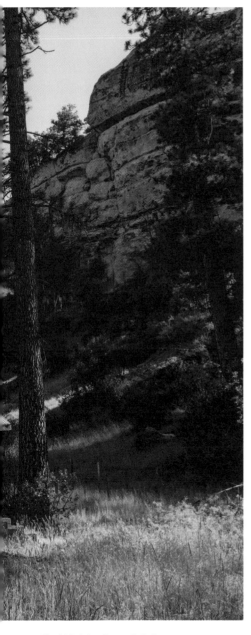

The wisteria plant growing across the front
porch was planted in the 1990s. The flowers
bloomed for the first time in the spring of 2013.

redwood frame and wire screen, Jack started creating two separate piles of gravel and sand by the creek. Gradually, they hand-carried the sand and gravel in 5-gallon buckets back to their site.

Whenever Jack came across a larger stone he liked the look of, he'd grab it and put it on a pile by their tent. On the trail, if he spotted a handsome stone, he'd toss it into his pack and bring it to Pine Valley.

Each weekend, father and son packed in more tools and materials: Jack carried a 25-pound Alaskan chain saw mill on his back, while Dennis carried the mill's two 22-pound Husqvarna powerheads in one trip. When something was too big or cumbersome to carry or strap onto their backs, such as a gas-powered generator, they used a wheelbarrow or a makeshift cart. Over the course of many trips, Jack and Dennis hand-carried several hundred feet of ½-inch-thick rebar in bundles that weighed 80 pounds each. They'd wrap both ends of a 12-foot-long bundle in foam, then each of them would shoulder an end and head out onto the trail. "It bounced and would beat you up," recalls Dennis, who was a lanky teenager. "Your shoulder started aching pretty soon, and then you'd switch to the other shoulder and go back and forth." At the site, as piles of rebar grew, so did bucketloads of sand and gravel. "I knew all the heavy work was making me stronger," Dennis says.

In 1976, Jack and Dennis felled mature ponderosa pine trees that were newly dead or dying from infestations of pine beetle. The following spring, they milled the lumber. To dry the wood, they built racks using rebar, and piled up the boards with sticks in between to ensure that air could pass between them. While they waited for the lumber to dry, they continued multitasking. Jack's collection of eye-catching stones continued to grow.

Once they'd collected enough gravel and sand, Jack and Dennis began to haul in a substantial supply of Portland cement. On one occasion, they lead a train of at least ten mules and horses, each carrying two bags of cement. Jack used the cement to hand-mix his own mortar. He cast the cabin's foundation wall and footing for the fireplace in solid concrete and rebar. The foundation was finished in the spring of 1977. That summer, they finished the framing, outside sheeting and siding, and roofing.

For the next three years, the family spent most of their weekends in Pine Valley. Mary planted a garden. They experimented with grapes, blackberries, raspberries, and various fruit trees. Jack labored on the cabin's interior. Once, when he stumbled across a felled black oak tree a quarter mile away from the cabin, Jack convinced Phil to help him lug the mill over to the tree. Jack knew the wood would be both beautiful and durable, so he used it for the floorboards. One larger piece became the fireplace mantel. To do away with the chain saw marks on the wood, Jack resurfaced the wood using a broadaxe and adze. The technique involves first striking the beam with the axe to create a series of parallel crosscuts on the surface. Next, the adze is used to smooth out those cuts. The mantel took Jack two or three hours to finish. He used that same technique on the ceiling beams, which took even longer.

After the four bunks were built and the kitchen was set up and the windows were in place, Jack began the stonework on the chimney, foundation, and fireplace. He would work a little bit at a time. By then he'd gathered stones from riverbeds and trails all over the valley. The stonework was purely cosmetic. But it helped give the cabin a detailed level of craftsmanship deserving of the area's natural beauty. Over the years,

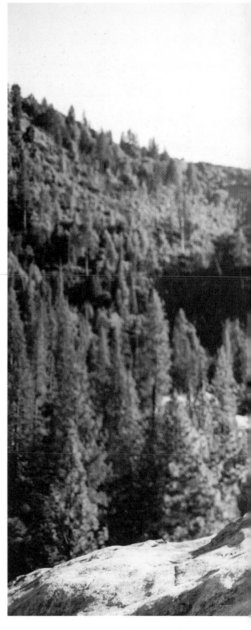

When he was a teenager, Dennis English helped his father build the small cabin on the valley floor below.

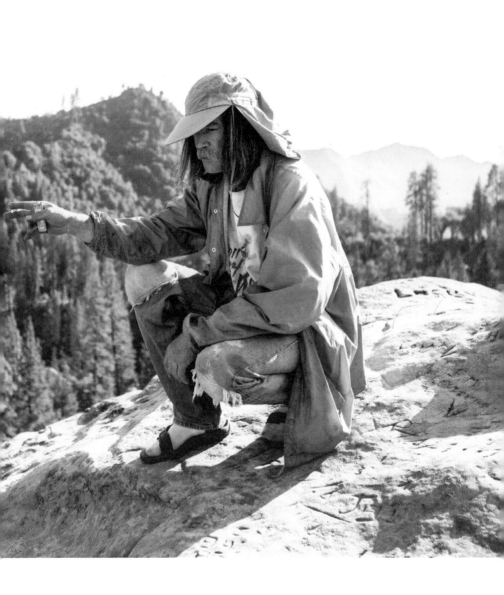

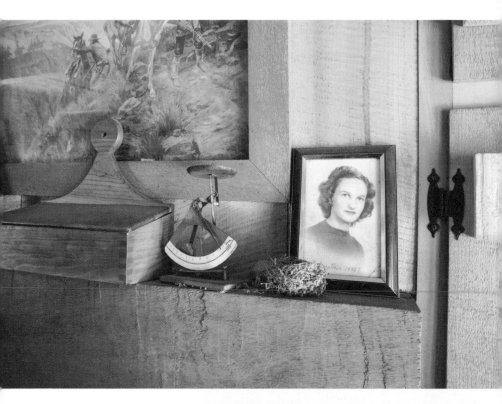

A portrait of Jack English's wife Mary, who was nicknamed Scrumptious, sits on a mantel cut from a black oak. The mantel's hand-hewn finish was achieved by scoring the wood with a broadaxe, then smoothing those cuts with an adze.

ʀ In 1976, the planning commission stipulated that the dimensions for this load-bearing carrier beam be calculated by an engineer. Jack hired a friend, who did all the calculations in one afternoon. The fee: $75.

ᴏᴘᴘᴏsɪᴛᴇ The wood-burning stove was helicoptered to the cabin for $250.

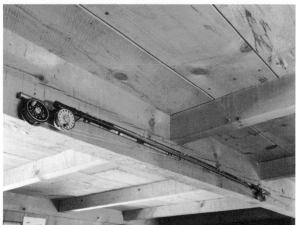

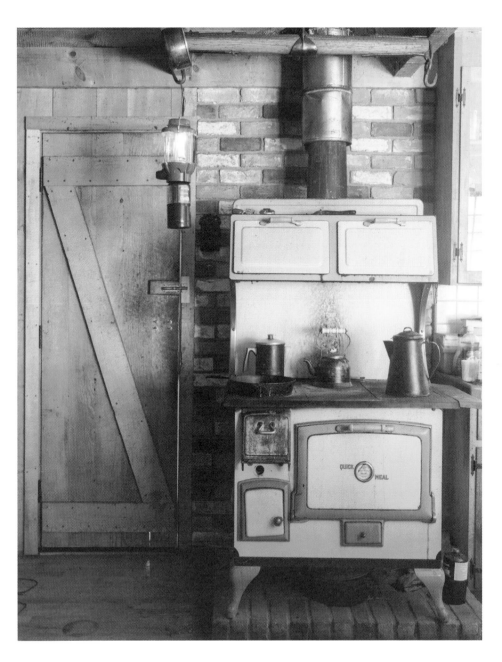

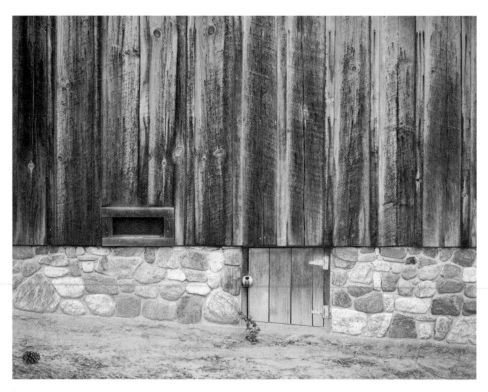

The exterior boards were never planed, so the patterned cuts from the chain saw blade are still visible.

OPPOSITE Jack English spent several years collecting stones from the stream and along the trail in order to assemble the chimney.

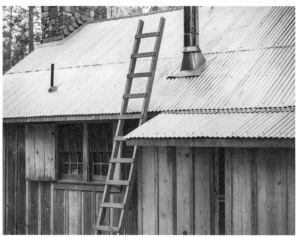

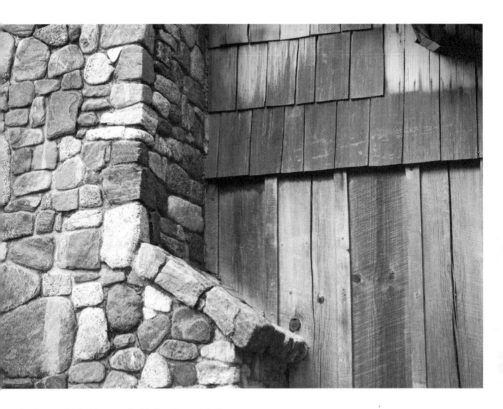

the 5-acre plot had become Jack's favorite spot in the
entire valley. He placed the final stone in 1980.

That same year, Jack and Mary began extending their
stays out at the cabin. Sometimes they'd hike in and spend
up to a month at a time, just the two of them. Having
retired, Jack had no obligation to be elsewhere. He took
up crafting bows for violins, cellos, violas, and basses. Out
in the woods, time seemed to stand still. Ever since the
1950s, Jack had grown increasingly disenchanted with
modern society. With the rise of commercialism, people
were turning away from farming and building and making
things. He believed that products were getting cheaper in
quality. "I don't care for progress. I'd rather go back. My
wife was the same way," Jack says. "When I lost her, it's not
been the same since."

In 2001, Mary died at the age of seventy-eight. Soon
after, Jack moved to the cabin and began to live there
almost all the time. Their home in Soquel reminded him

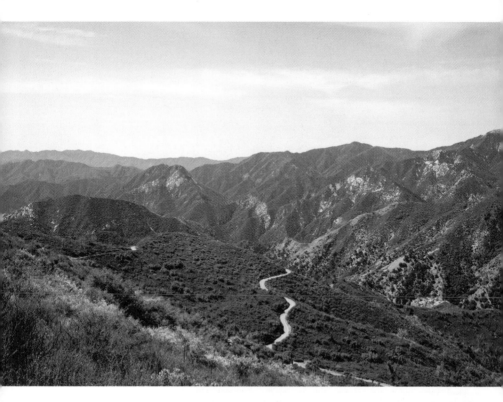
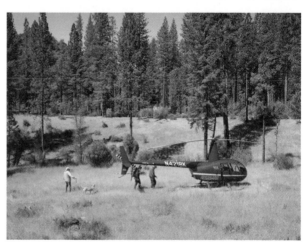

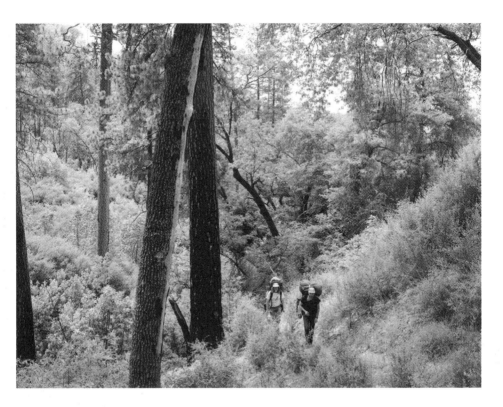

Jack English completed the five-hour hike the day before his ninety-third birthday.

OPPOSITE TOP The trailhead to the cabin begins at the bottom of a meandering dirt road.

OPPOSITE A local helicopter pilot volunteers to drop off Jack English near his cabin whenever he asks.

too much of Mary. He couldn't stand to be anywhere outside Pine Valley. He'd hike in alone and stay for a month, then head back into town to gather supplies, pay his bills, and visit with Dennis and the grandkids. Jack kept Mary's ashes in a small cardboard box. He carried her with him. "He didn't want an urn of any kind," Dennis says. "Because it would just be too heavy to be packing everywhere."

Around this time, Jack became a local legend among hikers and backpackers. Although there are two fences near the property, Jack always left the gate open. He welcomed all visitors. On one Thanksgiving, a camper caught in a rainstorm took shelter with Jack in his cabin. Jack fed the man and kept him warm. For the next eight years, the man returned to Pine Valley every Thanksgiving to hand-deliver Jack's dinner.

As the years passed, Jack remained physically strong, but he started to develop arrhythmia. So Dennis began accompanying his father whenever he'd hike in or out of

Pine Valley. The last time Jack hiked the trail was in 2012, the day before his ninety-third birthday. He made the hike in three hours and fifteen minutes, which is still faster than most novice backpackers.

Months later, Jack suffered a heart attack. Once he'd been released from the hospital, Dennis made the decision for Jack to move into his home in Soquel. But every month, Dennis makes arrangements for his father to visit the cabin in Pine Valley. A local helicopter pilot volunteers to fly Jack roughly 20 minutes from a nearby airport to his cabin so he can stay over for a couple nights. Dennis, now fifty-three, set up a makeshift heliport in a meadow less than 100 yards behind the cabin.

In May 2014, after his helicopter landed, Jack walked slowly toward the cabin he built four decades ago, on the land he first explored eight decades ago. He sat down behind the cabin, near the workshop where he had handcrafted dozens of violin bows. "It's a good place to die," ninety-four-year-old Jack said, exhaling. "I think my days are about done. But I've had a good life. I can't complain." He took a moment to look around before heading inside. Around the cabin, not much had changed. In 2011, a few enormous sandstone boulders had tumbled down a hillside a five-minute walk from the cabin. As of 2014, not one boulder had touched the cabin that Jack and Dennis built.

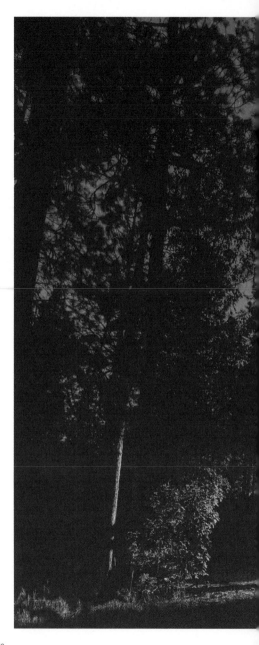

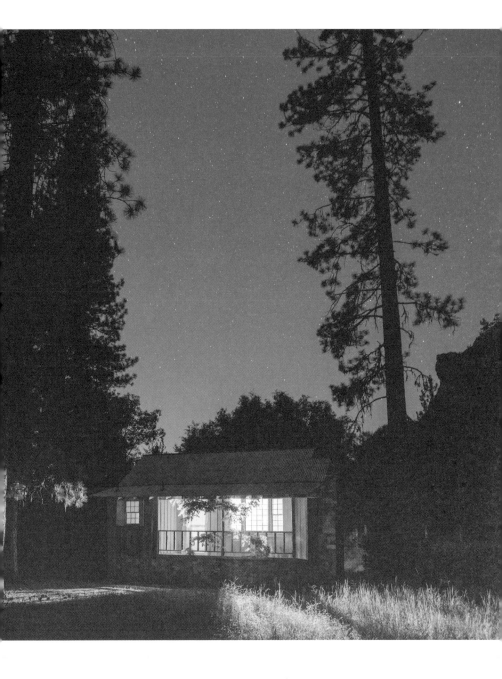

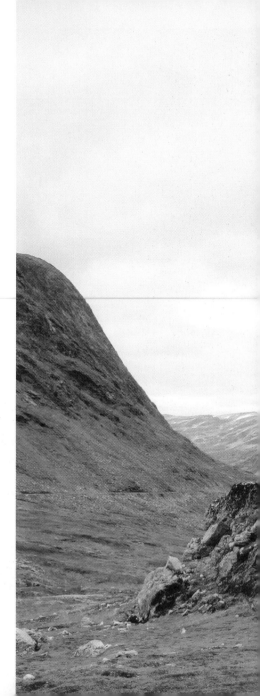

BACKCOUNTRY

ARCHIVE

Grotli, Norway
CONTRIBUTED BY
Anka Lamprecht & Lukas Wezel

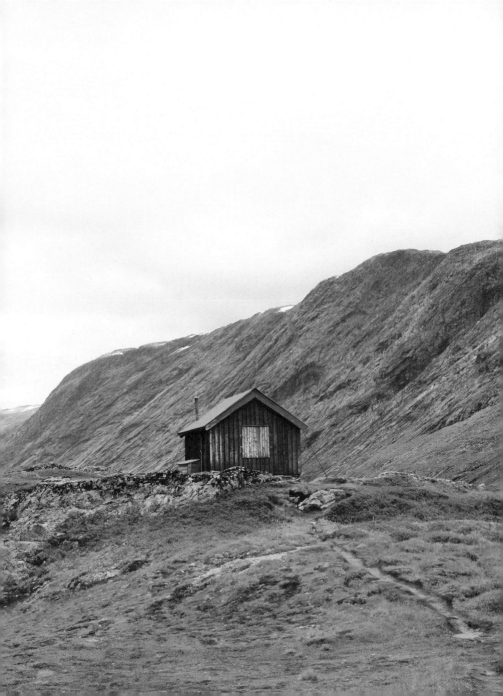

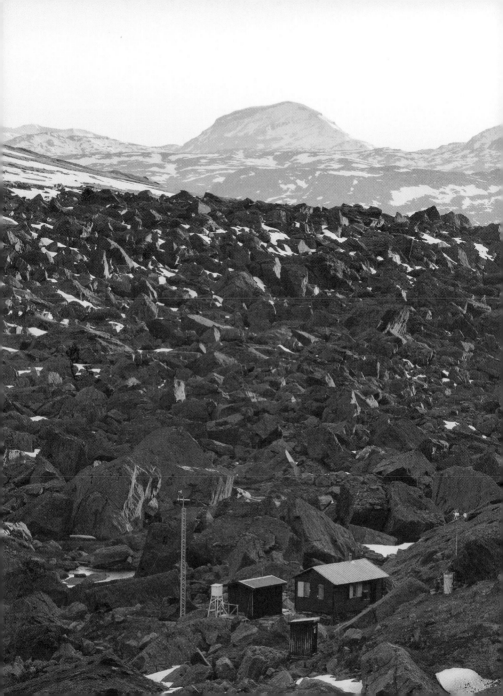

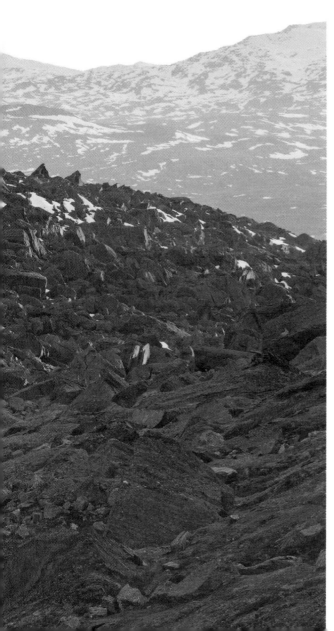

Hut in Kärkevagge, Swedish Lapland
CONTRIBUTED BY Henrik Bonnevier

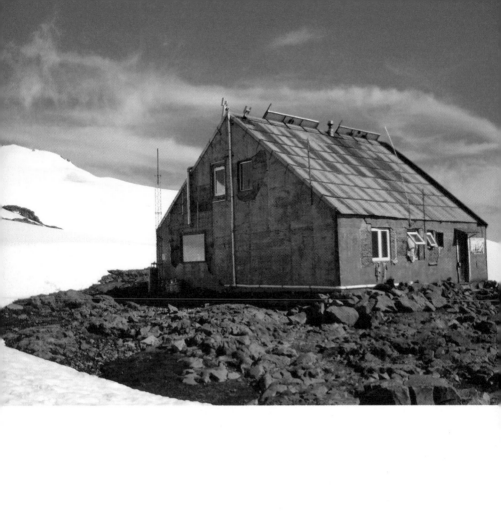

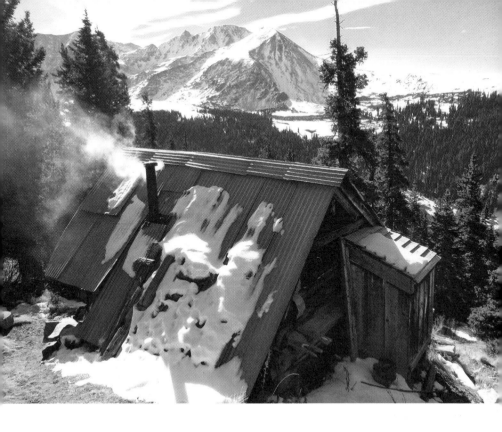

Patagonia, Argentina
CONTRIBUTED BY Dr. Julius Christopher Barsi

Just outside Leadville, Colorado,
in the Rocky Mountains
CONTRIBUTED BY Taylor L. Applewhite

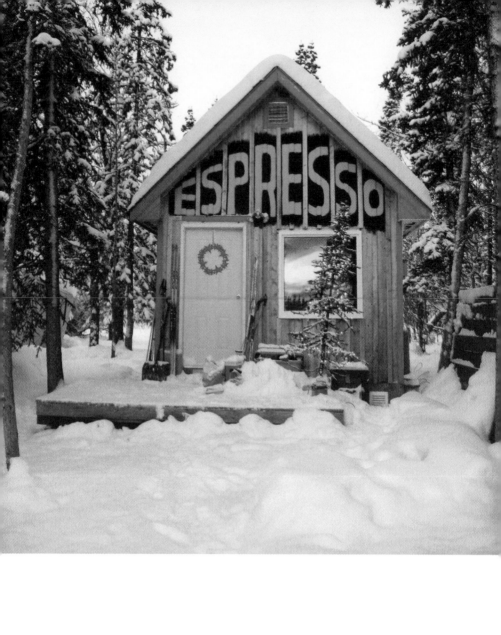

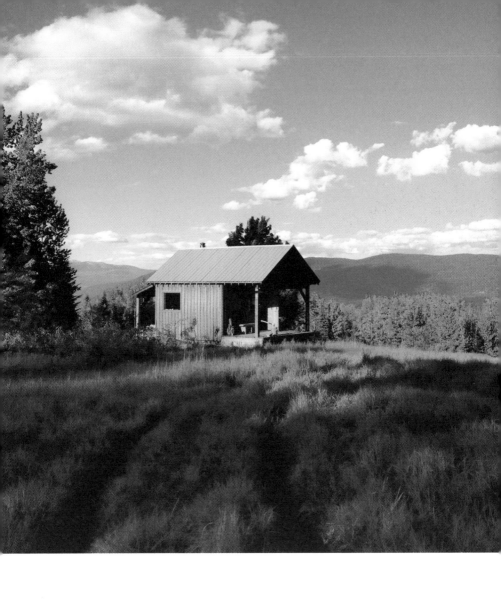

Echo Lake, Yukon Territory, Canada
CONTRIBUTED BY Peter Turner

Hemlock cabin in Rossland,
British Columbia, Canada
CONTRIBUTED BY Tyler Austin Bradley

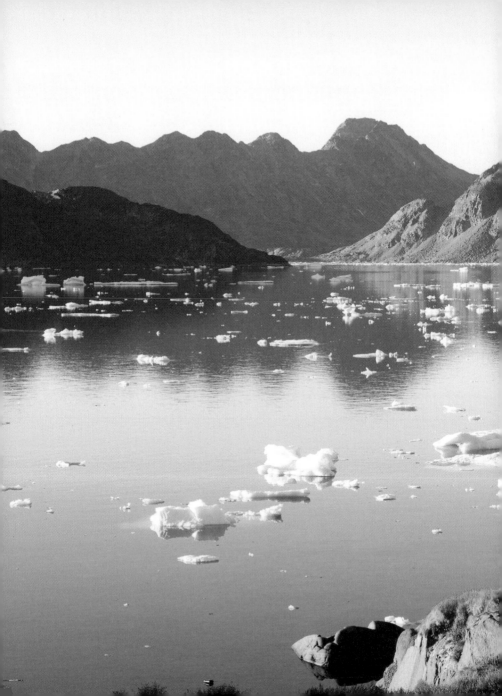

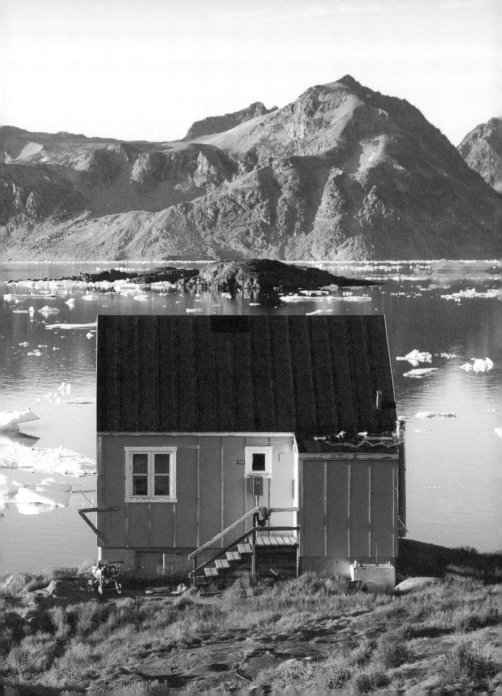

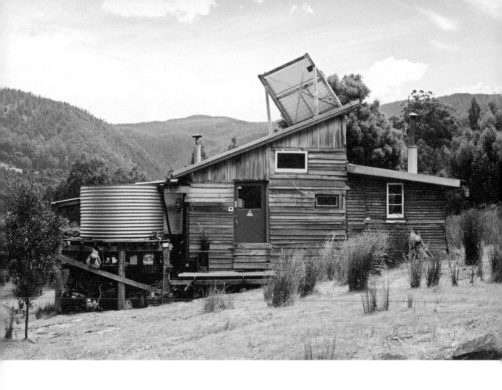

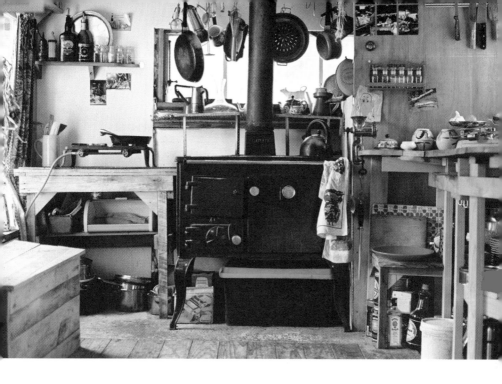

Axel's Humpy in Huon Valley, Tasmania
CONTRIBUTED BY Tom Powell

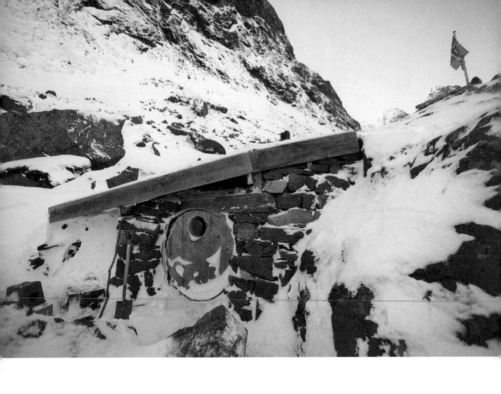

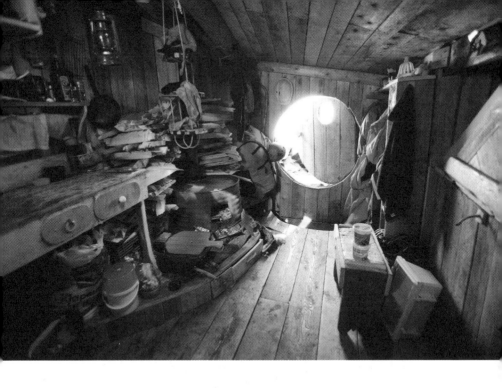

Cabin built out of driftwood, stone, and sea debris
in Northern Norway above the Arctic Circle
CONTRIBUTED BY Inge Wegge & Jørn Nyseth Ranum

NEXT Cottage on an island near Nora, Sweden
CONTRIBUTED BY Jonas Loiske

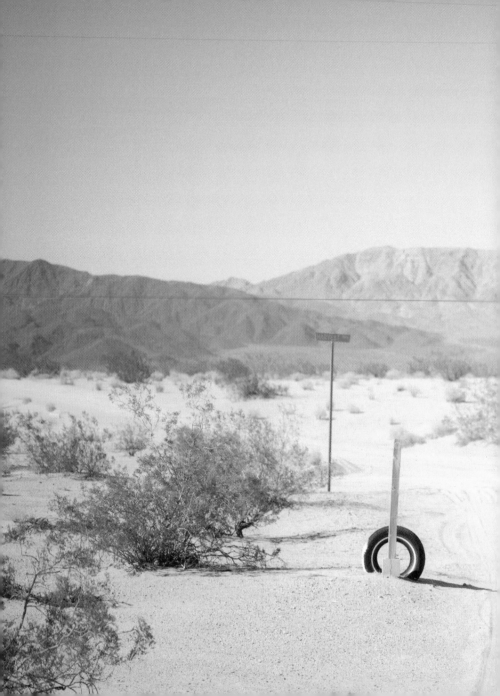

FIXER-UPPERS

2
FIXER-UPPERS

A couple overhauls a
dilapidated desert homestead.

How to Revive
a Bungalow

**Wonder Valley,
California**

Lisa Sitko and Douglas Armour studied the house in
the real estate listing and then looked at each other.
No way they'd ever buy it, they agreed. The one-story
bungalow had broken windows, peeling paint, and
a rickety vintage trailer parked on blocks beside it.
Nothing in the photographs appealed to the couple.
There was even a utility pole standing right next to the
structure, intruding on the landscape. Nevertheless,
the property was only a twenty-minute drive away, so
Lisa and Douglas hopped into their truck. They figured
they might as well see this place in person before
crossing it off their list.

In May 2006, Lisa and Douglas were crisscrossing
Wonder Valley, California, determined to find and buy
a parcel of land with a cabin they could renovate.
Located in the Mojave Desert north of Joshua Tree
National Park in a flat sandy basin surrounded by bar-
ren, craggy mountains, Wonder Valley is home to hundreds of deserted little dwellings that began popping
up in the 1950s. After the passage of the Small Tract

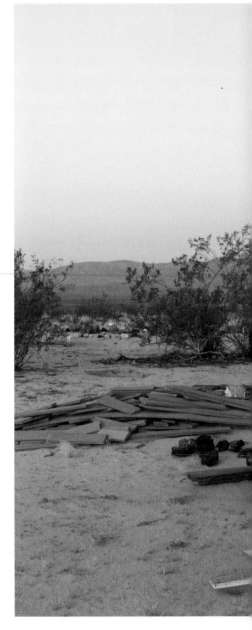

The front yard doubles as a supply
depot for materials they've salvaged.

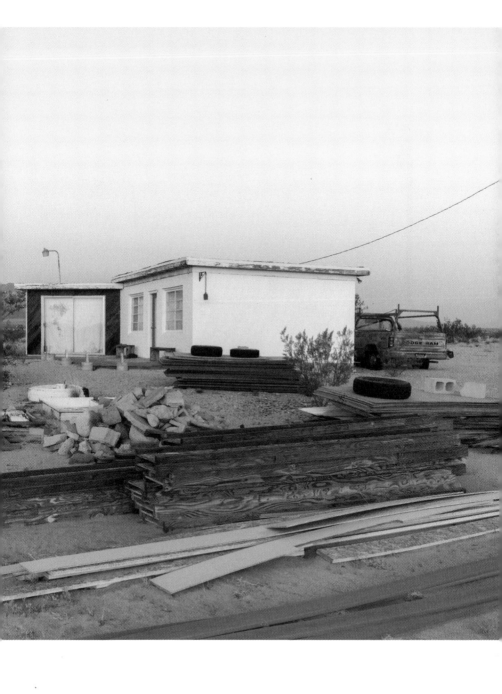

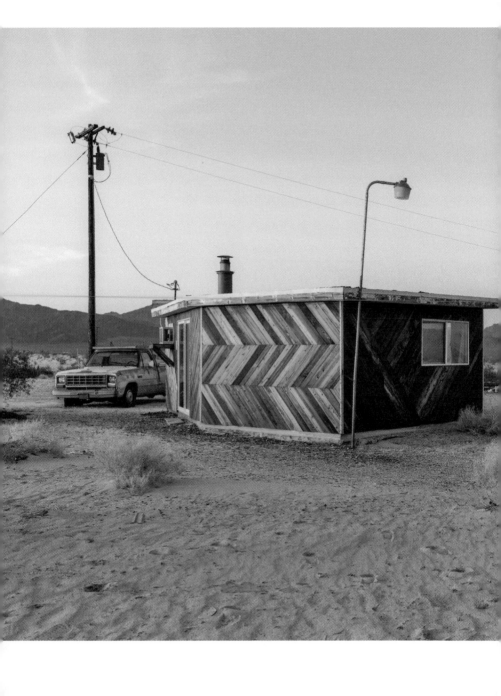

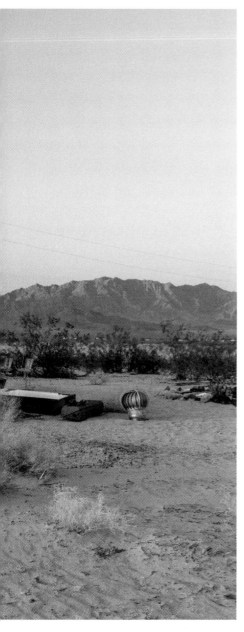

Act of 1938, the Bureau of Land Management parceled out several thousand acres of federally owned desert. Two varieties of plots—5 acres and 2½ acres—were sold for $10 to $20 per acre on one condition: prospective landowners had to build a structure that was at least 12 by 16 feet. Southern Californians, mostly World War II veterans and suburbanites, flocked to the desert to claim land and construct cheap vacation cabins—what would become known as jackrabbit homesteads. But the area features peak temperatures that can approach 120°F and heavy winds that send dust storms blustering through the valley. In time, many of the homesteaders abandoned their properties, leaving the shelters to contend with the elements. Today, there are shacks in all states of disrepair: some are boarded up; others are burned out. Many cracked concrete slabs are surrounded by piles of trash and debris.

Lisa and Douglas discovered Wonder Valley in 2001 when they house-sat for a photographer friend with a second home there. At the time, they lived in Los Angeles. During the four months the couple spent in Wonder Valley, they fell in love with the desert's intense sunsets, bright night skies, and sprawling emptiness. The way they perceived the dry, inhospitable ecosystem began to change. "It's an area where on the surface it seems like everything is dead and there's no life. But you start to notice life everywhere," Lisa says. "The longer you're here, the more your senses start opening up." They spotted birds' nests up in telephone poles. They snapped photos of purple wildflowers blooming. Along with coyotes trotting by at dusk, there were sightings of snakes, scorpions, and vinegaroons, scorpion-like arachnids with sharp, pinching claws. Lisa and Douglas fantasized about buying land in Wonder Valley, but soon they relocated to New York City, and then to Berlin and Detroit. After returning to Los Angeles in 2004, they bought a book of road maps for the desert and started hunting for a homestead.

As soon as Lisa and Douglas pulled up to the available property in their Ford Ranger, they noticed that the home was perched above the surrounding land. The view to the east, facing away from the utility pole, was remarkable. They walked around the property and took stock. Attached to the original 400-square-foot cinder block structure, which was built in 1958, was a 300-square-foot add-on. The bungalow had no front door. Inside, everything was covered with a thick layer of sand and dust. The burgundy shag carpet was stained and sun-bleached. There were dead appliances, including a rusty fridge. Along the back wall was a short partial breezeway that had been hastily framed out with plywood. It was attached to the trailer, which was filled with stuffed animals and plush toys. The bathroom sink overflowed with pink bunnies and teddy bears. Lisa and Douglas later learned that in remote areas like Wonder Valley, it's easier to use a trailer with a septic tank as a bathroom than to run actual plumbing. Although this property didn't include a well or indoor plumbing, it did have electricity, which meant Douglas would be able to use his power tools. "This is it," they agreed. That evening they made an offer.

Two weeks later, they were in their truck bouncing on the dirt road that leads to the homestead. In the distance, they spotted a flowing river where there had been none before. Flash-flood waters 20 feet wide and 3 feet deep were raging right at the bottom of their driveway. They finally understood why the previous owner had marked the property with an old tire painted with the words high 'n' dry. The homestead was literally on high, dry land. "Just gun it!" Lisa

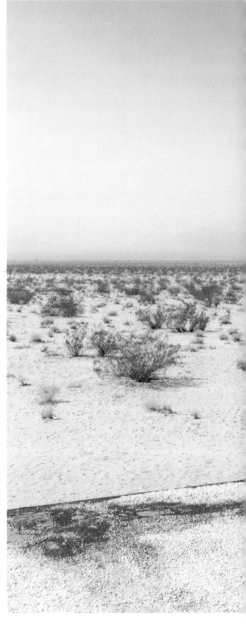

Lisa Sitko and Douglas Armour began renovating their bungalow in 2006.

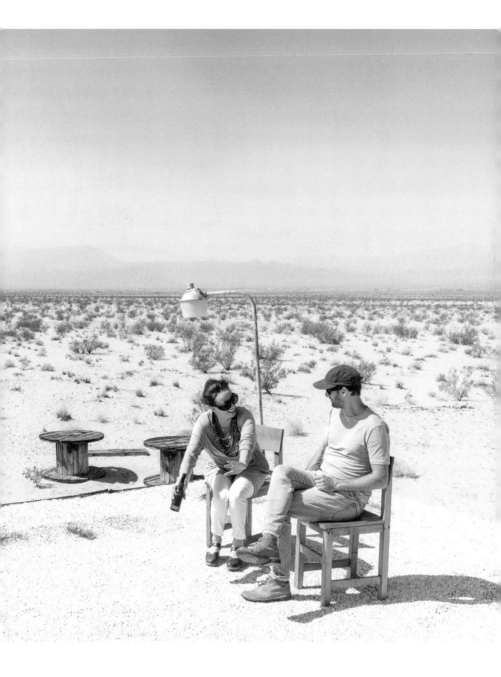

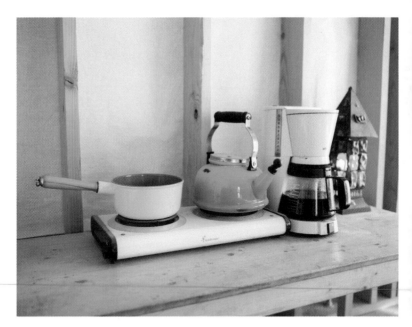

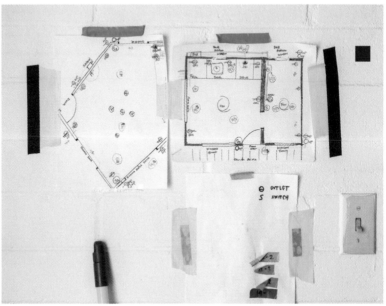

A diagram of the electrical wiring.

OPPOSITE The owners brought this unpermitted add-on up to code, by adding extra rafters and studs.

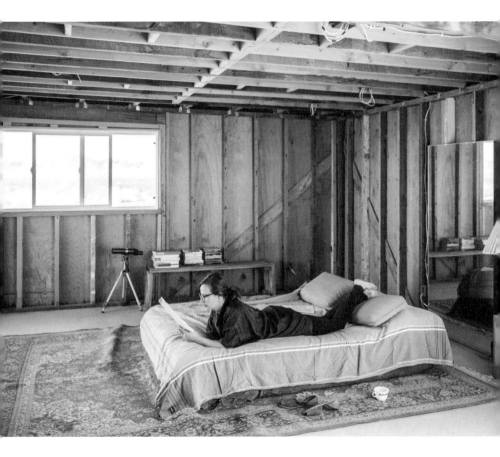

yelled. Douglas backed up, then put the Ranger in drive and accelerated. The truck managed to ford the waterway. Later, after studying the flood patterns, they understood that their property sits right where various impromptu streams all converge after heavy rain. Occasionally, these tributaries gather to form a small lake off in the distance.

Lisa and Douglas began by sorting the junk inside the bungalow into three piles: usable, cool to keep around, must go. They spent hours sweating in the summer heat as they filled up no fewer than forty-five black contractor trash bags. It took at least fifteen runs to the dump, which was 10 miles away, to remove all the junk. Douglas tore down the breezeway to the trailer and then paid $300 to have it towed off the property. They stripped the carpet

and found that the concrete slab was still intact. They bought three windows and a sliding glass door from Home Depot. Before framing out and installing the windows, Douglas found birds' nests inside the walls. He removed them only after determining that all the eggs had hatched.

After a month of off-and-on work, they installed a front door, which Douglas had bought at a salvage yard in East LA for $75. Being able to lock up their home for the first time was a big moment. From there, the couple settled in. They dug a fire pit thirty-four paces from the house. Forty-two paces behind the bungalow, they nailed up a handful of boards to create three privacy walls for an open-air outhouse.

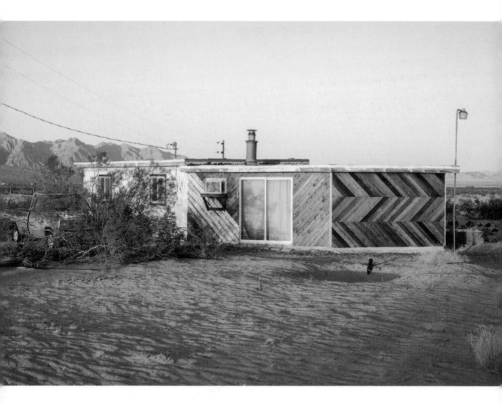

Lisa, an artist, created decorative piles of broken pottery and glass in the sand. They started to understand the unorthodox layout of the two conjoined structures, which create one seven-sided building. "It's a bizarre shape. I never would've done that in a million years," Douglas says. "But you get the sunrise through the bedroom windows and the sunset out the back."

Moving forward, the couple had no plans, no budget, and no timetable. They agreed to take time acclimating to the space, working on projects whenever it made sense. Often, that has meant waiting until they stumble on something that inspires. "We definitely come from the standpoint of doing things with materials that just happen to come our way," says Douglas, a musician who works as a carpenter and frequently builds sets for advertising campaigns.

In 2007, he did a job for a lumber company that wanted to showcase its new weather-resistant siding with before-and-after photographs. He built a wall featuring untreated, weathered old wood juxtaposed with the company's bright baby-blue composite, which was stamped with a faux wood grain. To him, the old lumber looked better. After the photo shoot, when he was told to trash the lumber, Douglas hauled it out to Wonder Valley. After sorting the wood by size and color, he spent a day and a half nailing it up on the exterior of the bungalow. All the pieces were relatively short, so he couldn't cover the length or width of an entire wall. He arranged the pieces at 45-degree angles and created a herringbone pattern, mixing and matching the darker and lighter wood. He still doesn't know what type of wood it is. Along the way, he kept text-messaging pictures to Lisa, who was back in Los Angeles.

Not long after, they hosted a weekend party at the homestead for thirty-five people. During the day, everyone attended the High Desert Test Sites, a program that sets up

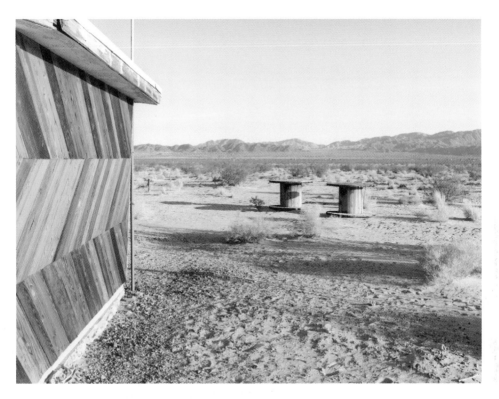

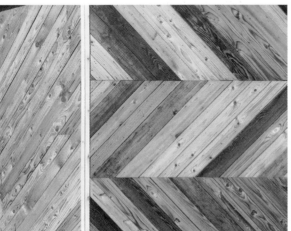

The salvaged boards were relatively short in length — making it impossible to cover an entire wall. To solve the problem, Douglas Armour decided to cut the boards and arrange them in a herringbone pattern. The wood is treated with a weather sealant every few years.

OPPOSITE An old trailer parked on concrete blocks used to connect directly to the structure through the sliding glass doors.

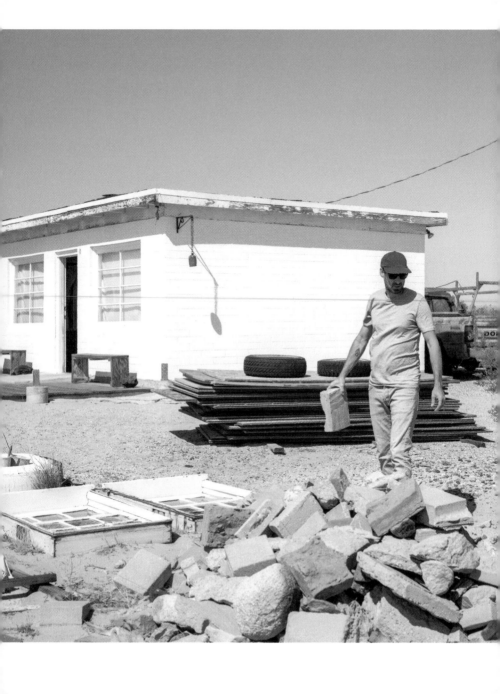

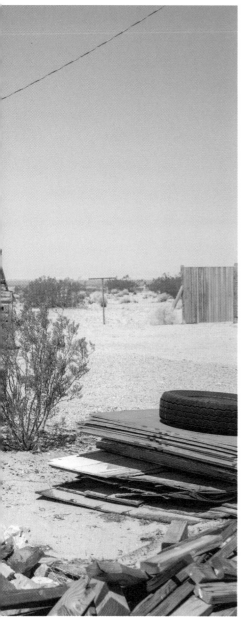

art installations throughout the desert. At night, they gathered around bonfires, drank beer from kegs, and camped in tents. Since then, friends have used the homestead to record albums, shoot music videos, and just get away from the city.

The building has evolved slowly. Lisa and Doug have amassed a small scrap yard with materials collected over the years. After building a patio with a composite material that eroded in the sun after a few years, Douglas rebuilt using another windfall of wood from an ad campaign. A denim company had hired him to build a cabin using $9,000 worth of salvaged wood from 1902. He wasn't sure what type of wood it was—only that its aged patina was beautiful. After the photo shoot, he was instructed to disassemble the cabin and discard the lumber. Once again, he hauled the wood out to Wonder Valley. In the spring of 2014, he spent two days crafting a new patio. Eventually, Douglas and Lisa plan to frame out their new patio and add an overhang made of corrugated metal or lattice wood. They also want to extend it so that the patio wraps around the house closer to the herringbone wall. They dream of creating a courtyard that will ultimately feature three 100-square-foot structures: one guest cabin, one office, and a bathroom that feeds into a graywater system they plan to install eventually. But there's no rush. "So many of our plans have changed. Slowing it down has been great for really understanding what's important to us," Lisa says. "A lot of people get wrapped up in thinking things need to be more grand than they have to be. If you keep things really basic, you can start to enjoy the place sooner."

Douglas Armour, a musician and carpenter, keeps a vast collection of materials for projects he's yet to imagine.

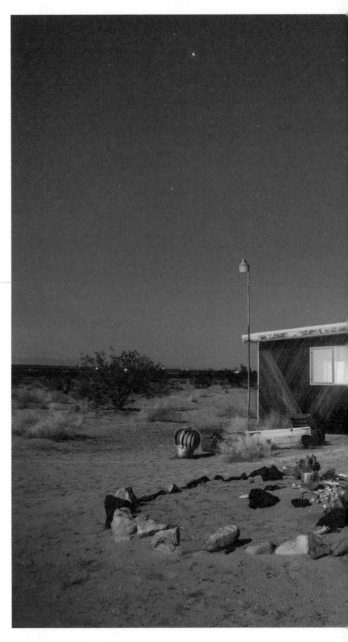

The two wings meet at a 135-degree angle.
From the bedroom on the left, the couple
has an unobstructed view of the sunrise.

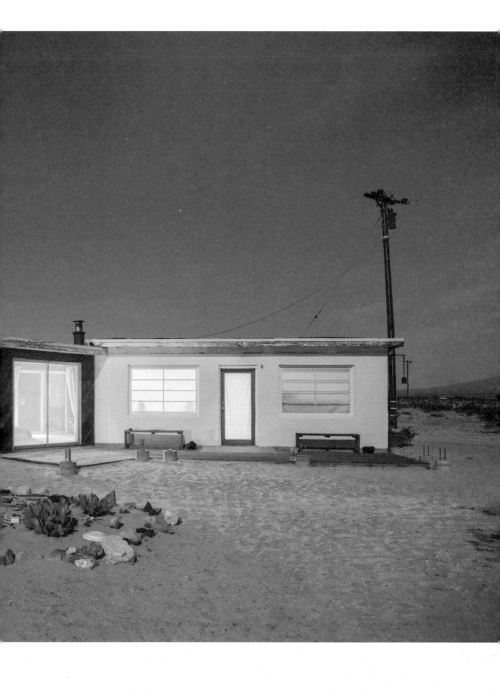

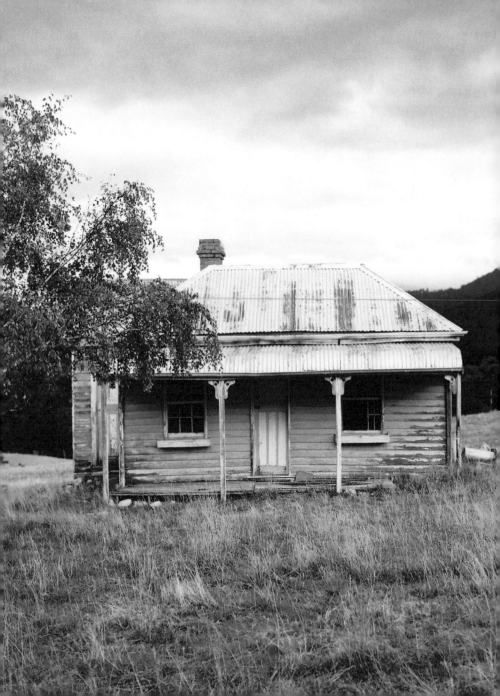

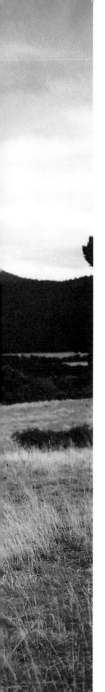

FIXER-UPPERS

ARCHIVE

Abandoned cabin in Lucaston,
Tasmania, Australia
CONTRIBUTED BY James Bowden

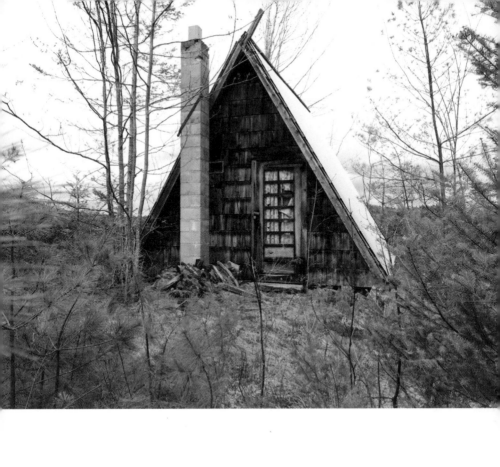

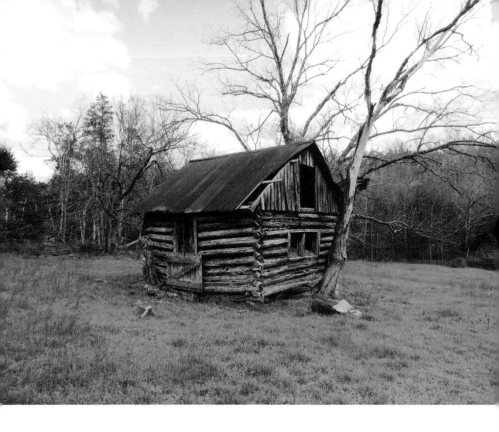

Abandoned A-frame in Bethel, Maine
CONTRIBUTED BY Joshua Langlais

Farmhand cabin in Madison
County, Missouri
CONTRIBUTED BY John T. Foster

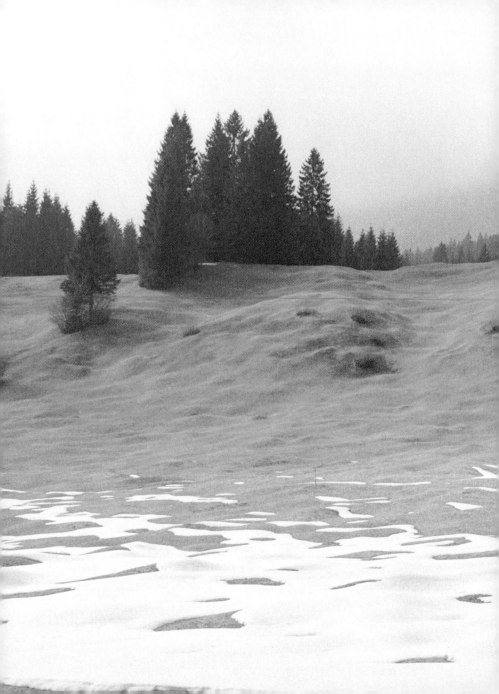

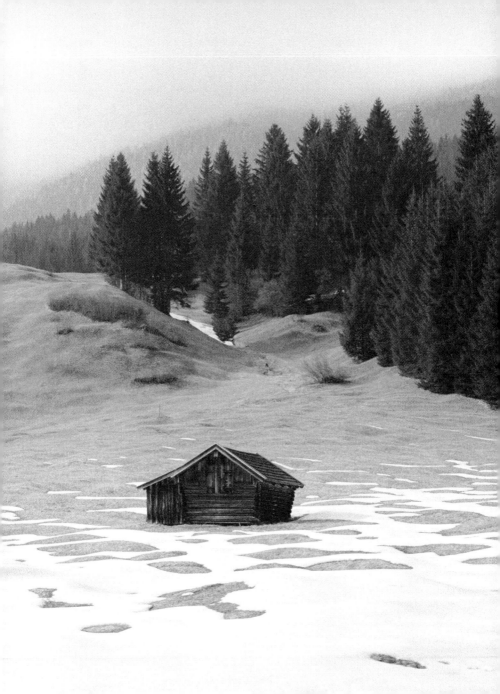

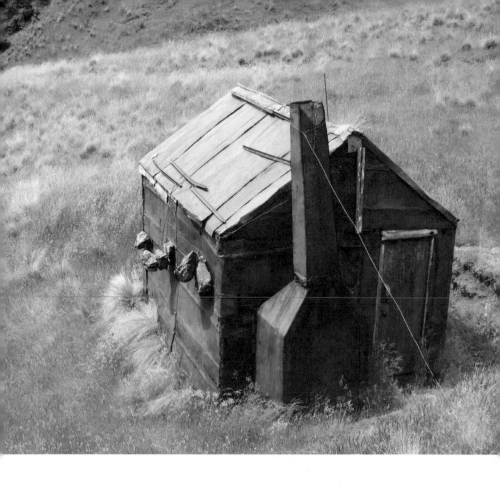

PREVIOUS Germany, near the Austrian border
CONTRIBUTED BY Maria Polyakova

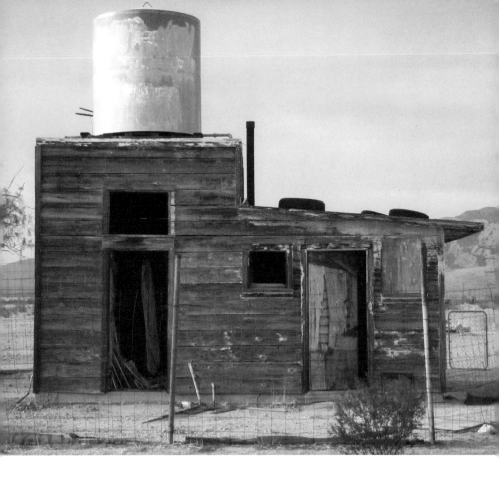

Mt. Judah, Glenorchy, New Zealand
CONTRIBUTED BY Rustan Karlsson

Twentynine Palms, California
CONTRIBUTED BY J. L. Kane

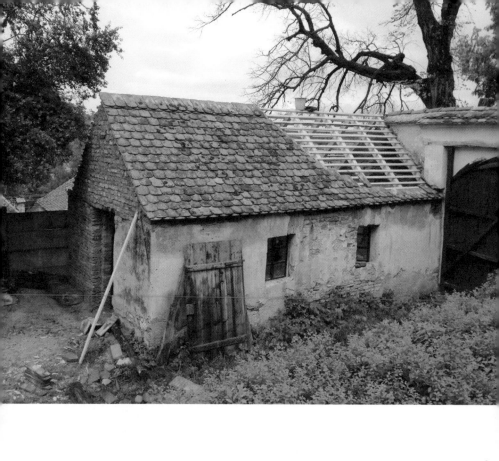

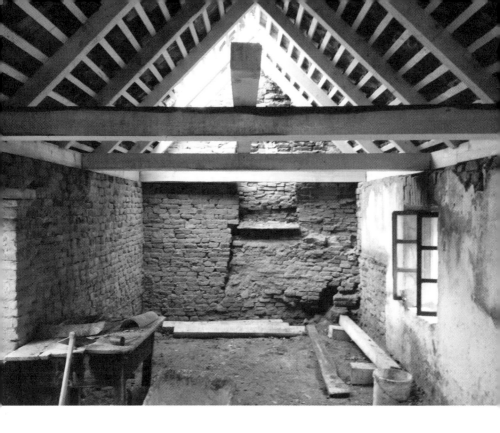

Reroofing an old bakehouse in
Holzmengen/Hosman, Transylvania, Romania
CONTRIBUTED BY Stefan Guzy

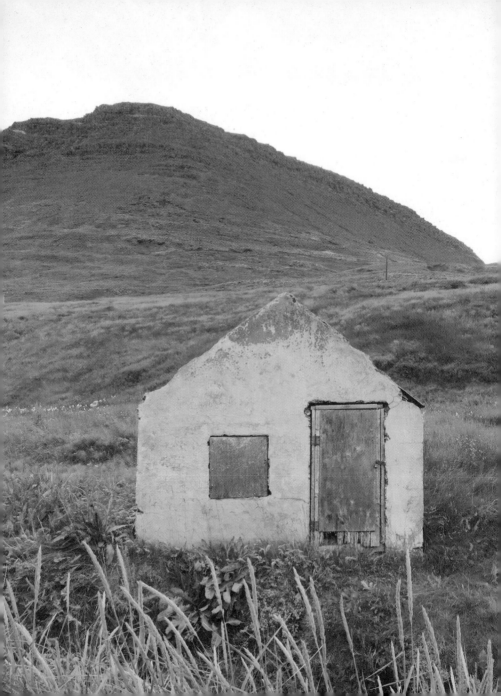

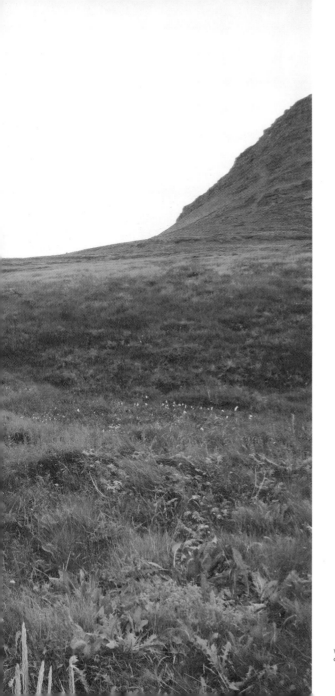

West Fjords, Iceland
CONTRIBUTED BY Kate Stokes

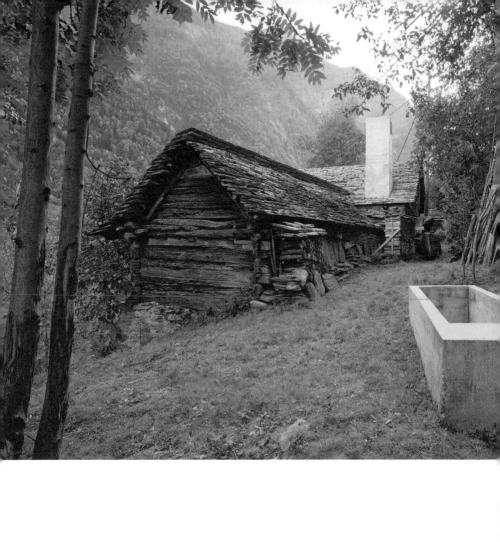

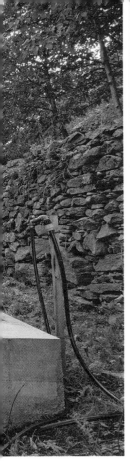
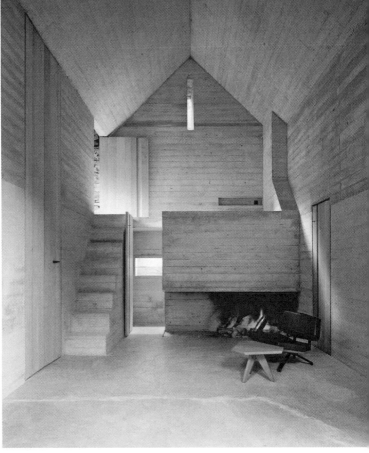

A 200-year-old stacked stone home in Linescio
Switzerland. Renovated in 2011 by Buchner Bründler
Architekten, the exterior was left untouched; the interior
was reconstructed layer by layer with poured concrete.
CONTRIBUTED BY Ruedi Walti

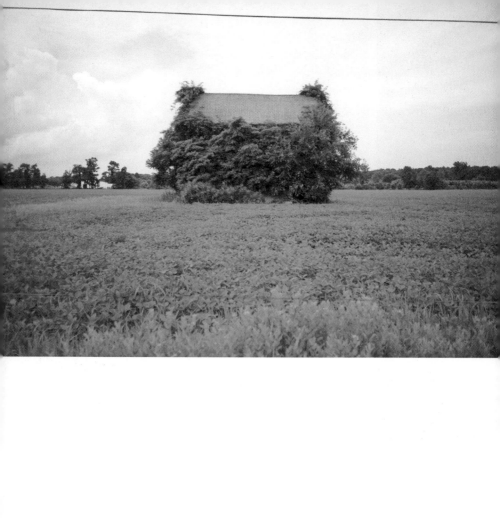

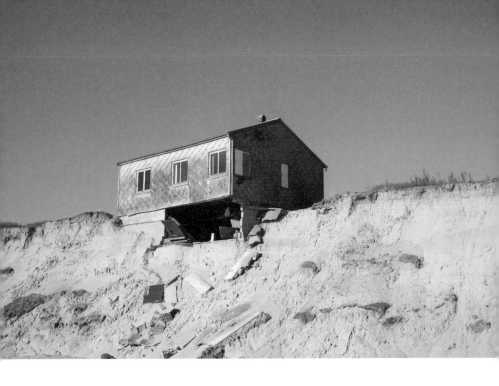

Farmhouse outside Berlin, Maryland
CONTRIBUTED BY Patrick Joust

Deserted home, Cotentin Peninsula,
Normandy, France
CONTRIBUTED BY Vincent Menu

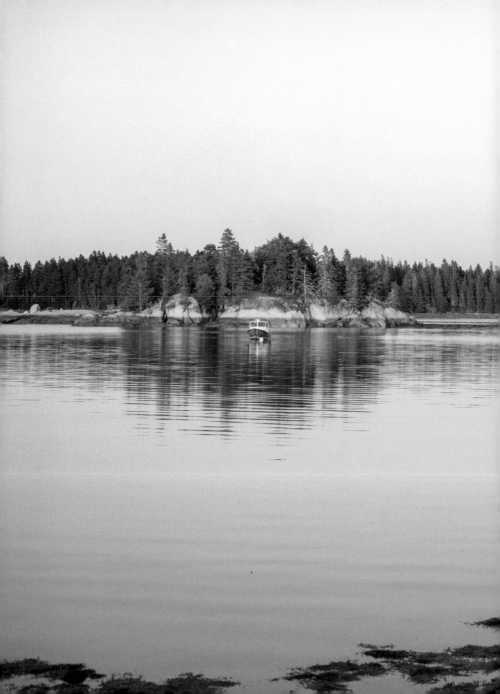

RUSTIC

3

RUSTIC

A couple crafts
a hostel reminiscent
of the seventeenth century.

How to Craft an Off-Grid Bunkhouse

Deer Isle,
Maine

All Dennis Carter knew for sure was that his building would have a stone foundation. It was 2006, and
after years of saving and planning, he was preparing
to break ground on a new structure on his wooded
17-acre property on Deer Isle, Maine. A tiny coastal
island hamlet that's accessible only by boat and a
narrow two-lane bridge, Deer Isle is known for its
abundance of lobster and granite. The region's quar-
ries have supplied raw materials for projects like the
Brooklyn Bridge and the Smithsonian Institution. In
the 1990s, Dennis worked his way up from slinging
a shovel to running his own business hand-laying
stone walls around town. He enjoyed stonework,
but the profession was merely a means to an end.
Before settling on Deer Isle, he'd spent three years
volunteering at a rural hostel in Brunswick, Georgia,
where travelers sleep in hand-built geodesic domes
and treehouses, and learn about organic agriculture.
Ever since, Dennis had dreamed of one day establish-
ing his own sustainable homestead with a dwelling

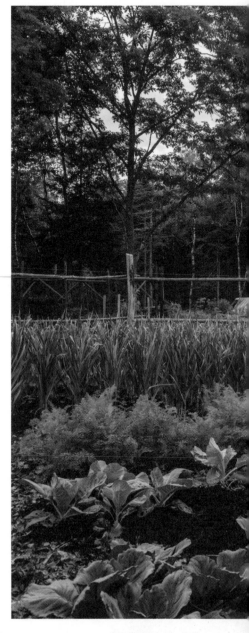

The builders imitated the gabled
dormers and overhanging second story
of colonial American architecture.

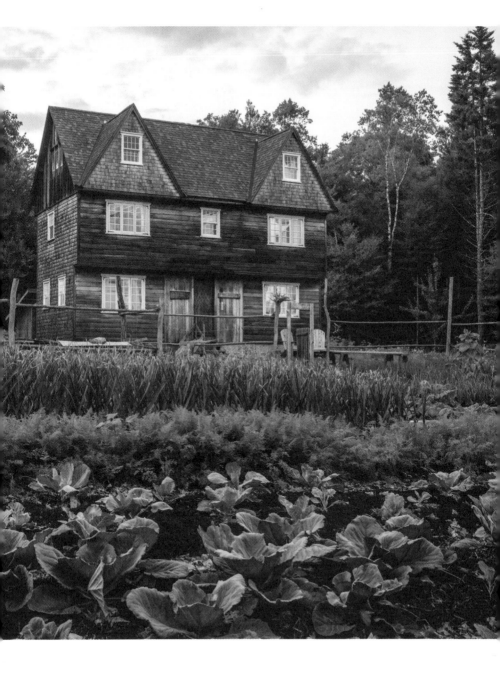

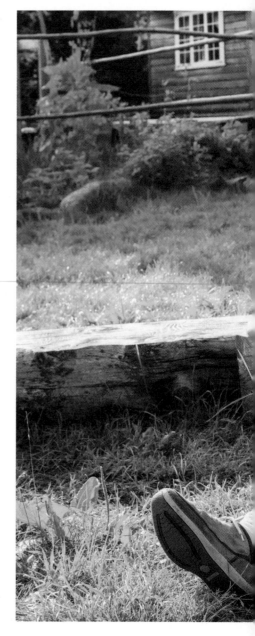

big enough to accommodate several travelers.

Early in the project, he'd decided on laying down a granite "cellar hole" foundation, but he wasn't sure how to design the structure. Something newfangled or experimental didn't appeal to him. He'd always liked the simplicity of American Colonial architecture, the classic style he'd grown up around in New England. But when it came to the timber framing, he was at a loss. He didn't want a traditionally constructed frame that would require a big crew or a crane to raise. He wanted something simple, yet still robust enough to stand the test of time.

Dennis headed to the public library in nearby Blue Hill, Maine. He thumbed through a handful of books, but nothing jumped out at him—until he stumbled on Abbott Lowell Cummings's *The Framed Houses of Massachusetts Bay, 1625–1725*. He flipped randomly to a page with pictures of the Boardman House: a two-story residence built around 1687 in Saugus, Massachusetts, that's intact today. The old building—with its commanding façade—appealed to him. Dennis stared at the book's detailed illustrations, which showed a conjectural sequence of how the house's frame must have been raised. "I had a feeling of déjà vu," recalls Dennis, whose family comes from a long line of carpenters, boat builders, and farmers with roots in New England since the 1600s. "My ancestors have been there in reality. They've done this. It's not far under the surface in me."

Dennis looked at the illustrations and intuited how he might be able to raise his frame in stages by installing one beam at a time—instead of pushing up several preassembled bents. After poring over Cummings's book from front to back, he continued researching. He learned that during the 1600s, there had been a lot of experimentation with materials

Dennis Carter spent years doing stonework in Maine before building the Deer Isle Hostel.

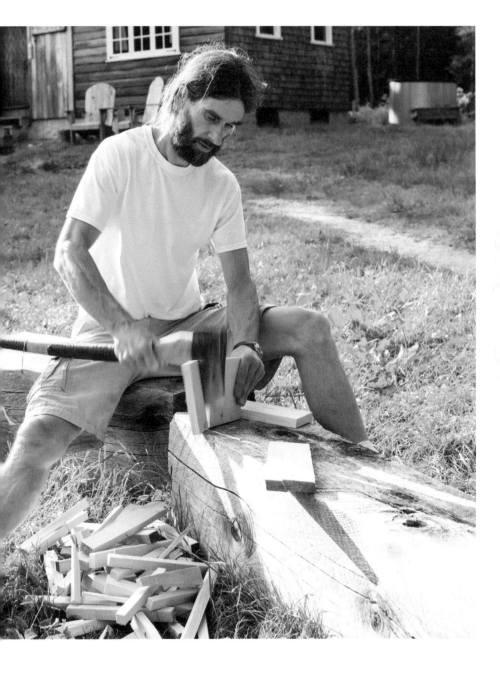

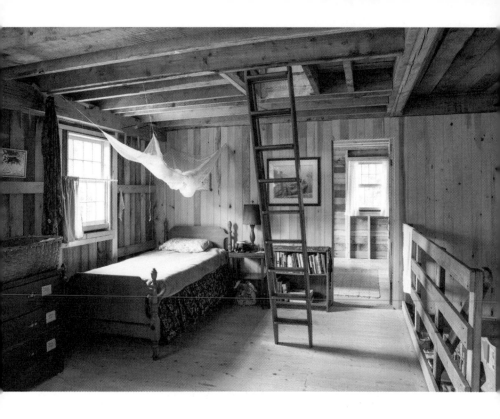

and techniques in New England, because carpenters from England were trying to adapt to the new region. Timber-frame buildings like the Boardman House, which were constructed with basic iron hand tools and traditional joinery, were still standing because they'd been engineered to last. By the 1830s, Dennis understood, carpenters were starting to build homes using cheaper materials and hastier methods, which partly explains why so many of those structures had since been rebuilt or demolished.

Modeling his hostel after the Boardman House— both in its aesthetics and in its engineering—was the way to go. The overhanging second floor, known as a jetty, would create additional square footage without changing the building's footprint. During the summer, the overhang would cast a shadow over the first-floor windows to help cool the house. By orienting his hostel to the south, Dennis would be able to take advantage of natural air-conditioning during the summer and maximize direct sunlight to help heat the house during the winter.

By January 2007, Dennis had been carving his frame using red spruce, a strong wood that's plentiful on his property, as well as salvaged Douglas fir, which is more rot resistant. Along with studying Jack Sobon's *Build a Classic Timber Framed House,* Dennis had received guidance from Jim Bannon, a professional timber framer who prefers using hand tools and local lumber. Together they'd carved the first two-thirds of the frame. Meanwhile, Dennis had already chosen a site and dug into the ground, cutting out what would eventually become his root cellar, a naturally cool and humid bunker for storing food. He began laying the granite for the foundation. Working alone, he took one hour to position each stone in its right place. Then, in late January, he hopped a bus and rode thirty-two hours to

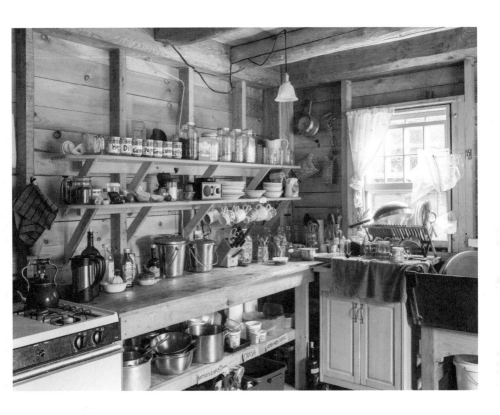

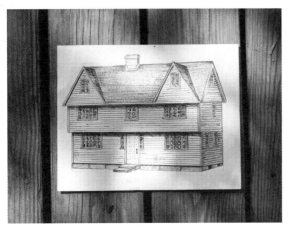

Communal dinners are cooked every
evening during the summer.

L Dennis Carter's drawing of the
Deer Isle Hostel.

OPPOSITE The ladder leads to
a third bedroom in the attic.

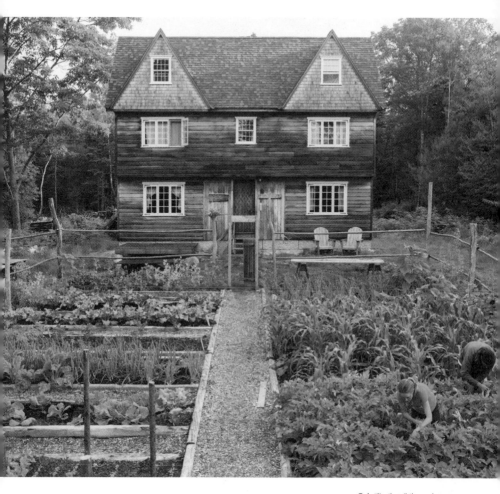

To fertilize the soil, the couple covers
garden beds with seaweed harvested
from the seashore. Along with
chickens, the couple also raises pigs.

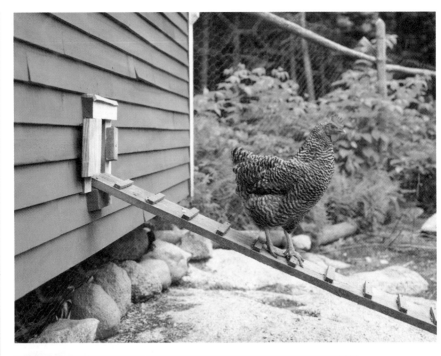

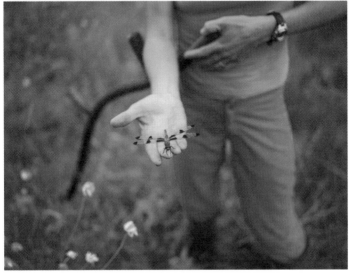

Brunswick, Georgia. He understood he couldn't build his hostel without help. He figured he might find a few volunteers at the hostel in Brunswick.

"I remember he had a big nose and a dorky backpack," Anneli Carter-Sundqvist says with a laugh. At the time, Anneli had been volunteering at the hostel in Brunswick for a month. For her, hostels were a great way for solo travelers to meet new people. A backpacker from Sweden, she was raised in Umeå, a city in the north of Sweden, but she had rural roots. Her dad grew up in the backwoods of northern Sweden on a homestead that didn't have electricity until the 1950s. Her mother grew up on a farm, where the family raised and butchered pigs.

It didn't take long for Dennis to see that Anneli was a doer. At the hostel in Brunswick, the pair would get up before sunrise and work on projects—just the two of them. They'd mulch a blueberry patch, or do carpentry odds and ends. There was no romance at the time, only a mutual love of maintaining the land and getting things done.

By July 2007, Dennis was back in Deer Isle working on his hostel with four volunteers from Brunswick. That month, he wrote a letter to Anneli and asked her to come help. Six months later, in February 2008, after jumping on a plane to New York and visiting friends in Asheville, North Carolina, she then hopped a bus to Maine. By that time, Dennis's four volunteers had all departed. They'd finished the stone work and much of the frame. That fall, Dennis had finally finished the roof framing on his own. Ultimately, his scheme for the frame had worked: only one part needed to be preassembled before being raised—three beams joined together forming an H. From there, Dennis and his volunteers installed every additional part of the frame, one beam and corner post at a time.

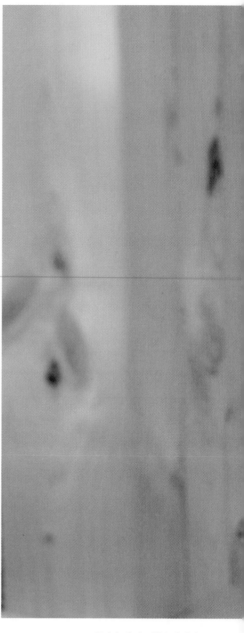

Born in Sweden, Anneli Carter-Sundqvist met Dennis Carter while she was backpacking through the U.S.

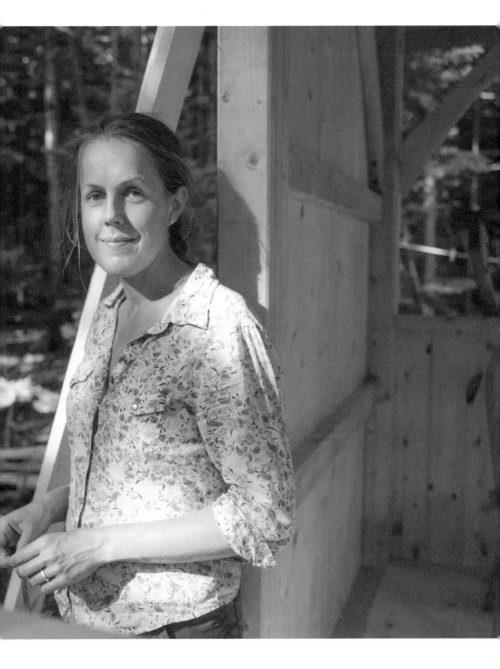

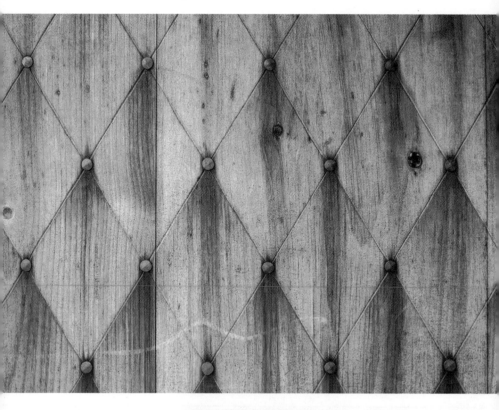

The rivets on the front door
are clinch nails, which were
hammered through the door
then fastened on the inside
of the door using hand tools.

R The hostel's mortise and
tenon joints are clinched with
handmade pegs.

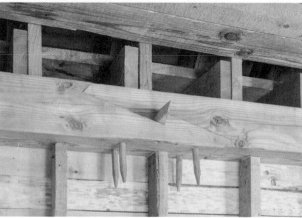

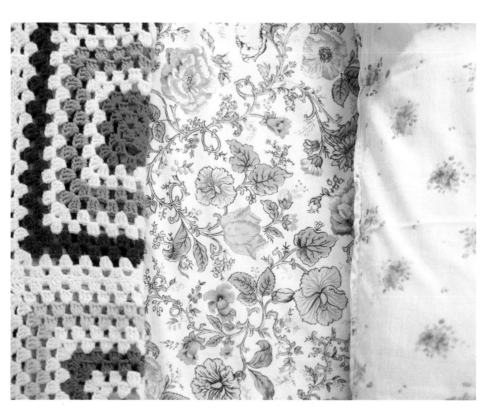

When Anneli arrived on Deer Isle in February, the bare-bones hostel had a roof and frame but no walls, floors, or finishings. She was underwhelmed. "When you don't know anything about timber frame, then it's like *whatever*," she confesses. "To me, at that point, it was like, Okay, it's the skeleton of a house. Can we now have a hostel?" The duo got to work, just the way they had in Brunswick. Within a week, a romance blossomed between them. What Anneli didn't know about carpentry, she made up for with enthusiasm and resolve as as they worked on the hostel. Dennis was a patient optimist. "It was tricky because she couldn't measure," he recalls. "But that's the great thing about doing the gables. Because in the end you have all different length boards, so you can take all the mistakes and make them into un-mistakes."

In April 2008, as Deer Isle sprang back to life after the cold winter, Dennis and Anneli managed to build out

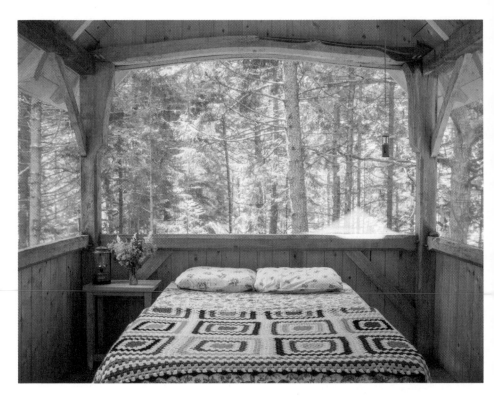

One of two screened-in sleeping porches on the property.

all four walls, using mostly pine. Getting to stand inside an enclosed space, Anneli finally felt excited. She could sense the building's potential to become a home. She set up a small table and chairs inside the hostel-to-be, and the couple ate their first meal there together.

From there, the couple divided and conquered. While Dennis concentrated on carpentry—installing cedar corner boards and white cedar shingles on the walls—Anneli moved on to the garden. She cleared the land, planted seeds, and built everything out slowly over time, eventually expanding to 8,000 square feet with an array of crops: carrots, beets, potatoes, lettuce, cabbage, beans, garlic, and more. In 2008, she also started doing fund-raising to help offset some of their start-up costs. In two years, Dennis had spent roughly $35,000 on materials. They found secondhand solar batteries and wired-up solar panels to generate enough electricity to keep the lights on.

There was still much work to be done—finishing the

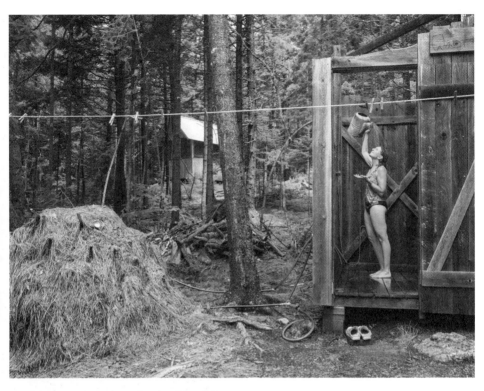

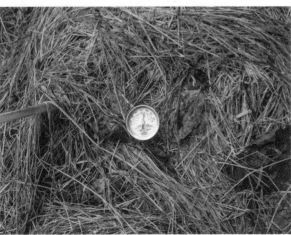

As aerobic bacteria break down the compost, the pile generates heat which warms the water pipes coiled inside. Depending on the season, the water temperature can hit 150°F.

kitchen, the windows, the solar-powered electrical system, and the composting outhouse. Nevertheless, in 2008, they publicly announced an opening date: June 21, 2009. "I was the catalyst. I rush into things," Anneli recalls. "Dennis is much more thoughtful. He could have spent years puckering away on details before opening."

On June 21, 2009, Dennis and Anneli had planned a big opening-night party and invited a dozen of their friends and kindest neighbors. They were proud but devastated—the hostel hadn't booked a single reservation for the entire summer. They officially opened at 4 p.m. Then, just before dinner, there was a knock on the door. Two backpackers from Switzerland had just arrived in town and needed a place to stay. Someone had suggested they try the hostel. That night, everyone gathered inside at the big dining room table and feasted on pancakes, whipped cream, and organic strawberries from the garden. Since then, hundreds of travelers from all over the world have stayed at the Deer Isle Hostel. In 2011, Dennis and Anneli were married.

When you set foot on their property, it almost feels as if you've traveled back in time to a bygone era. "I've always asked myself if we're traveling backward or forward," Dennis says. "And really, I feel in my heart that we're traveling forward. But I've also come to another conclusion, which is that good ideas are timeless. Our 1946 Speed Queen washing machine is an awesome washing machine. Solar panels made in the United States in the late 1990s and early 2000s are excellent. And timber-frame joinery from the late 1600s is the height of carpentry."

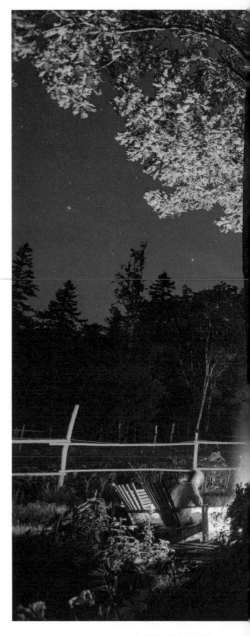

The hostel uses solar panels to generate all of its electricity.

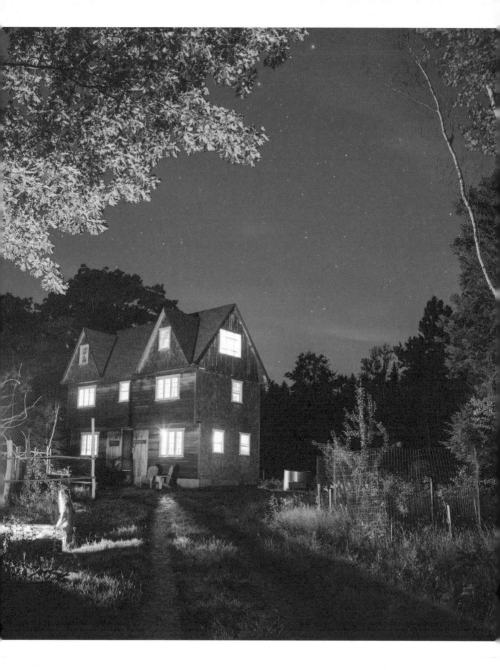

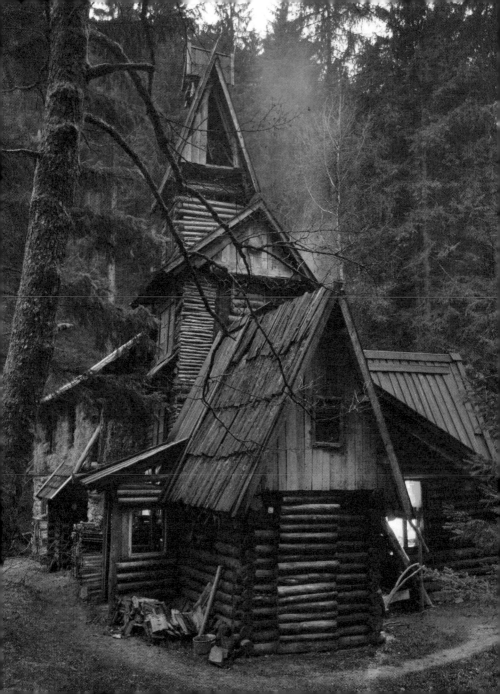

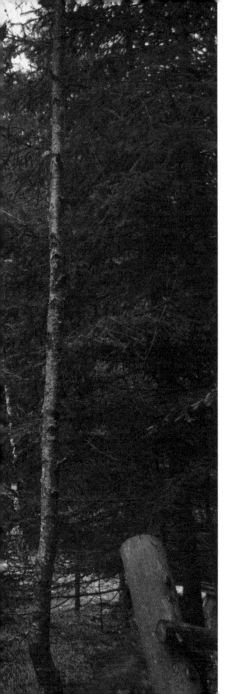

ARCHIVE

A magical cabin converted from a water
mill. A Serbian painter built several wooden
cabins along this river in the Bosnian village
of Zelenkovac, transforming the mills that
belonged to his father.
CONTRIBUTED BY Brice Portolano

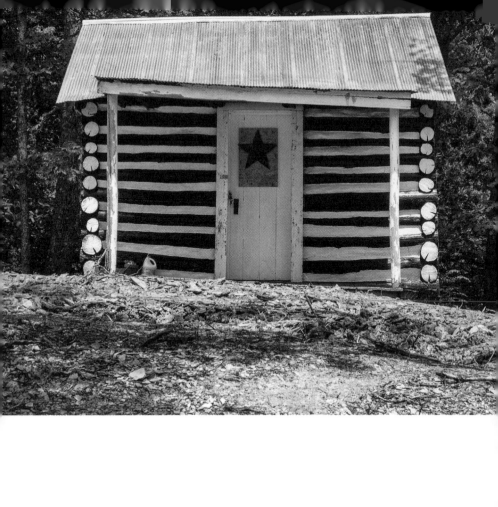

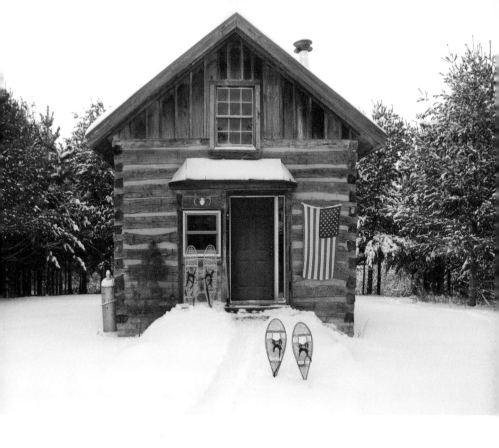

"Black and white" cabin
in Irvine, Kentucky
CONTRIBUTED BY Randel Plowman

Hunting cabin
in northwestern Wisconsin
CONTRIBUTED BY Stephanie Schuster

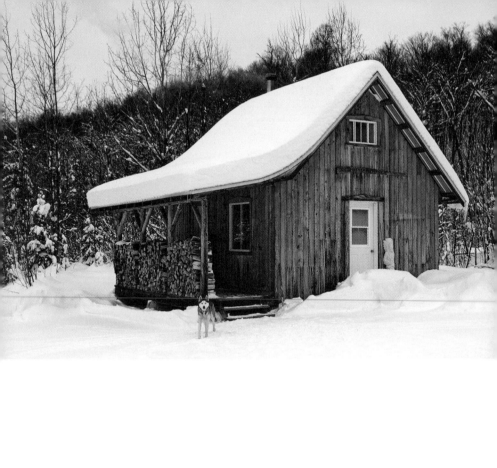

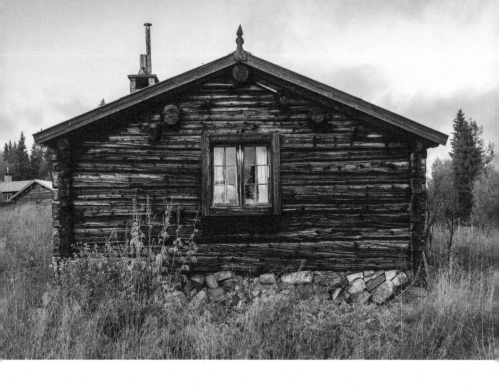

Kanatha-Aki in Quebec, Canada
CONTRIBUTED BY Mina Seville

Sörvallen Härjedalen, Sweden
CONTRIBUTED BY Kristoffer Marchi

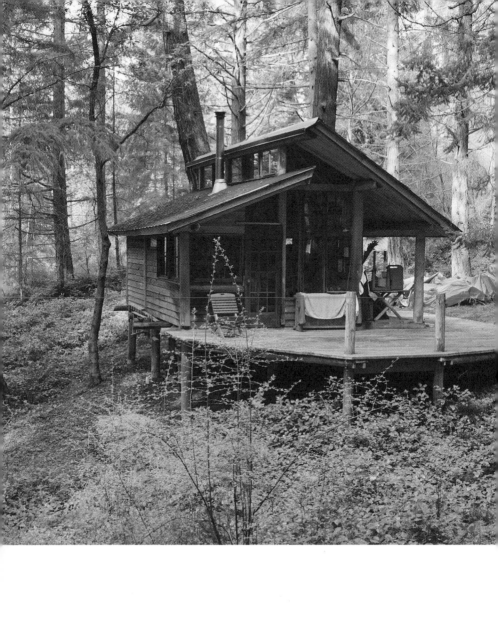

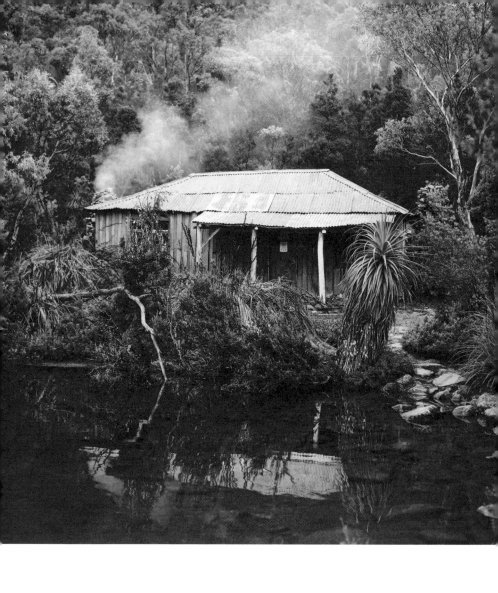

San Juan Island, Washington
CONTRIBUTED BY Kate Barrett

Mt. Field, Tasmania, Australia
CONTRIBUTED BY James Bowden

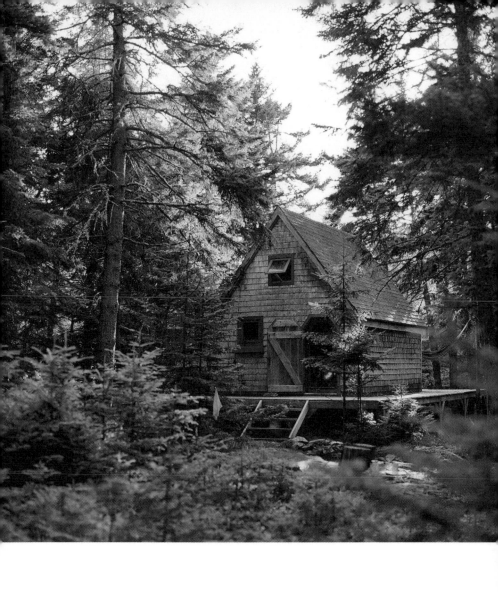

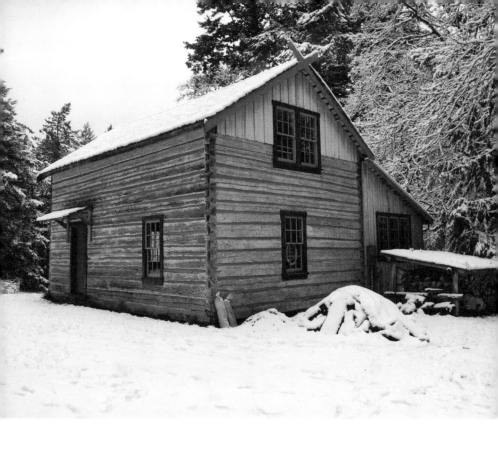

Islesboro, Maine
CONTRIBUTED BY Scott Meivogel

Circa 1880's homesteaders cabin
on Orcas Island, Washington
CONTRIBUTED BY Brittany Cole Bush

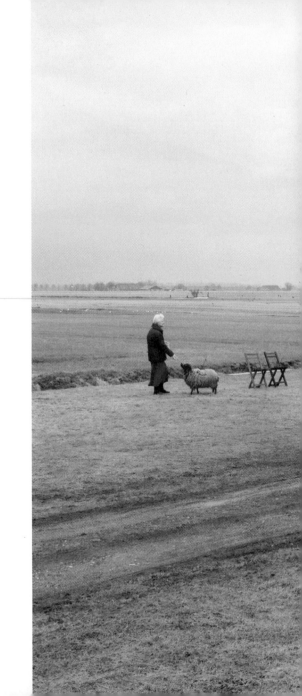

Holiday house in winter, Ten Boer, Netherlands
CONTRIBUTED BY Marieke Kijk in de Vegte

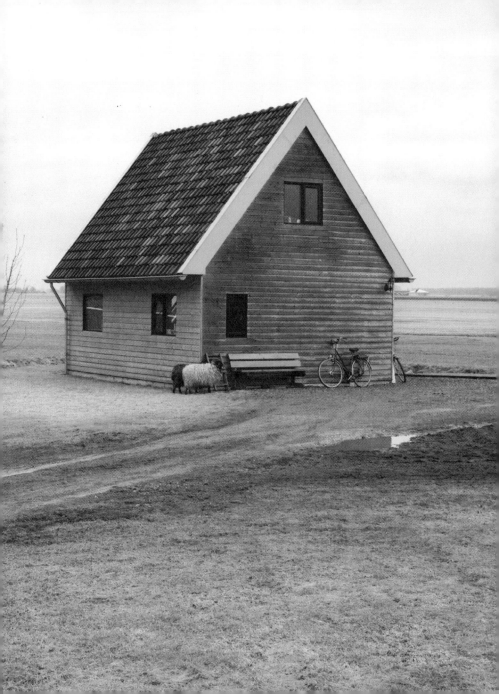

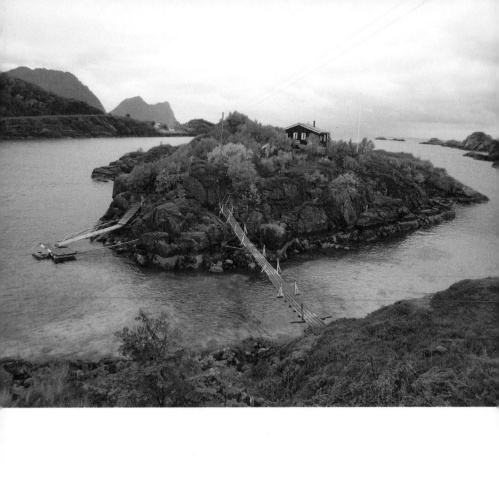

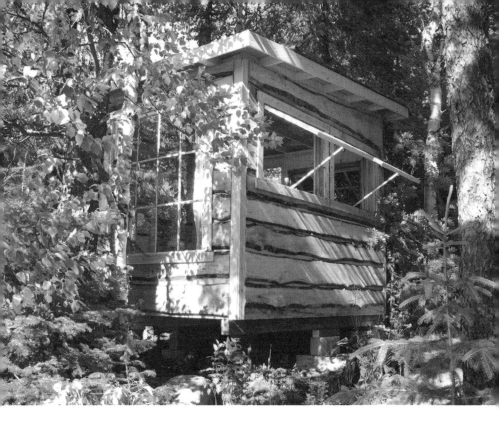

Arctic Ocean near Senja Island, Norway
CONTRIBUTED BY Nicolas Schoof

Cabin built with repurposed windows,
skylight, and palettes for the floor, near
Nellie Lake in northeastern Ontario, Canada
CONTRIBUTED BY Donna Irvine

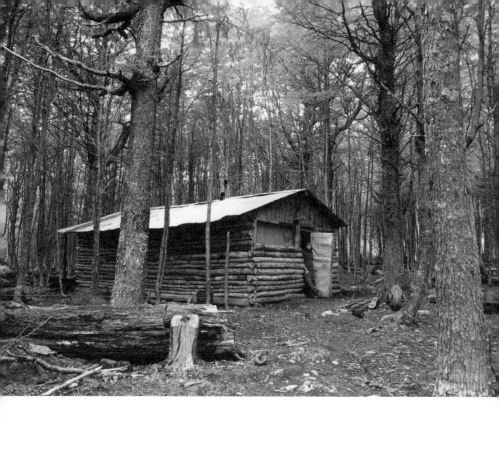

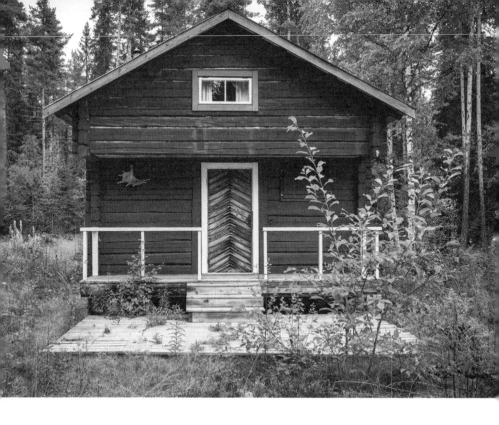

Tierra del Fuego, Argentina
CONTRIBUTED BY Haukur Sigurdsson

Stavselforsen Jämtland, Sweden
CONTRIBUTED BY Kristoffer Marchi

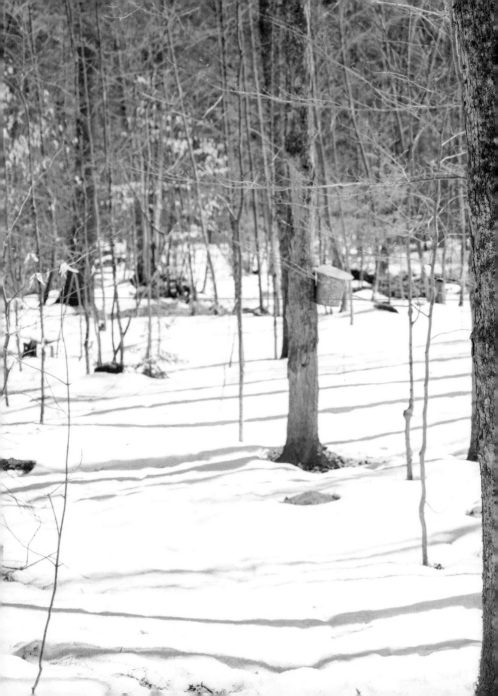

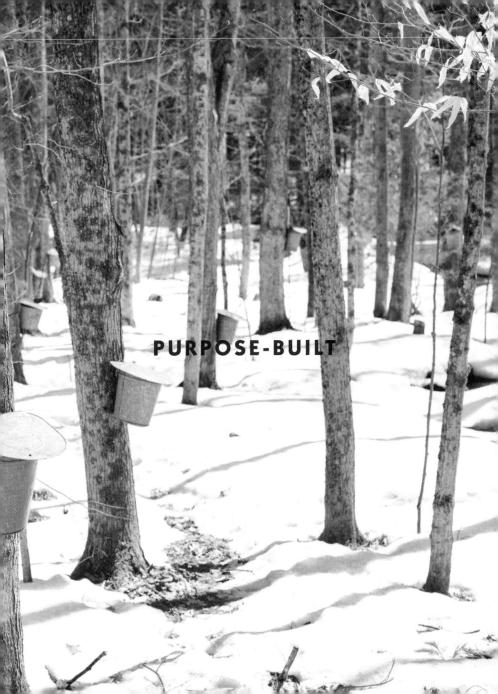

PURPOSE-BUILT

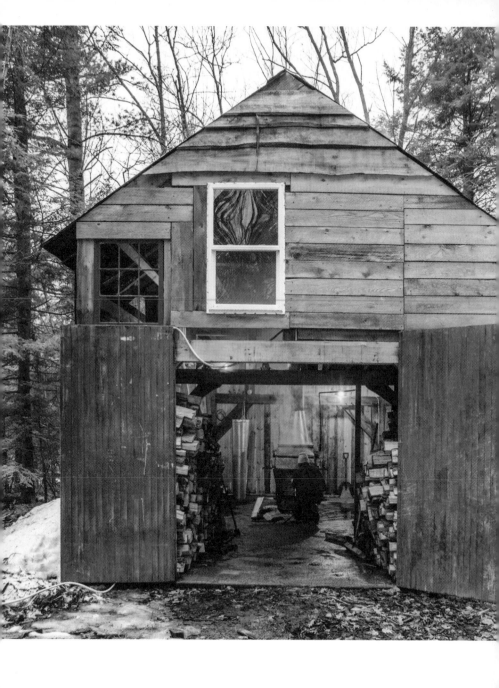

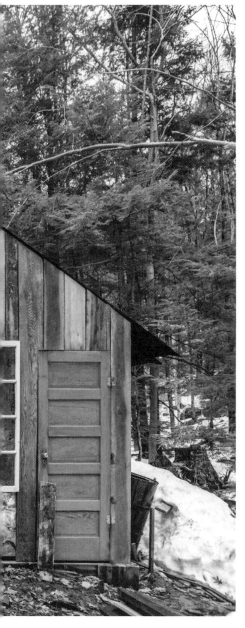

Sugar cabins or *cabanes à sucre* are typically constructed with gabled roofs that open to vent steam.

A team of friends construct
a shanty for boiling sap.

How to Make Maple Syrup

**Bolton Landing,
New York**

Sam Caldwell was nailing up boards as fast as he could. In December 2012, he was determined to finish his new sugarhouse, a 20-by-30-foot post-and-beam structure on a concrete slab with no insulation and one primary function: boiling sap foraged from maple trees. Sam was working into the night in the hills above Bolton Landing, New York, a lakeside town in the northeastern Adirondack Mountains near Vermont. Having grown up there, where an average of 70 inches of snow falls every year, Sam knew he had to get his roof on and walls up before any serious weather came through. Otherwise, he'd have to wait until spring to complete construction, which meant that it'd be a full year—early 2014—before his sugarhouse would produce a drop of syrup. Sam continued hammering.

Sugar cabins, or *cabanes à sucre*, became popular in Quebec, Canada, starting in the early eighteenth century. As is generally the case with structures built for one specific use, sugar cabins share a single dominant architectural feature: a gabled roof, often capped by a cupola, with vents that can be opened to allow steam to escape. Inside, gallons of raw sap are heated in a large metal pan atop a furnace called an arch. As water evaporates from the sap, the sugar concentration increases. The longer the sap boils, the darker it becomes. The process itself is relatively straightforward. The complication is in the timing. Maple trees can be tapped only during a short window in time when the air temperature swings between 40°F during the day and 20°F at night. This delicate freeze-thaw cycle creates a pressure differential between the inside and outside of a maple tree that stimulates the flow of sap. The sugaring season generally starts in early March and lasts for only a few weeks.

To spend time inside a sugar shack is to revel in the change of the seasons and the coming of spring. Friends, neighbors, and family members gather at these shacks to socialize and enjoy the fragrant steam boiling off the sap. "It's a good cure for cabin fever," says Sam, who has been sugaring since childhood (and notes that he doesn't get cabin fever). Back in the early 1980s, he and his older brother, Ruben, started helping their father produce 6-gallon batches of maple syrup. Instead of a shack, the family would congregate in the driveway and burn wood inside a 55-gallon metal drum with a sap pan on top. "For as long as I can remember, we were doing that," Ruben says. "I really liked it at first because when I was little it meant hanging around this fire and cooking marsh-mallows or hot dogs, and getting to stay up late with the adults. But then, like all things, it became work. Like, Oh, great, gotta help Dad carry the buckets. And so we'd have to tromp through the woods and collect sap."

Bolton Landing is a good place for sugaring.

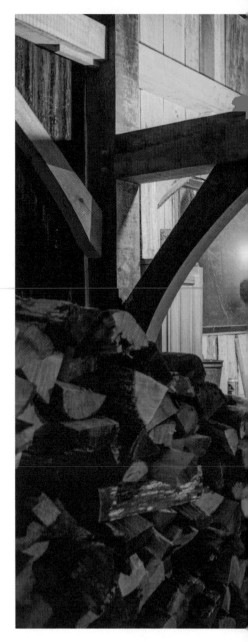

Sam Caldwell examines his arch, a wood-burning furnace used to boil sap from trees.

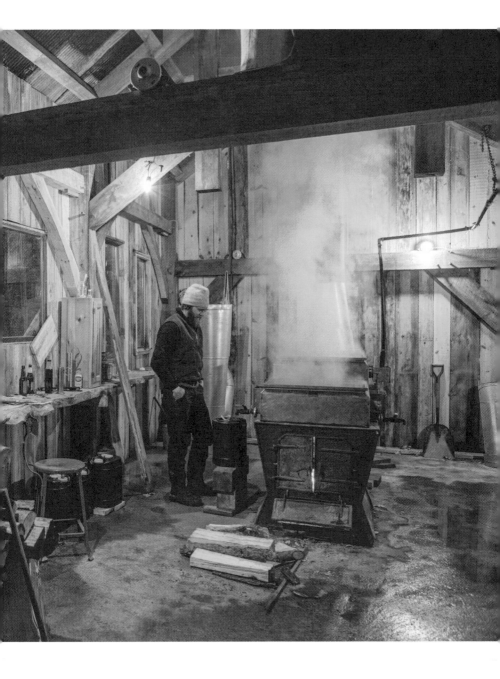

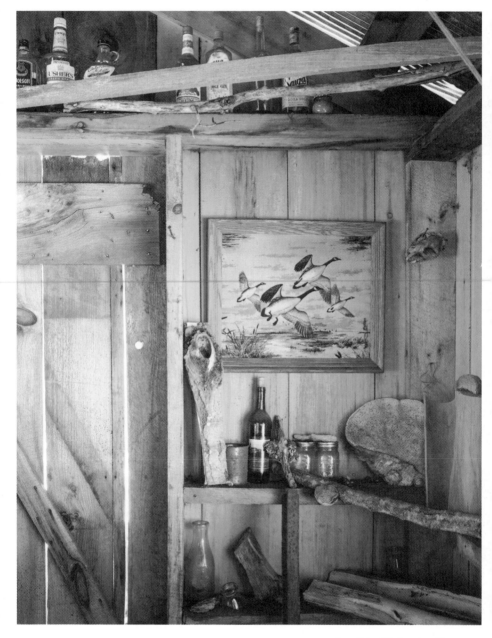

Sam and Ruben Caldwell's great-grandfather
built a 12-by-15-foot sugar cabin in the 1930s.

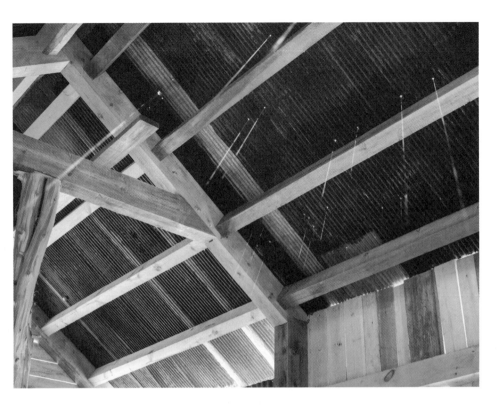

Beyond the weather, the region's rolling forests contain sugar, red, and silver maple trees, three of the most common species used for syrup production. Long before French Canadians began tapping trees, Native American tribes were collecting sap and bartering with maple sugar. Sam and Ruben's ancestors, who settled in Bolton Landing in the 1700s, have been boiling sap since at least the 1930s, when their great-grandfather Harold Bixby built a 12-by-15-foot sugar cabin. Nestled in a sugar bush a couple miles from where Sam and Ruben's parents still live, the shack features an arch and chimney that were hand-built with bricks. Their father used the sugar cabin in the 1970s, but by the 1980s, he'd relocated syrup production to his driveway. In the 1990s, Ruben and Sam helped him build a proper shack on his property. Not long after, an eastern white pine tree fell on Harold's deserted sugar cabin, destroying the entire front end of the building.

Eventually, after returning from college in 2001, Ruben and his cousin James "J" Harrison decided to repair Harold's shack. They wanted to see if they could boil enough syrup to launch their own small-batch syrup label. That fall, they took a chain saw to the felled pine. Then they rebuilt the doors, took down the water-damaged chimney, and added two wooden fold-down benches—one on either side of the shack's interior—which they occasionally used for sleeping. By spring 2002, Ruben and J and their friends were spending long nights boiling in the old shack. That season they made 13 gallons of maple syrup, which were sold locally in bottles labeled BIXBY'S BEST.

Around that time, Ruben was living in an 8-by-12-foot shack with no heat or electricity. He didn't have an e-mail address. His neighbor David Cummings was also living in a shack. Eventually, Sam would

Eastern white pine was used to build the newer sugar shack's frame.

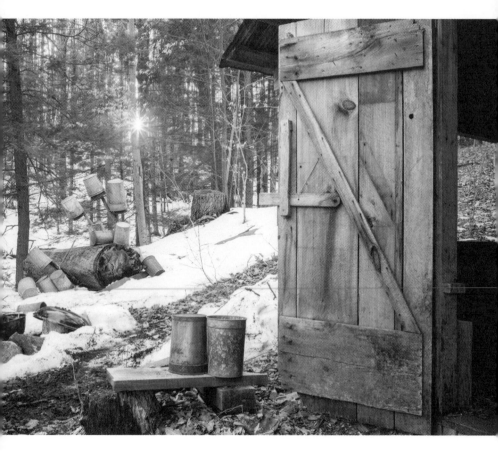

set up one of his own, as well. The friends dubbed their woodsy pocket of Bolton Landing Shack Valley. Throughout the year, they worked carpentry jobs. Every winter, they'd collect sap and make maple syrup. Around 2005, Sam returned to Bolton Landing from Northern California, where he'd been working on a farm. He started doing carpentry and hanging around the old sugar cabin. Huddling inside the shack, drinking cans of Genesee Cream Ale and staying up until dawn with his brother and Dave, Sam started to gain a new appreciation for sugaring. In 2007, when Ruben moved to Brooklyn to work for an architecture firm, Sam took over Bixby's Best. Sugaring became less of a casual hobby. He read articles in *The Maple*

News and attended maple syrup conferences. He learned how to cut back the forest to encourage sap production and how to drill and insert taps—small tubes or spouts that extract and conduct sap—into trees without harming them. In time, he wanted to grow his operation, but he needed an arch that could burn fuel more efficiently. Busting up the old shack's brickwork didn't seem right. "There was a sentimentality of just keeping that whole place as a kind of time capsule," Ruben says.

In 2011, Sam asked Ruben to design a new shack for him. Sam planned to build on a 14-acre plot he'd just bought, which neighbors Dave Cummings's land. Sam wanted a saltbox, a type of frame dwelling much used in Colonial New England that has two stories in front

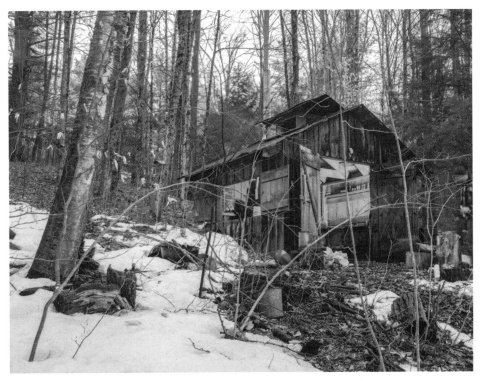

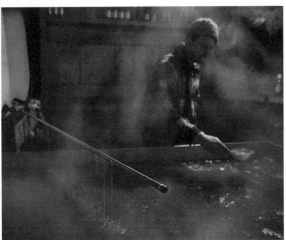

The family's older sugar shack was rebuilt in 2001.

ʟ Dave Cummings filters the evaporating sap.

ᴏᴘᴘᴏsɪᴛᴇ Sap buckets sit idle for most of the year until syrup season arrives at winter's end.

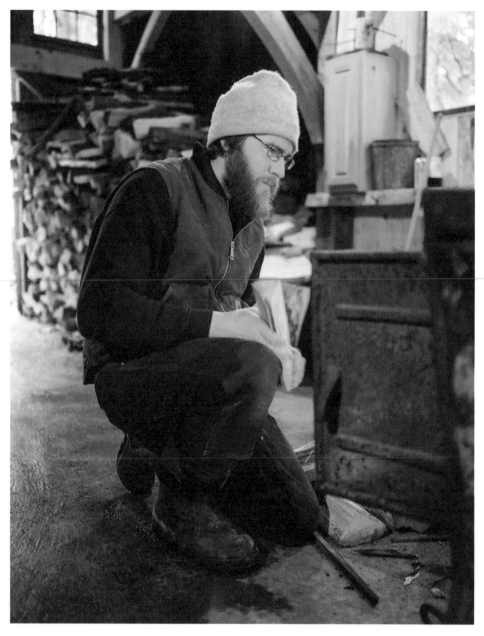

Sam Caldwell was born and raised
in Bolton Landing, New York.

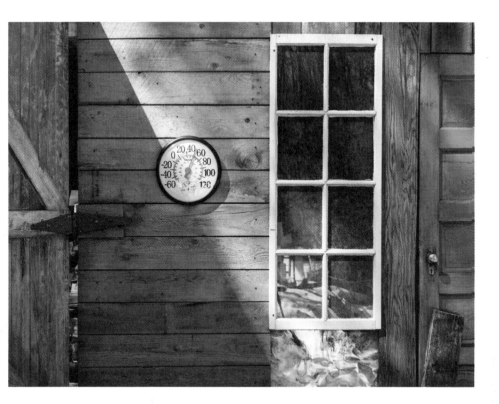

and one behind, with the roof double-sloping so the longer and lower slope is to the rear. Otherwise, Ruben, who completed his master's in architecture at Columbia University in 2011, had free rein. He began sketching and experimenting with abnormal geometry. Ruben wanted the trusses, the structural supports for the roof, to be asymmetrical. "It was more for my entertainment than anything else," he says with a laugh. The rest of the structure had no specific design. Ruben didn't specify where any doors or windows needed to go. The idea was to create an attractive, simple frame that could be added onto and rejiggered over time to accommodate Sam's needs. "Living in a city now," Ruben says, "it drives me completely insane that I don't have access anymore to a space to sort of experiment."

One afternoon in October 2011, Sam, Ruben, their father, and Dave poured the cement foundation, leveled it off, and celebrated with beers. The timber frame's four main bents were assembled using traditional mortise and tenon joints with hardwood pegs. They chose eastern white pine, one of the most abundant fast-growing species found in Bolton Landing. That December, Sam and Dave managed to gather an impromptu group of five or six friends to help them raise the first bents. "We always try to time it so it's appropriate to have a beer afterwards," Dave says. "Otherwise you're not gonna get anyone to help you."

Construction continued, progressing in what Sam calls Adirondack time, meaning slowly. He drove to Vermont and bought a used Small Brothers Lightning arch and a 2½-by-8-foot stainless steel pan. He hauled the gear back to his unfinished sugarhouse, put the rig on the concrete, and covered it with a blue tarp. Sam did another season in the old family shack. As

The door on the far right was salvaged
from an old boathouse on Lake George.

the seasons changed from summer to fall 2012, his desire only grew to get his new sugarhouse to the point where it was at least functional. He continued gathering leftover white pine from his father's sawmill, as well as scrap metal roofing. He found other odds and ends, including an old unused door from his family's boathouse.

By early December 2012, time was running out. They used Dave's tractor to pull up the rest of the frame. From there, Sam did much of the labor by himself. He spent two weeks slapping together the roofing and siding with little thought or planning. After he ran out of boards, he covered a big portion of the façade with a scrap sheet of corrugated metal.

Sam finished, and in February 2013, as the snow began melting and the sap began flowing, he boiled his first batch of maple syrup in the sugarhouse his brother had designed and his friends had helped him build. That year, he ramped up production. He tapped 800 trees—39,200 less than New York's largest maple syrup producer. Bixby's Best continues to be bottled in Sam and Ruben's mother's kitchen. "Making syrup is in our bones," says Sam, who still earns his living as a carpenter. He and Ruben, who is now a partner at Studio Tack in Brooklyn, often talk through ideas about how to reconfigure their shack. "I'm sure if you go back there in a year, it'll look completely different," Ruben says. "That was always the point."

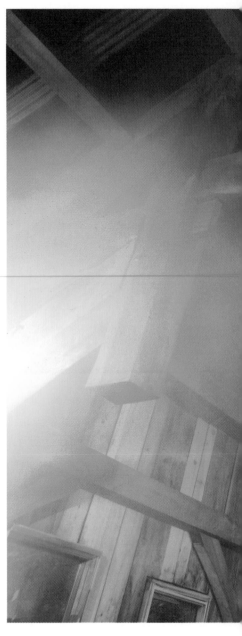

During a maple syrup boil, the column of steam billows out of the venting cupola.

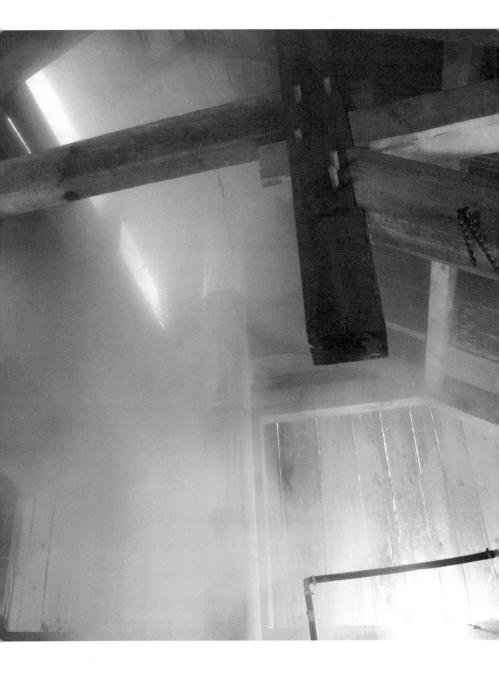

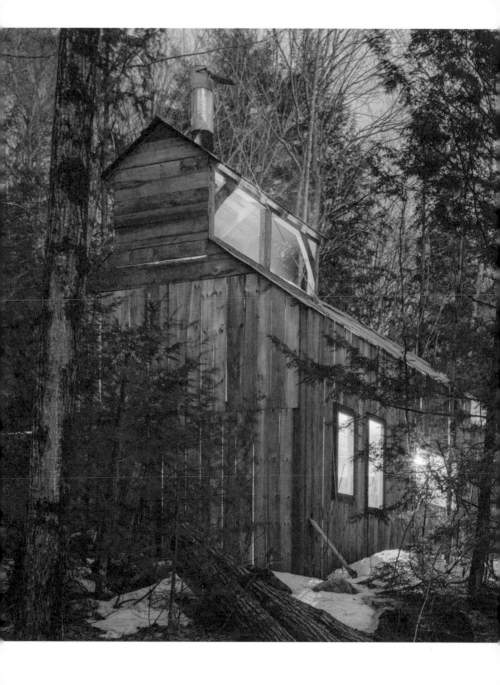

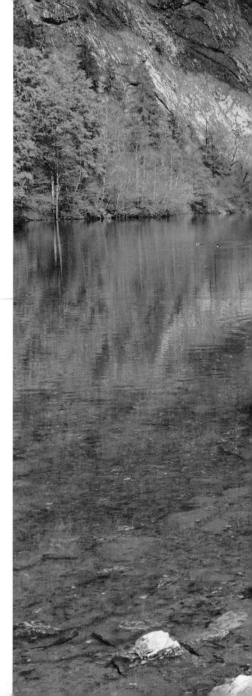

PURPOSE-BUILT

ARCHIVE

Boathouse on the Obersee in Bavaria, Germany
CONTRIBUTED BY Jenn & Willie Witte

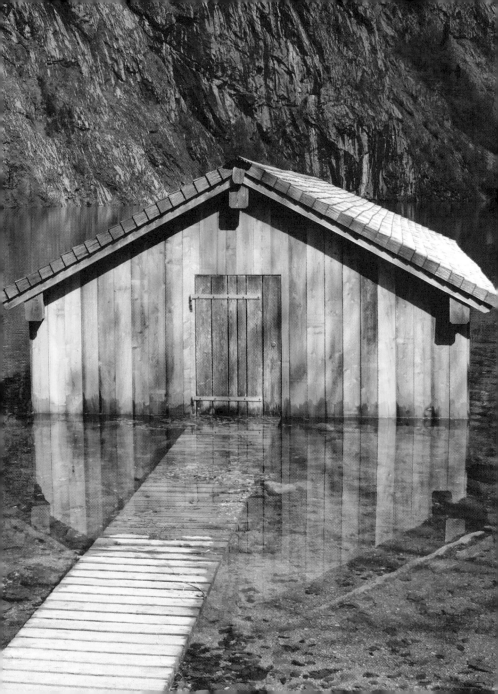

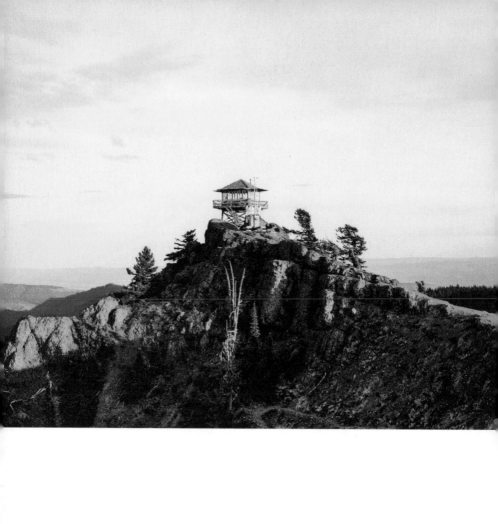

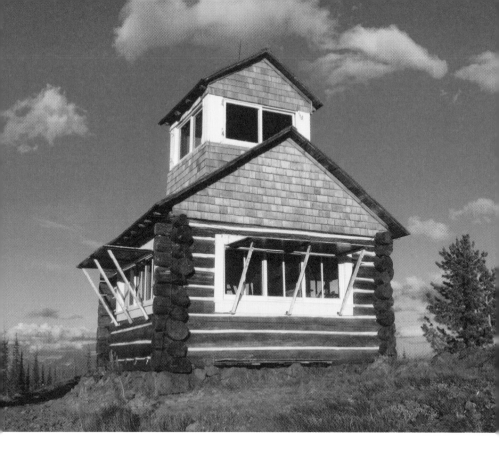

Red Top Fire Lookout in Eastern
Washington. From the Fire Lookout
Project, an attempt to document all 92
remaining lookout towers in Washington.
CONTRIBUTED BY Kyle Johnson

Hornet Lookout, near Polebridge, Montana.
Captured during a ten-day bikepacking tour
of fire lookouts in Idaho and Montana.
CONTRIBUTED BY Casey Greene

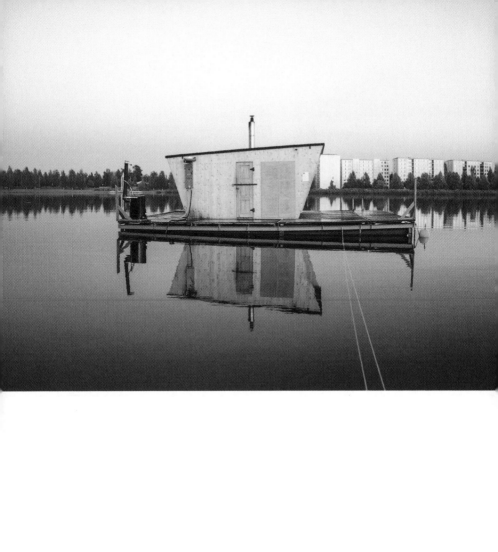

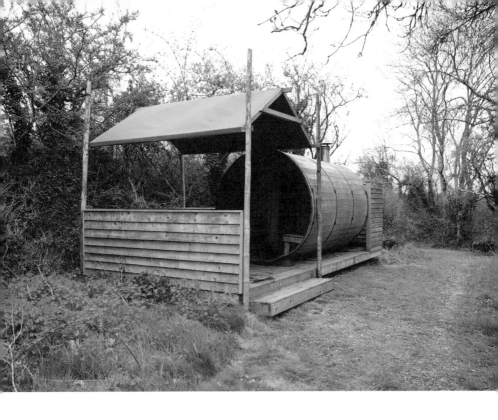

Kesän Sauna, a public sauna on
Tuira Beach in Oulu, Finland
CONTRIBUTED BY Joonas Mikola

Dome and sauna at fforest Camp
near Cardigan, Wales
CONTRIBUTED BY Jonathan Cherry

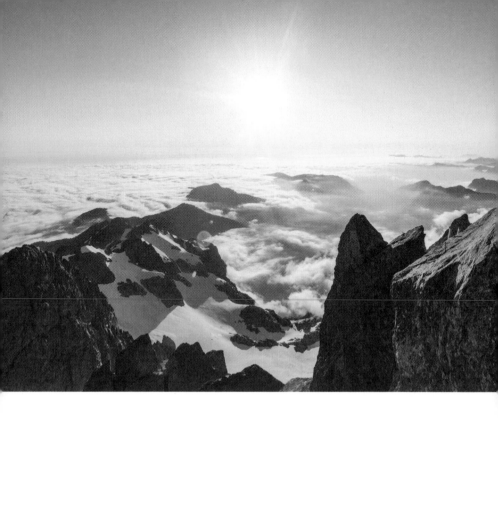

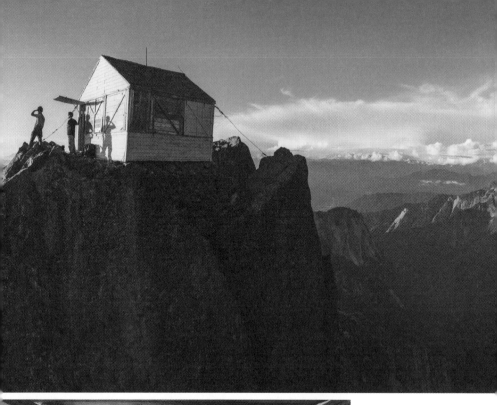

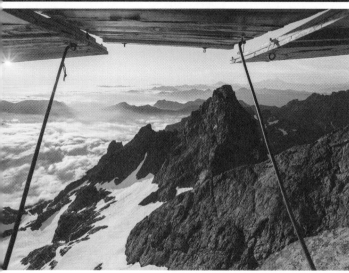

Three Fingers Mountain Lookout,
Boulder River Wilderness, Washington
CONTRIBUTED BY Ethan Welty

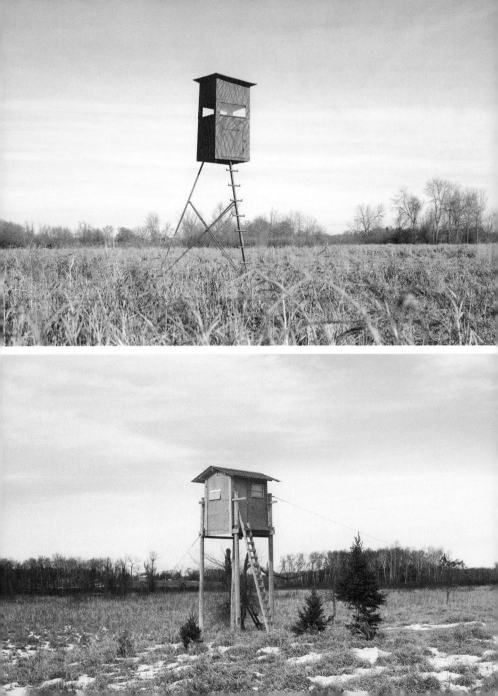

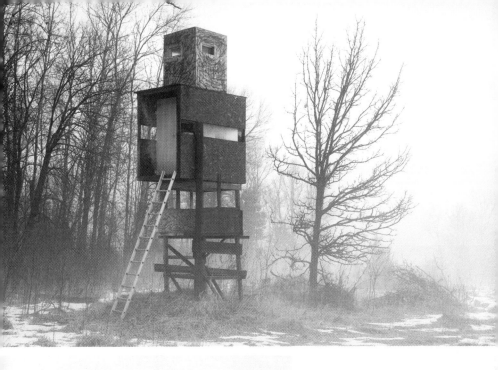

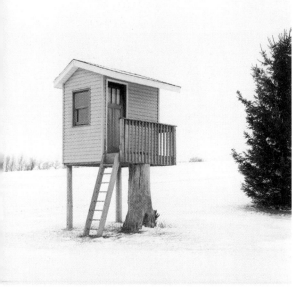

Selections from "Hide,"
a series documenting deer
stands in Wisconsin
CONTRIBUTED BY Jason Vaughn 149 PURPOSE-BUILT

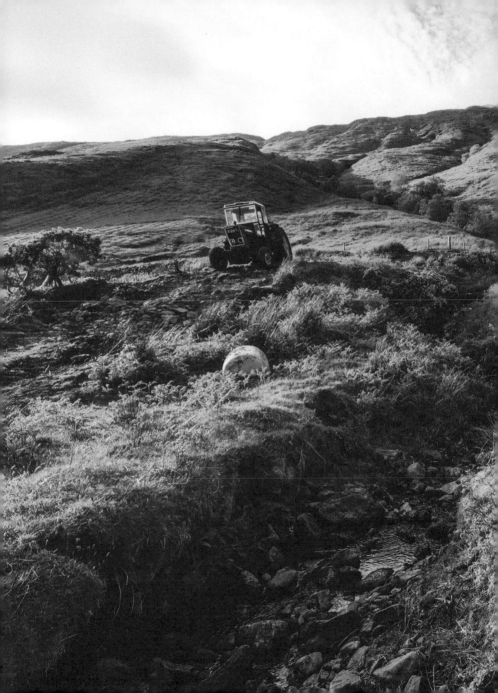

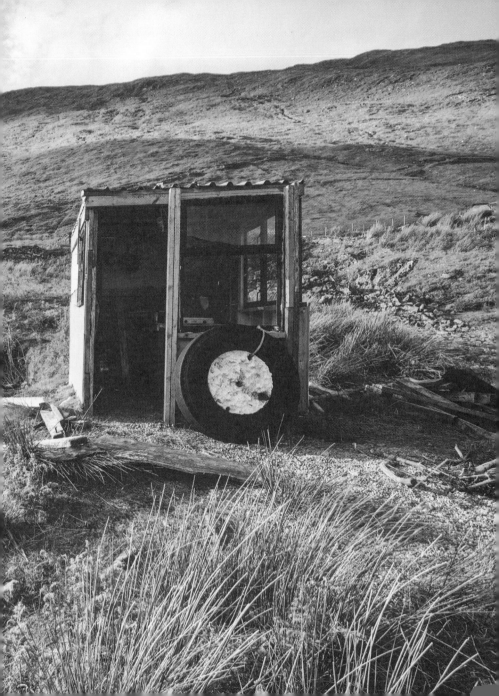

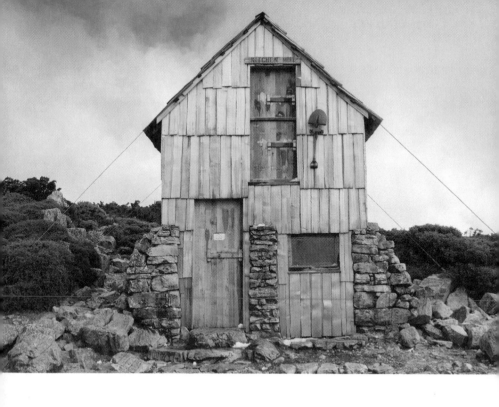

PREVIOUS Fisherman's cabin alongside
Killery Harbour in Leenane, Ireland
CONTRIBUTED BY Stu J. Beesley

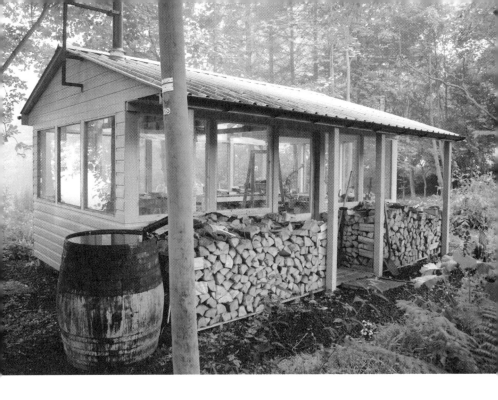

Kitchen Hut, which has been used
by hikers since the 1930s, in Cradle
Mountain-Lake St. Clair National Park
in Tasmania, Australia
CONTRIBUTED BY Jaharn Giles

Glassmount House, an artist's studio,
near Kirkcaldy, Scotland
CONTRIBUTED BY Peter McLaren

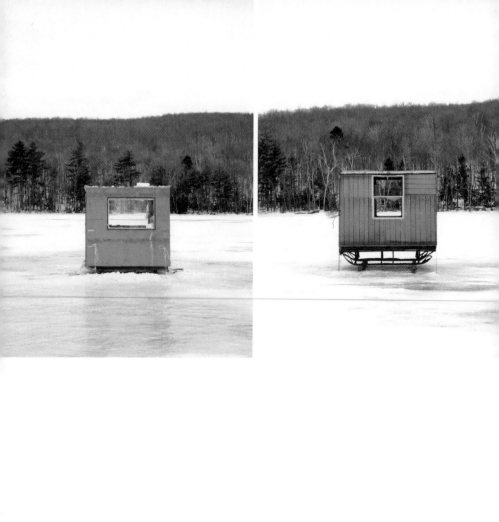

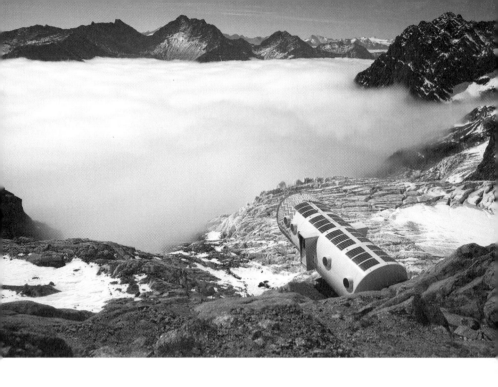

Ice shanties in New England
CONTRIBUTED BY Foster Huntington

Zero impact climber's cabin on Mont Blanc, Italy.
Designed by LEAPfactory.
CONTRIBUTED BY Francesco Mattuzzi

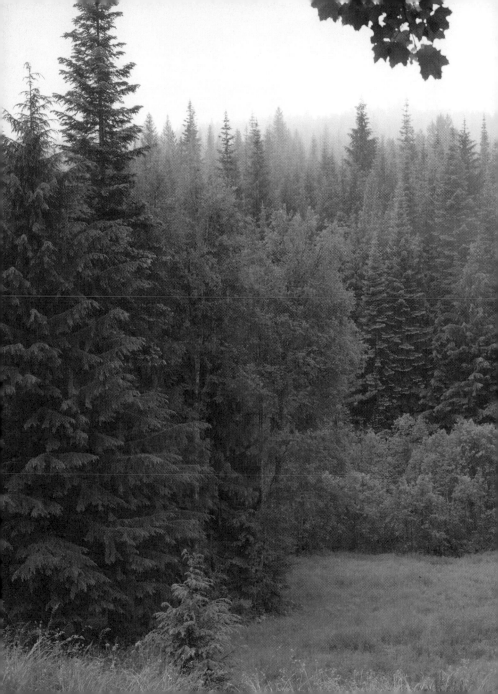

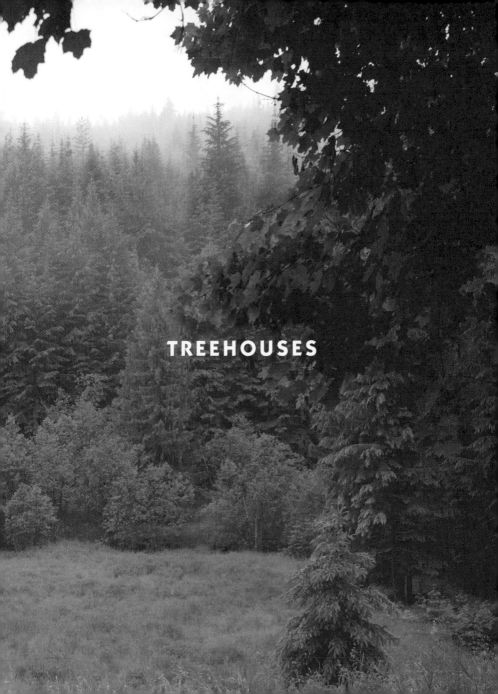

TREEHOUSES

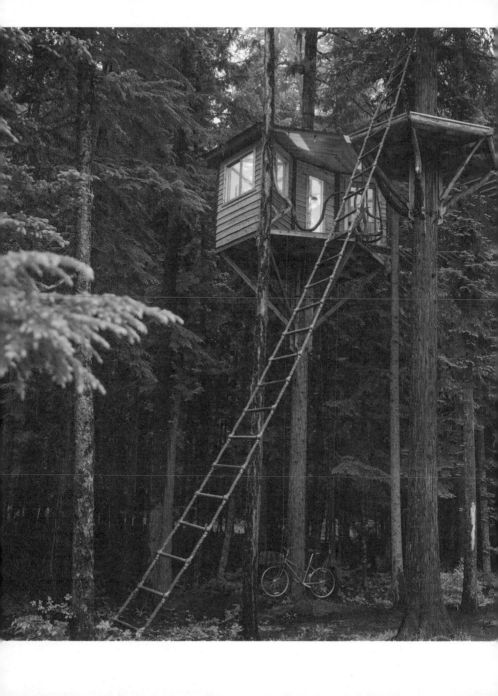

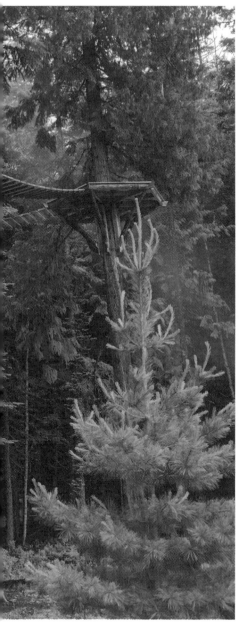

The builder chose western larch,
a strong, slow-growing species.

5

TREEHOUSES

A thrill-seeker engineers
a backyard bedroom.

How to Live
30 Feet in the Air

Sandpoint,
Idaho

Ethan Schlussler laid down his axe. He stood back
and looked at the mammoth pile of firewood sitting on
the hill behind his mother's barn. After four hours of
bucking grand fir, he'd finished splitting enough wood
to last them a month. It was an early afternoon in June
2013, and the summer sun wouldn't be setting until
close to 9 p.m. Now what? Ethan wondered. Glancing
up at the trees, he suddenly remembered that when
he was younger he'd dreamed of building a treehouse.

In 1999, when he was eight years old, Ethan and
his family moved to an 8½-acre plot on the outskirts
of Sandpoint, Idaho, near the Kaniksu National
Forest, a lush 1.6 million acres that spill across Idaho,
Washington, and Montana. Nestled along a creek, the
family's land was full of fragrant evergreens, conifers,
and deciduous trees: grand fir, white pine, hemlock,
western larch, western redcedar, cottonwood, Douglas
fir, Engelmann spruce, and Rocky Mountain maple.

By the time he was ten, Ethan was a proficient
climber. At twelve, he hammered together his first

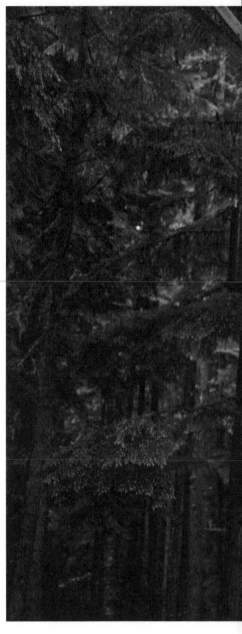

"treehouse," a modest little platform with no walls or roof that still sits 20 feet up in a birch tree near his mother's cabin. The family lived in a two-bedroom A-frame with a corrugated aluminum roof and wood-burning stove. It was cozy but small. So when he was eighteen, Ethan began fantasizing about constructing a separate bedroom for himself in a towering grand fir neighboring the cabin. He grabbed a pencil and started sketching. He drafted a few floor plans but then got distracted and left for college to study photography. When he returned home a few years later, he started working for a local contractor: felling trees, landscaping, renovating homes, and constructing guest cabins. He also helped his mother maintain their forest, which included clearing trees and chopping a lot of firewood.

As Ethan chopped firewood that afternoon in June 2013, he thought about time. It had been five years since he'd abandoned his plans to build a new bedroom. "A lot of people have dreams; then they get a job and have a family. And then they get to be forty or fifty and suddenly realize all their dreams just fell by the wayside. I didn't want that to happen to me," he recalls. "Twenty years from now, I didn't want to be like, Why didn't I ever build a treehouse when I had the chance? I realized I had the time and the energy and the resources. So I just decided right there: Okay, I'm gonna do this."

Ethan walked around, surveying the trees. He climbed a few before settling on a tall, healthy larch. He found his original drawings and started sketching new ones. The experience of working for the local contractor had increased his knowledge of construction. He wanted to avoid drilling holes and inserting bolts into the tree. A common and dependable way to fasten lumber to a trunk, bolting doesn't necessarily

The pedal-powered bicycle elevator is counterweighted by an old black water tank on pulleys (above left).

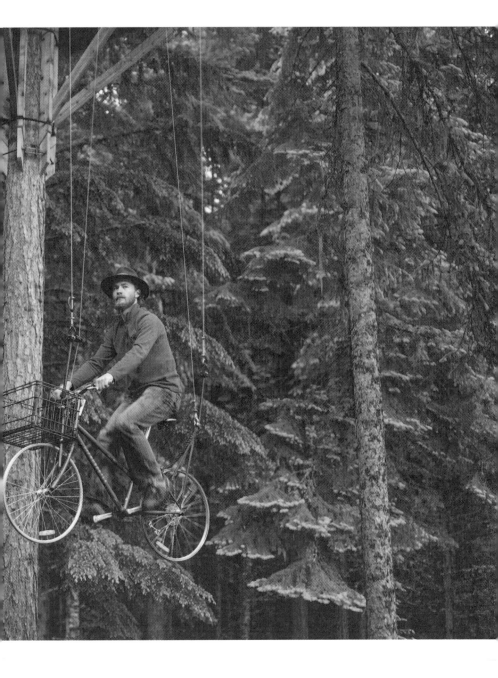

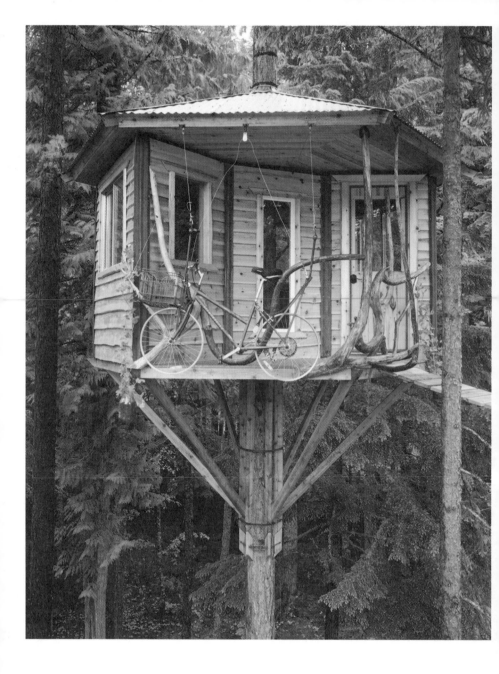

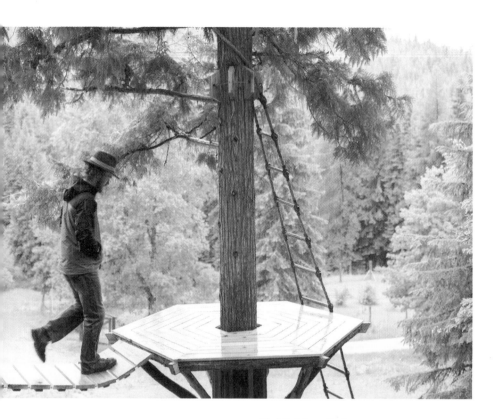

Ethan Schlussler has considered installing rope handrails across the bridges.

OPPOSITE The walls are made from western redcedar, a light wood that's highly resistant to rot.

harm or stunt a tree's growth, but it can. Ethan was determined to find an alternative. He was also determined to engineer something unique. "I intentionally ignored the rest of the world when it comes to treehouses," he says. "I did no research whatsoever. I wanted to build it entirely from my own ideas. I wanted it to feel like it was entirely mine. If you're not looking at a book telling you how to do it, then every possibility is open to you."

That afternoon, he quickly got to work sketching ideas. He devised a clamping system—a series of two-by-fours arranged vertically around the trunk and held in place by a metal cable. With enough pressure and friction, the two-by-fours would stay fixed, at least theoretically. From there, the boards would become an anchor—the skeleton to which he could attach the frame of his treehouse.

Ethan hacked together a small prototype to test his clamp design on a little tree, 3 feet off the ground. He

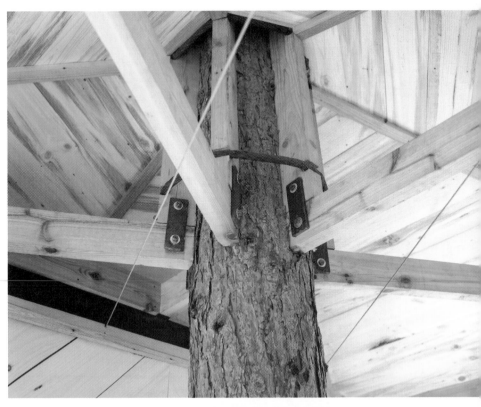

Instead of bolting into the tree, this anchor system is held in place by a thick steel cable that "hugs" the tree.

ʀ The bicycle elevator operates on a pulley system.

ᴏᴘᴘᴏsɪᴛᴇ The door features a spruce branch. The interior siding is made from white pine.

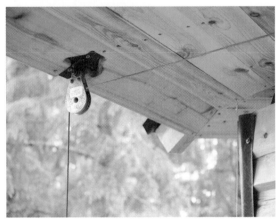

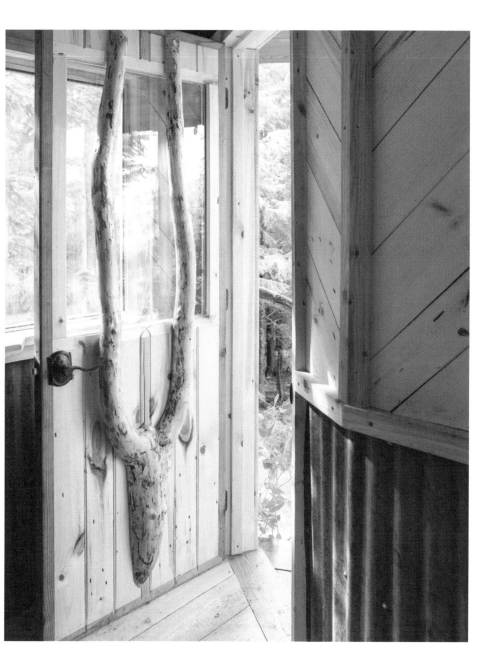

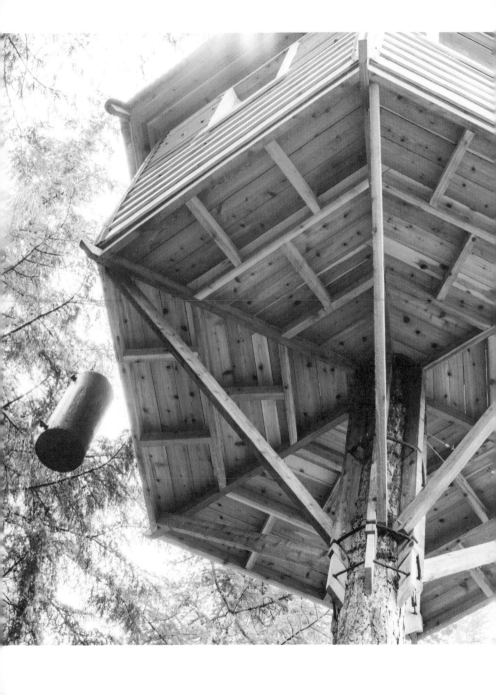

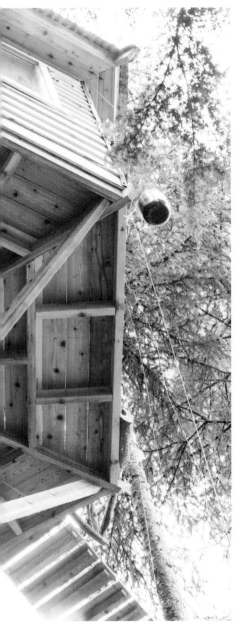

The builder considered a circular floorplan before deciding on a hexagon for its simplicity.

drilled a small hole into each board, threaded the cable through, pulled it tight, and then welded a bolt to the cable ends. The boards didn't budge. So he climbed on top of the boards, hugged the tree, and jumped up and down over and over. The boards still didn't budge.

Ethan returned to his larch. He measured the trunk's circumference and began calculating the specifications for a larger clamp. With the sun starting to dip behind the tops of the evergreens, he moved inside and began drawing floor plans. In time, his design evolved from a circle to an octagon, and then to a hexagon. Fewer sides would make for a lighter, less complicated frame.

For two weeks, Ethan worked his job five days a week from 8 a.m. to 3 p.m. Every afternoon, he'd return home and work on the treehouse until 9 p.m., or whenever it got too dark to work. He borrowed a lumber mill from his childhood friend Aza, who helped him cut some of the boards. Ethan opted for cedar, because it's lightweight, highly resistant to rot, and one of the prettier woods available on his mother's property. He built the clamp and six triangular support braces to hold up the floor and walls. Then he borrowed a 32-foot extension ladder, which determined the height of the treehouse; he simply climbed to the top of the ladder and marked a spot on the trunk. A rock climber and self-described adrenaline junkie, Ethan has little concern for heights.

He slung each of the 60-pound support braces over his shoulder and carried them up the ladder one at a time. He used a ratchet strap to hold everything in place on the tree until he was ready to secure the clamp permanently with logging cable and bolt the braces to it. It took a week of afternoons to get everything installed, then a day and a half to lay the flooring just right. He wanted the floor to echo the treehouse's hexagonal shape. To create the right pattern, he needed to adjust the lengths and angles of the boards gradually. Getting all the angles to match was maddening; every tiny little variation from the previous cut just kept getting exaggerated. On day one of the flooring, Ethan spent more than eight hours in the tree. Without walls or a roof, the treehouse was so light that the platform swayed back and forth whenever he moved. When he got back down on solid ground, he felt seasick.

Once the flooring was finished, he started hosting treehouse parties. Around the edge of his 100-square-foot platform, he constructed a temporary railing. Sometimes six friends would join him to sleep in the tree.

Throughout July and August, the rest of the treehouse was designed on the fly. Ethan built the roof before the walls. He decided to include a porch. Most important, he thought about having to climb that 32-foot steel ladder repeatedly. In three months, he'd already ascended and descended the ladder hundreds of times. His knees were tired. And it was boring. What he needed, he realized, was some kind of elevator. Maybe a small platform with a hand crank and winch? Ethan wasn't sure. He kept thinking.

His friend Aza suggested a pedal-powered elevator. Aza thought it'd look cool to orient the bike vertically with both wheels touching the tree trunk—the cyclist would literally ride up the tree. Ethan thought a horizontal orientation would be easier to build and operate; plus, it'd still look cool to sit on the bike and float upward, almost as if he was defying gravity. He commandeered his mother's old Diamondback and bought five large pulleys and about 150 feet of metal cable. He built most of it in a day and then tinkered

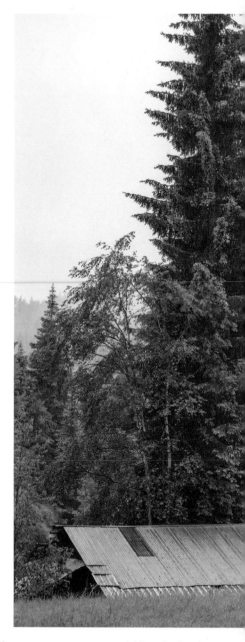

A zip line runs from the treehouse to a Grand Fir by the barn.

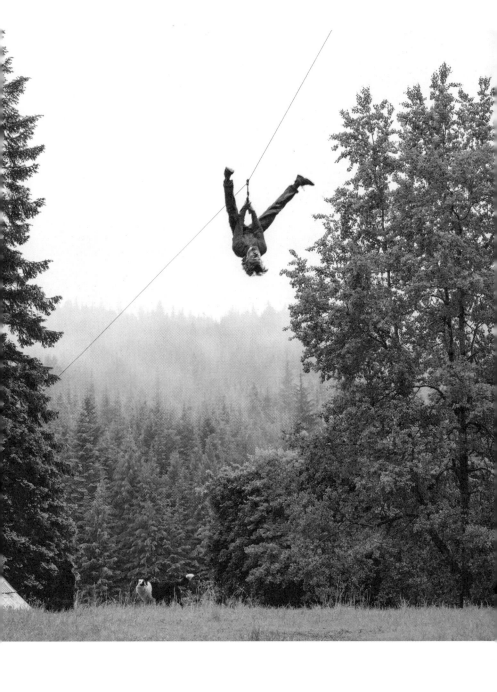

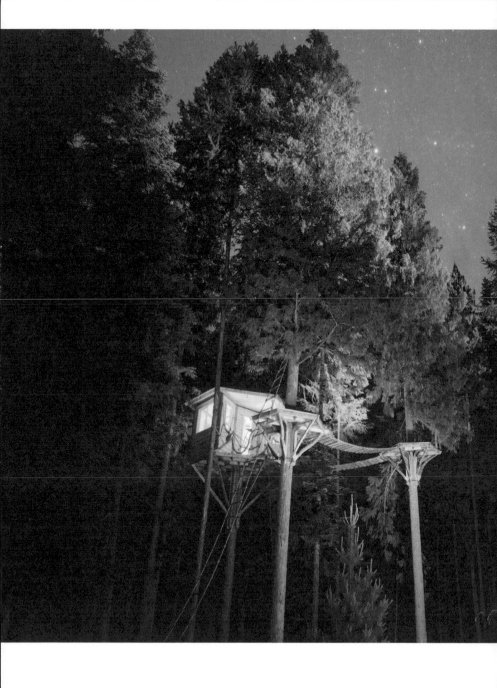

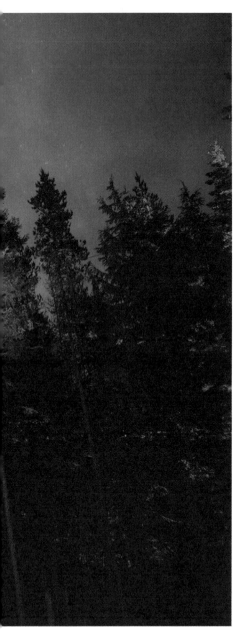

for a week. He attached two cables—one to the front of the frame and one to the back—so that the bicycle wouldn't tip forward or backward. At first, pedaling was exceptionally difficult. So Ethan removed the big sprocket from the crankset and welded it onto the back wheel hub to make the gearing lower. He also found an old water tank sitting in a junk pile along with scrap metal near his mother's garage. He attached the tank to the cabling, figuring that with enough water, it'd be heavy enough to function as a counterweight to help pull the bike up as he pedaled. He was right. It worked.

Watching visitors pedal themselves up into the treehouse is gratifying for Ethan. He knows the elevator adds a sense of whimsy to the whole structure. But he's equally thrilled about his one-of-a-kind clamping system. Although the treehouse has gradually inched down the trunk—2 feet in one year—the structure itself is holding up just fine. Plus, he's made adjustments that have slowed its descent. As the treehouse keeps settling, Ethan believes, the trunk will grow around the clamp, helping to prevent further sliding and keep everything in its right place. "And, you know," he says, smiling, "only time will tell if I was right or wrong."

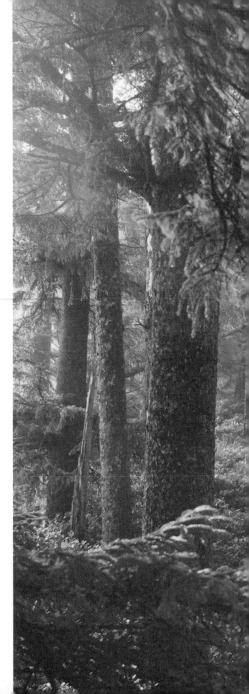

TREEHOUSES

ARCHIVE

Surf cabin on Nootka Island,
Canada
CONTRIBUTED BY Dean Azim

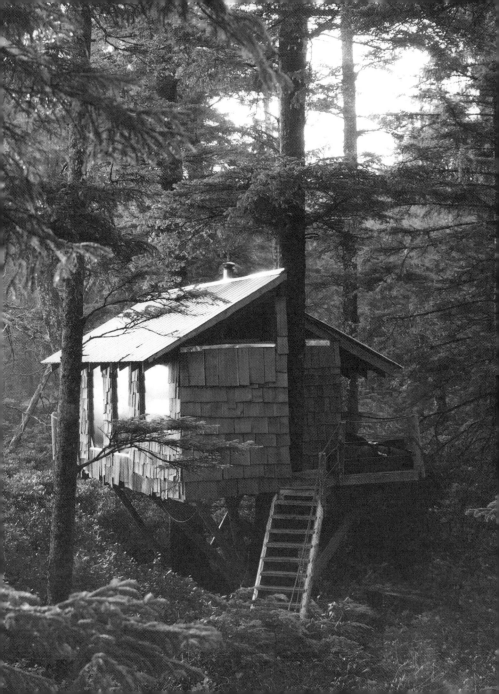

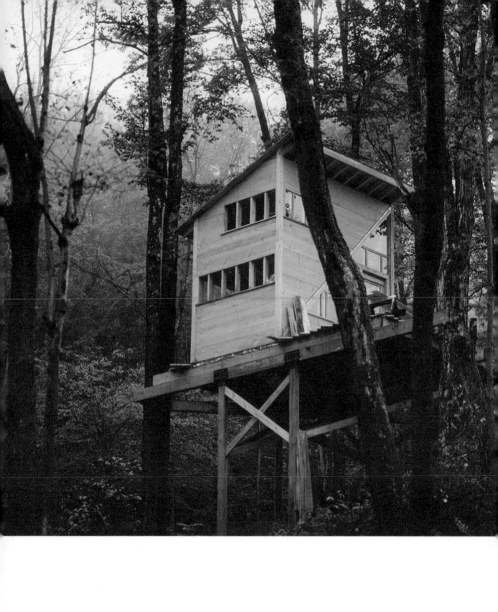

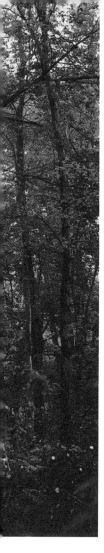

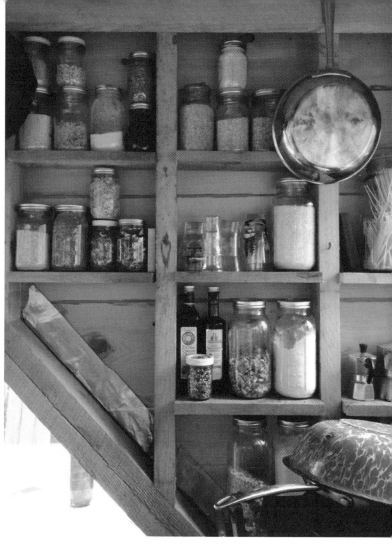

Bovina, New York
CONTRIBUTED BY Kursten Bracchi

Interior, Bovina, New York
CONTRIBUTED BY Linda Aldredge

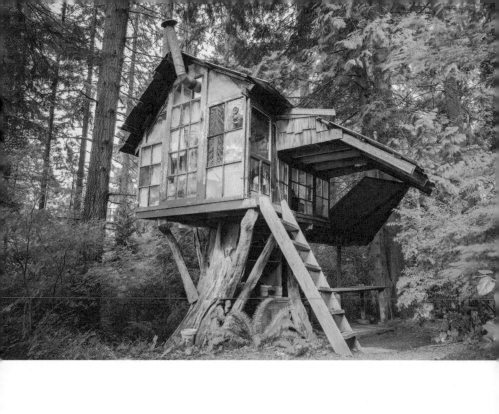

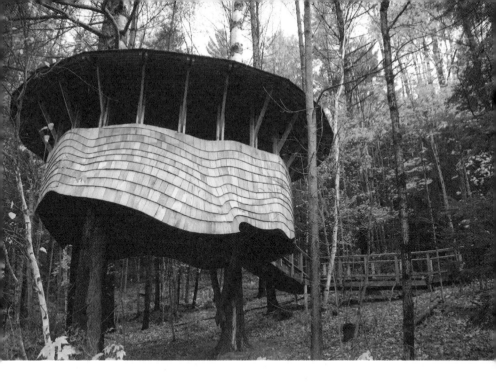

Buster Simpson Treehouse at Pilchuck Glass
School near Stanwood, Washington
CONTRIBUTED BY Alec Miller

YestermorrowDesign/Build School
in Waitsfield, Vermont
CONTRIBUTED BY YestermorrowDesign/Build School

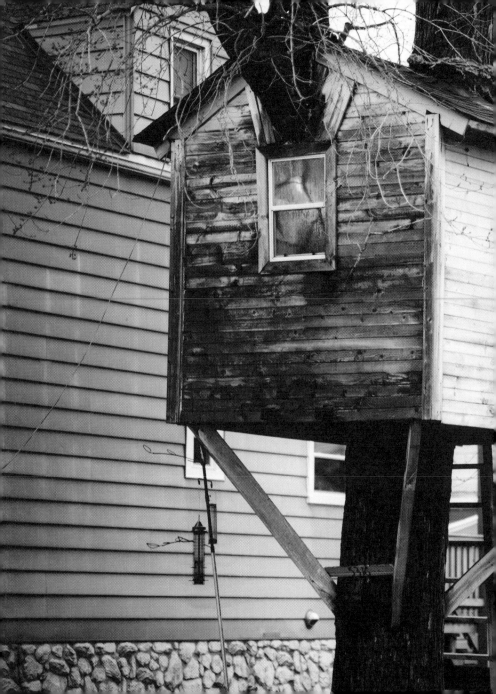

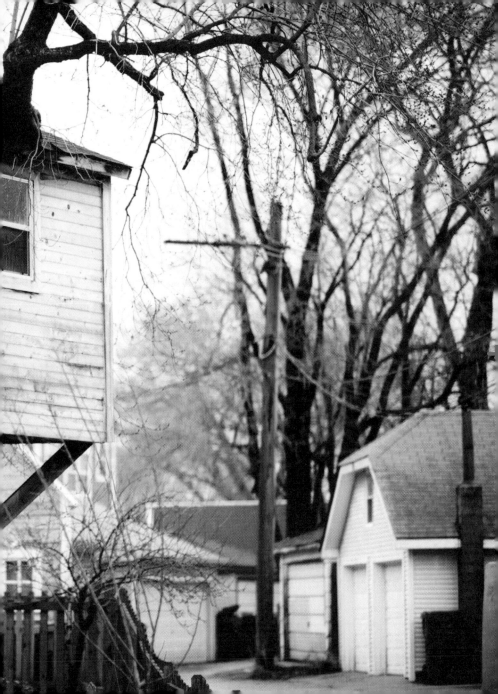

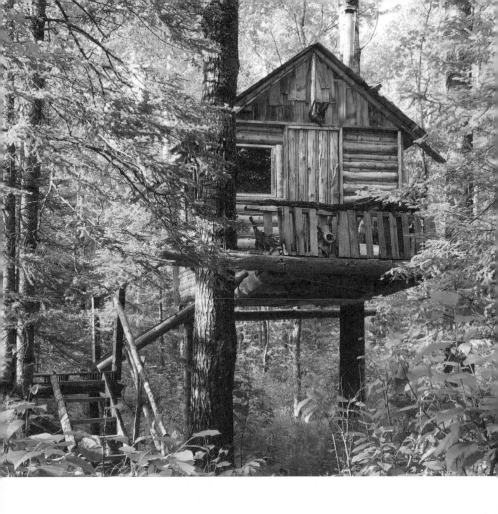

PREVIOUS Bell Avenue in Chicago, Illinois
CONTRIBUTED BY Erik A. Jensen

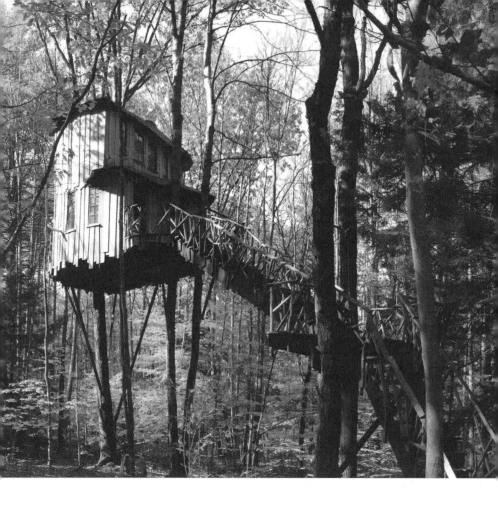

Wynn Kinsley's cabin
in Cotton, Minnesota
CONTRIBUTED BY Katy Anderson

An office and guest cottage with a loft attic,
two small balconies, and a wood pellet-burning
stove in Swanzey, New Hampshire
CONTRIBUTED BY Matt Beckemeyer

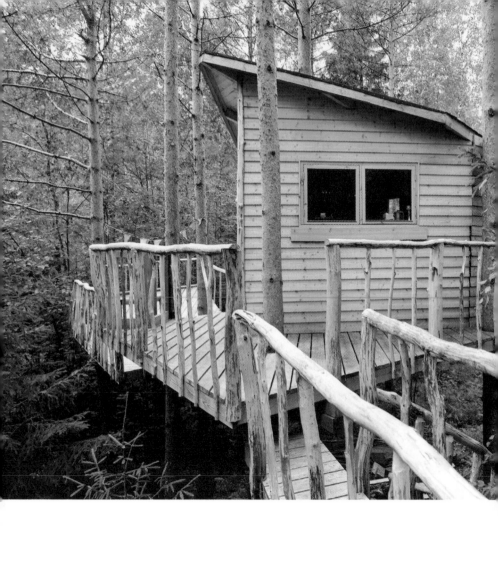

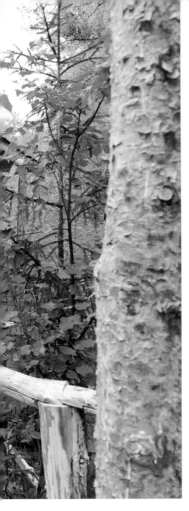

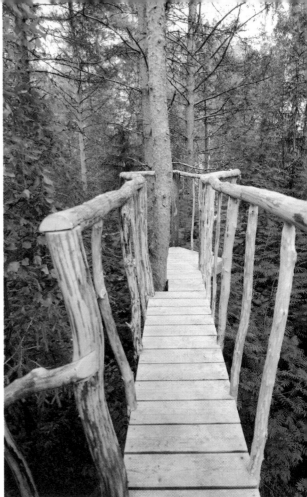

Puumaja, a seven-tree installation in a
forest in the Lakeland area of Finland
CONTRIBUTED BY Andrew Ranville

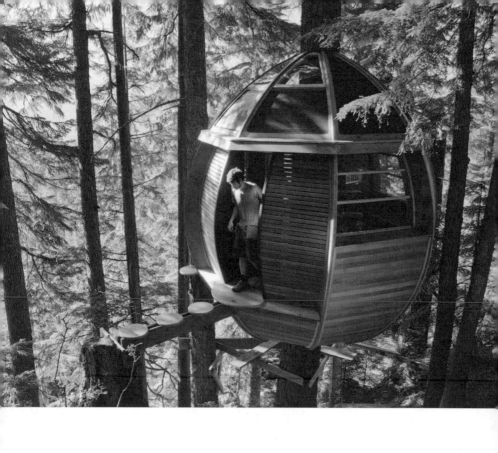

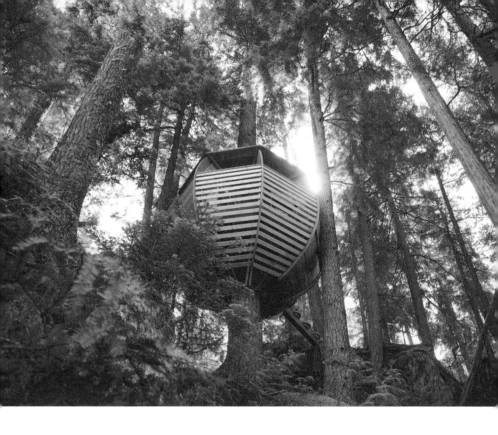

HemLoft, which was constructed primarily
with free materials found on Craigslist,
in Whistler, British Columbia, Canada
CONTRIBUTED BY Joel Allen

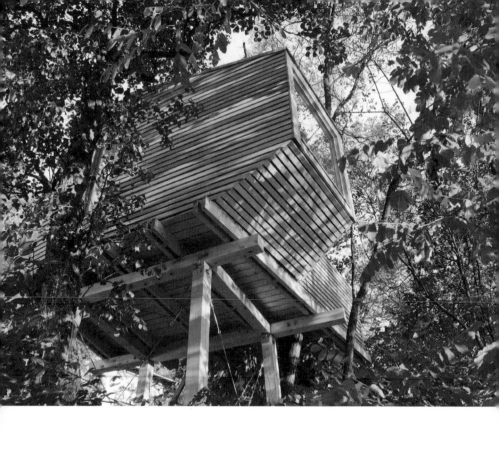

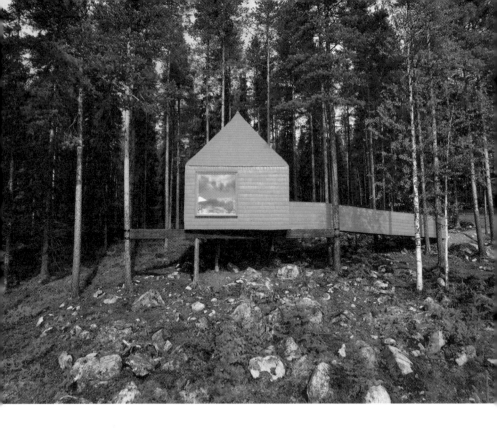

Lukovica, Slovenia
CONTRIBUTED BY Rok Pezdirc

Little Red Treehouse in Norrbotten,
Sweden, at the Blue Cone Treehotel
CONTRIBUTED BY Peter Lundström/WDO

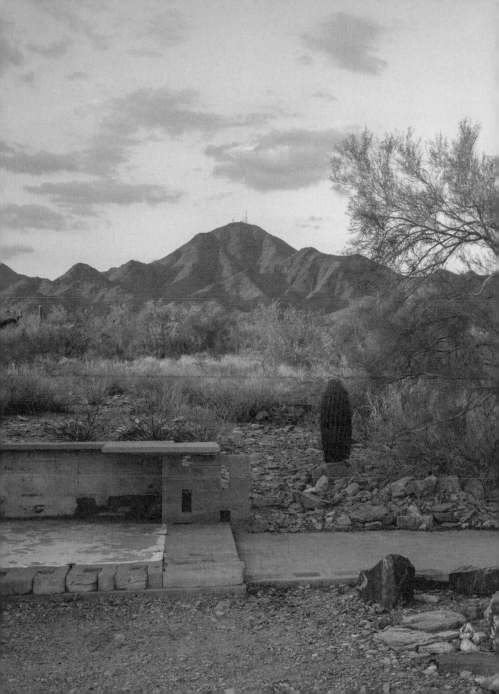

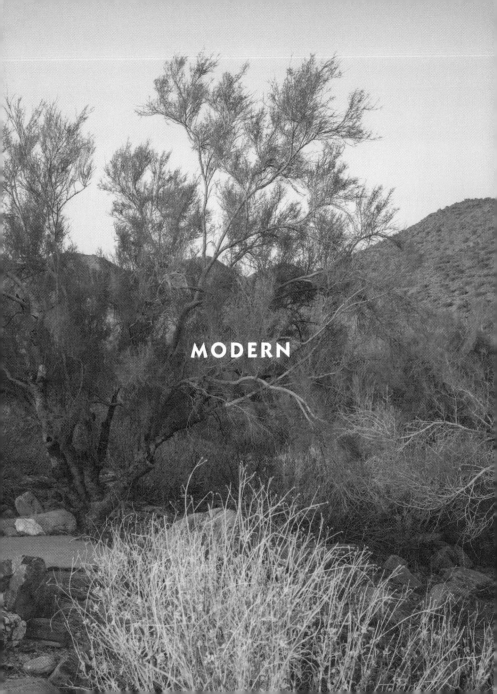

MODERN

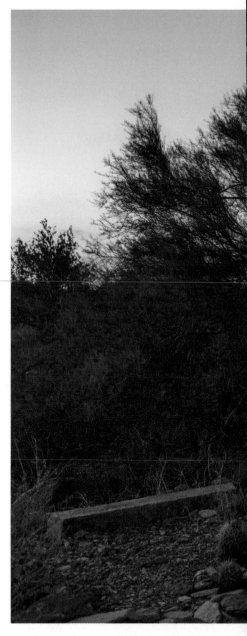

6
MODERN

An architecture student
continues a legacy in the desert.

How to Build
a Simple Shelter

Scottsdale,
Arizona

The heat was unforgiving. Beads of sweat descended
Dave Frazee's forehead. He was alone on foot, explor-
ing a 500-acre swath of desert along the northeastern
edge of Scottsdale, Arizona. As the afternoon temperatures climbed, Dave couldn't believe it—somehow
he'd forgotten to carry water with him. Born and
raised in the suburbs downriver of Detroit, Dave had
never been to the desert. So in the fall of 2007 when
he arrived in Scottsdale to attend Taliesin West, an
architecture program founded by Frank Lloyd Wright,
twenty-one-year-old Dave wasn't just underprepared;
he was anxious. "I thought there were snakes and
scorpions everywhere," he recalls. "It was like, This
is crazy. I can't believe I'm gonna live out here."

In 1937, Wright purchased the rugged, undeveloped land and built himself a winter home with a
drafting studio sizable enough to accommodate a
dozen apprentices, the beginnings of a campus in the
desert. Wright and his students would spend part of
the year at his compound in Wisconsin and the rest

Dave Frazee spent more than two
years designing and building his
shelter in Scottsdale, Arizona.

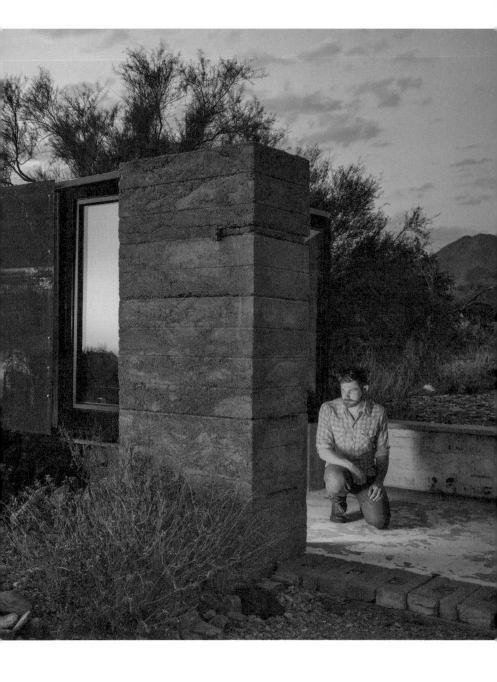

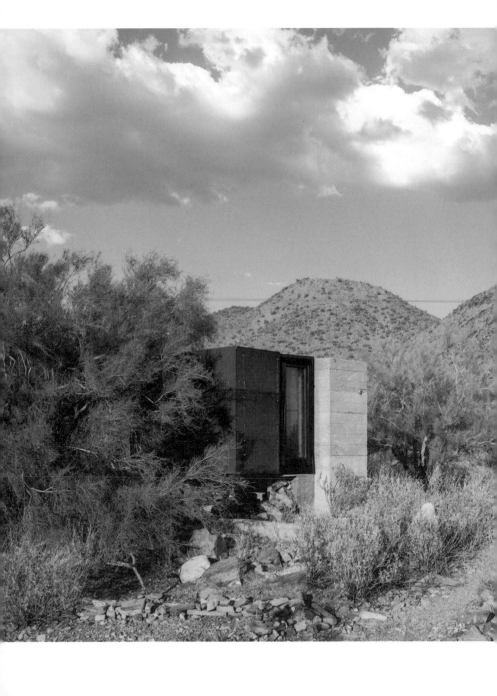

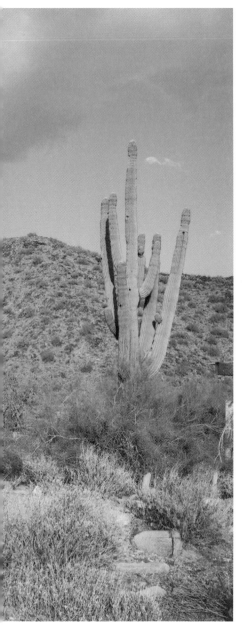

Cold-rolled steel was chosen for strength, durability. Also, the rusting patina resembles the desert's red rocks.

in Scottsdale. Instead of dorms, students at Taliesin West camped in tents. In keeping with Wright's affinity for patterns and his ethos of "organic architecture"—in which a building exists in harmony with the natural environment—the architect originally designed a campsite to be composed of three triangular concrete pads (one per tent). Over the years, dozens of campsites were set up throughout the property and connected by a network of dirt footpaths lined with stones. Instead of triangles, Wright's tent-bound apprentices decided on using square concrete pads.

In time, his students would conceive and build their own more semipermanent shelters at the campsites. After Wright died in 1959, the program soldiered on. For nearly eighty years, the shelter ritual has endured at Taliesin West. There are now approximately 80 campsites, where students continue to test a range of forms and materials. While many of the experimental structures are intact, several have been torn down to recycle materials and clear space. If you walk the desert, it's easy to stumble upon the decayed remnants of old structures.

As the sun beat down on Dave that afternoon in 2007, he looked up toward the horizon and spotted a white chimney in the distance. The 7½-foot chimney was situated beside a palo verde tree and a concrete pad with a pair of foot-high white brick walls, and nothing else. Dave surmised that the chimney's concrete had probably been mixed by hand and poured on-site in sections, building up the chimney mass slowly over time. Jutting out between two sections of the concrete was a broken sheet of corrugated metal, which had likely been a roof. Dave sat there all afternoon observing and wondering—not realizing what the dry desert heat was doing to his body. That evening, after waking up feverish and nauseated in a

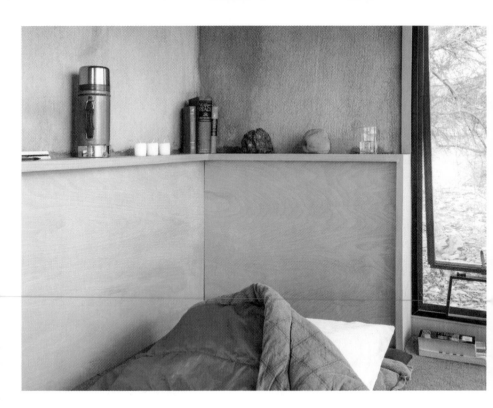

temporary bedroom near Taliesin West's dining room, he was rushed to the hospital and treated for dehydration.

Dave wasn't disheartened. A week later, he walked back out into the desert—this time with water—and built a small fire in the chimney. He was transfixed. Soon after, he started sketching ideas for a shelter that would make use of the chimney. His first draft was literally a pile of rocks—the desert's version of a log cabin, as Dave saw it. During study breaks, he would hike up into the nearby mountain range and gather volcanic black rocks, which he'd hand-carry one or two at a time, a half mile to the chimney. Dave did his collecting quietly. He hadn't yet asked for permission to develop the site. After one month, he'd amassed a pile of thirty rocks.

Then, during a lecture on desert ecology, one of his professors explained that moving even one rock in the desert could have an environmental ripple effect on the surrounding flora and fauna. Dave decided to press Pause on his shelter. He figured he had a lot more to learn. Growing up, he'd spent summers doing rough carpentry, framing houses, and learning masonry and roofing with his brothers-in-law. He understood how to build things. But he needed to improve his understanding of design. So he focused on his studies. For the next two years, during his semesters at Taliesin West, Dave kept returning to the chimney. He'd sketch possible shelters, light bonfires, or just sit and observe the desert. Sometimes he'd set up a cot beside the chimney and crawl into his sleeping bag for the night. Other times, he'd camp nearby, unfurling a yoga mat across the roof of his silver Jeep Liberty. Any sense of elevation—of being lofted above the desert floor away from scorpions, snakes, and pack rats—appealed to Dave.

In October 2009, when he advanced into the graduate program at Taliesin West, Dave felt he was ready to

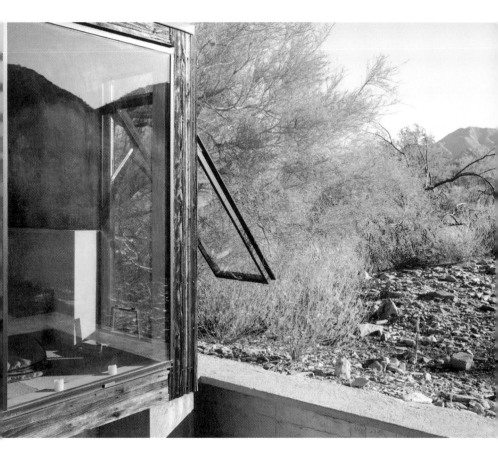

undertake designing a proper shelter beside the chimney.
He began researching the site's history. He wanted to consider the intentions of the previous architects rather than
dominate the site with his own independent scheme. "The
beautiful thing about architecture is there is a constant
dialogue *inside* the work itself," he says. "You don't have
any choice but to embrace that."

Dave mentioned his obsession with the chimney to
one of his mentors, Aris Georges, a professor at Taliesin.
As it turned out, when Aris was a Taliesin student in
the 1980s, he'd also fallen in love with the chimney site.
Aris explained that he was the one who'd laid a second
concrete slab for the patio and re-created some of the
L-shaped concrete blocks to extend one wall. But as Aris

Custom windows, which open wide,
remind the builder of a spaceship.

OPPOSITE Birch plywood shelves were
given a light stain.

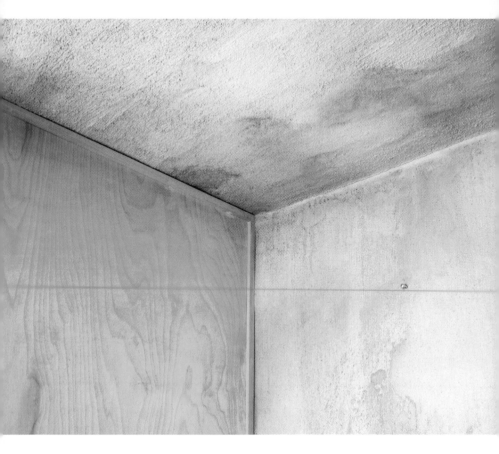

The builder dressed up two rough materials: plywood was coated with a light natural stain, and Durock was resurfaced with plaster.

OPPOSITE The concrete chimney dates back to the 1950s.

confessed, like many students, he'd gotten sidetracked on his graduate thesis and never completed the project. Dave became inspired to finish. He and Aris dug deep into the school's archives and found a few old slides of the original site. They discovered that the shelter was originally built by Aubrey Banks, a Wright apprentice who'd arrived in 1952. At some point, there had been a sheet metal roof extending from the chimney, attached to two steel columns embedded in the pad. Banks had intended to create a dual indoor-and-outdoor patio space.

Dave sketched a new shelter based on that original design. But simply reconstructing another architect's shelter didn't excite him. He did a geometric study of the original site and chimney. He broke down the proportions

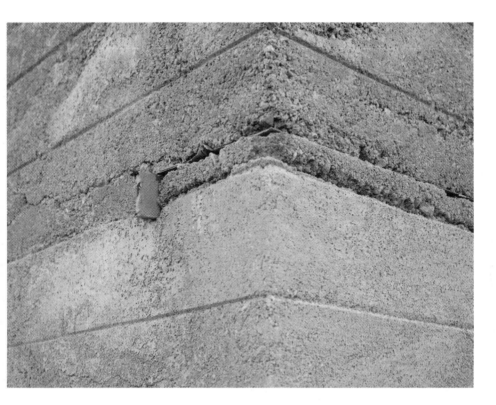

of each element, examining the individual shapes of the chimney, the pad, and the walls. Then he started sketching each of those forms and playing with their scale. He worked through hundreds of drawings, ultimately arriving at five main designs, which he drew both by hand and as computer models. He was particularly fond of one design, in which the entire patio was encased in free-cut glass with a sheet metal roof. He wanted to give occupants the illusion of being in the desert, but with the comfort of being protected from the elements.

He stared at the design. Something didn't feel right. Dave wanted to channel Wright's idea of *eliminating the insignificant.* "During that time, I was studying his Usonian houses, and I spent a lot of time in the archives," Dave says. "It started to really sink in that Wright would give himself so much information, and then he would just start pulling it all, removing it and taking the design back down to the bare essentials." So Dave began trimming back the

roof, allowing more and more of the patio to remain outdoors. Eventually, he stripped down his entire design into one "sleeping box" just large enough to fit a queen-size mattress.

In early 2010, he started scavenging for materials in Taliesin West's "boneyard," an outdoor space where students discard leftovers from other builds. He picked through piles of rusted, beat-up tube steel and set aside four 12-foot pieces, which he stashed at the workshop on campus. That February, he and a friend welded together a box frame using a 5-by-9-foot piece of sheet steel. Dave intended to weld the box frame to metal plates he embedded in one of the original brick walls. The sleeping box was supposed to float, cantilevered out from the wall. But he hadn't considered that the gauge of the box's steel was thinner than the plates. The acetylene torch kept melting holes into the steel. Had he used a MIG welder, he would've been

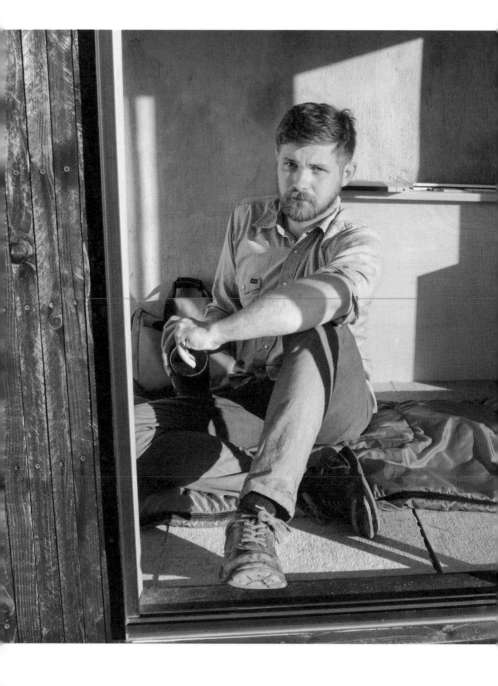

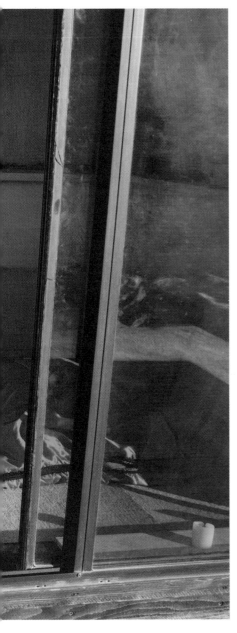

Dave Frazee designed a
floorplan just large enough
for a queen-size mattress.

able to dial back the heat to the right temperature. However, that would have required more power than their portable generator could handle. Dave had no choice but to bolt his box to the plates in the wall and weld two steel posts to the opposing side of the box.

In March 2010, he started sleeping on the platform. He'd lie there watching the stars, questioning his design, wondering if he'd made a mistake by adding the posts. Some of his professors felt he had screwed up. Dave knew the posts were a big aesthetic compromise, but he was determined to push on. In a matter of weeks, he'd be leaving Scottsdale to return to Taliesin's Wisconsin campus. That was why he chose to frame out the sleeping box using two-by-fours and plywood—he knew he could get it up fast. He and a friend assembled the frame in one week. He drove to Habitat for Humanity's local ReStore and bought one sliding glass window for $300. He salvaged two more pieces of glass from the boneyard. He applied white roof (a heavy-duty liquid polymer coating) and added black flashing and drip edge to protect the roof from rain, then wrapped the plywood in roofing felt (a heavier-duty, more expensive moisture barrier than Tyvek). With everything in place, he crossed his fingers and hoped for the best.

Seven months later, in October 2010, Dave returned to find the sleeping box intact. During his time in Wisconsin, between sessions of course work, he continued thinking about the shelter. He'd settled on using fifteen sheets of 1/8-inch steel as a finishing on at least part of the exterior. The thickness was overkill (each sheet weighs about 30 pounds). But Dave knew the steel wouldn't warp, bend, or budge after exposure to the harsh sun. He wanted his shelter to survive the desert. Although cutting such thick steel would be too complicated for him to do by himself,

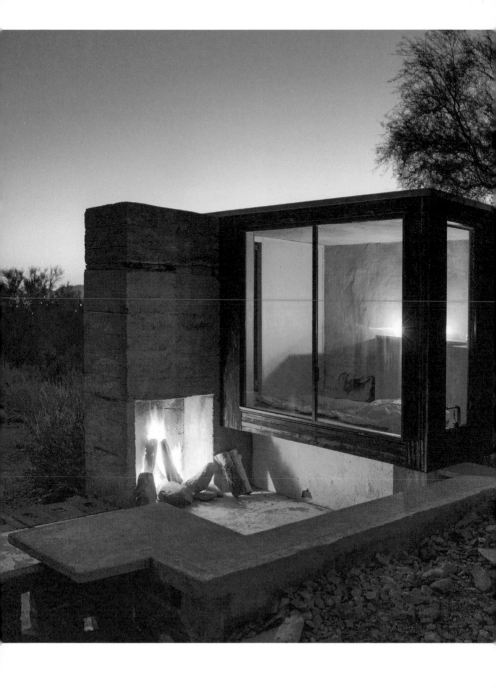

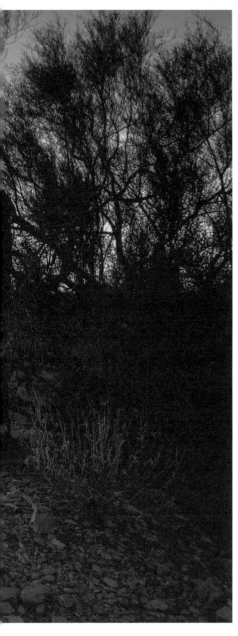

he was adamant about using the smaller panels. "The chimney has these nondescript lines, which create a horizontal feel out of a vertical mass. I wanted to echo that," he says. "So the steel would be talking a little bit to the concrete, saying, 'Okay, we're not the same material, but we're having the same conversation.'" He'd phoned a steel fabricator, who'd agreed to cut the sheets to his dimensions. Dave had also researched rain and air wall systems, a method of insulating a structure by creating a gap between the exterior and interior walls. Instead of attaching the steel directly to the frame, Dave installed metal strips called "hat channels" and then affixed his exterior steel panels to those strips. Thus, any heat generated by the exterior steel would dissipate before reaching the interior.

Dave had always planned to take out the static windows on the sides. In his mind, he kept picturing awning windows that could open wide—so wide that they would resemble wings. He wanted his pod to look like a spaceship. A contact at Taliesin arranged for the Architectural Window Manufacturing Company to donate two huge custom-order windows cut from insulated glass. Dave installed them in early 2011. The awnings open up to 2½ feet—so wide that he can exit the pod through the windows.

By March 2011, Dave had installed the exterior wood finishing—cheap redwood lap that he'd stained ebony. He knew it would fade considerably over time. That was the point. As with the rusting steel, he wanted the box to show its age.

The exterior was completed. But Dave wasn't excited. He was stressed. He'd assumed the entire project would be done by now. After all, he was only making one little box. Not only was he heading back to Wisconsin, but he still needed to complete the

The shelter was planned perpendicular to the chimney in order to create a cloistered outdoor space.

shelter and his final portfolio if he wanted to graduate in December.

When he returned to Scottsdale in October 2011, Dave hit the ground running on his shelter's interior. He wanted to find a few simple ways to tie the exterior to the interior. So he built shelving using birch plywood, which he stained lightly. Each shelf is L-shaped to echo the white bricks.

For the back interior wall, side wall, and ceiling, Dave decided to use Durock, a cement board typically used for tile work. A local mason, Ron Boswell, who repairs all of Wright's original desert masonry at Taliesin West showed Dave how to apply smooth plaster over the Durock. Even with this instruction, Dave intentionally left certain parts of the plaster on the rough side. He wanted the interior of his box to feel like a cave. He wanted his shelter to channel Wright's concept of the "cave dweller" and "nomad." Wright saw society as defined by these two opposing types of people; Dave wanted his shelter to marry the two. The interior box was a cave. But you could open the windows and door to experience the extensive outdoor patio space, which connects the structure to the open desert.

One week before graduation, Dave was nearly finished with his shelter. He still had that big pile of black rocks lying around. He felt compelled to put them to use somehow, so he placed them around the two steel posts holding up his box. Then he threw a party with cheese and crackers, craft beer, Tecate, and a bottle of Angel's Share barleywine. All the students at Taliesin West popped by to celebrate.

Since graduating in December 2011, Dave has returned to Taliesin West just once. In the summer of 2014, he walked back out into the desert, excited but nervous, to survey the condition of his shelter. Everything was intact.

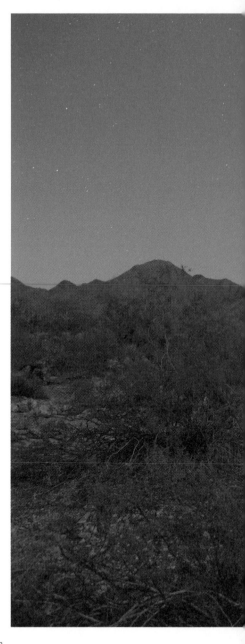

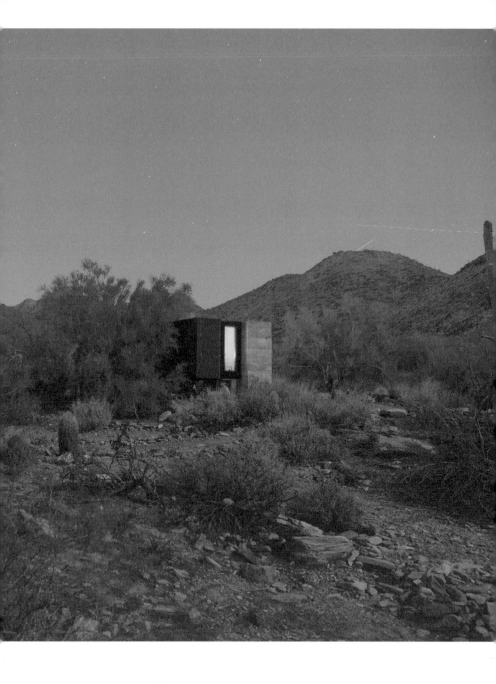

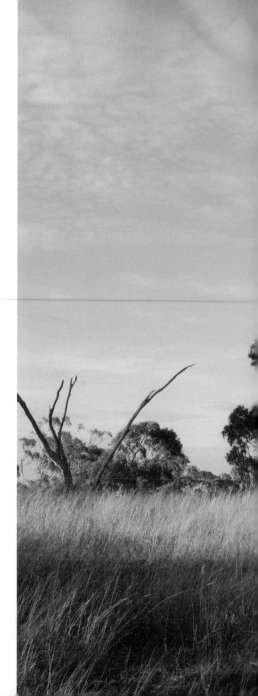

MODERN

ARCHIVE

"Permanent Camping" in Mudgee,
Australia, by Casey Brown Architects
CONTRIBUTED BY Penny Clay

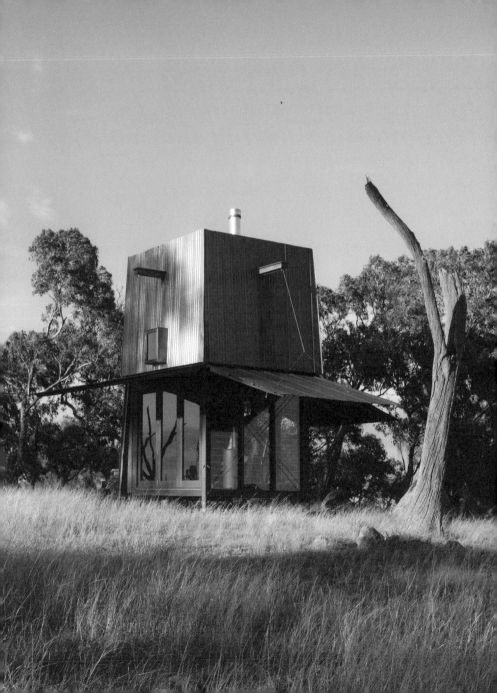

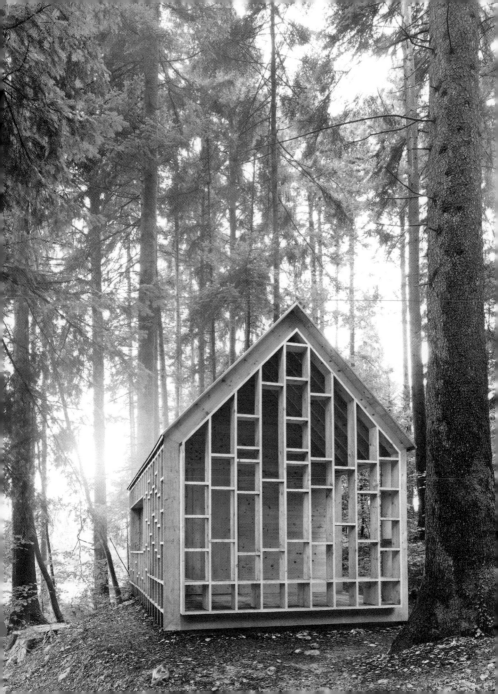

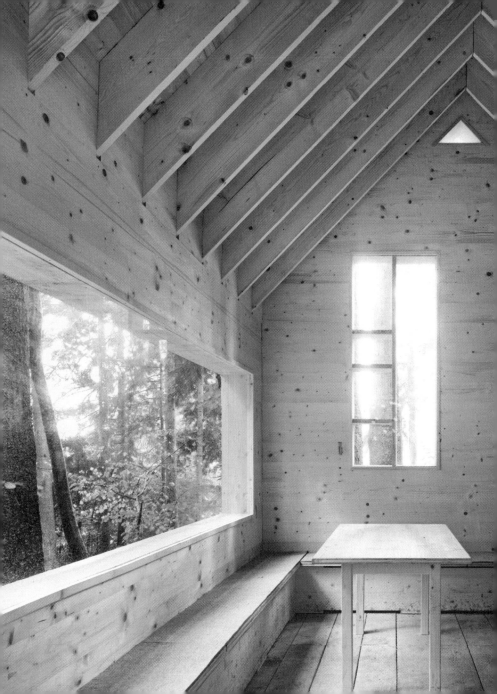

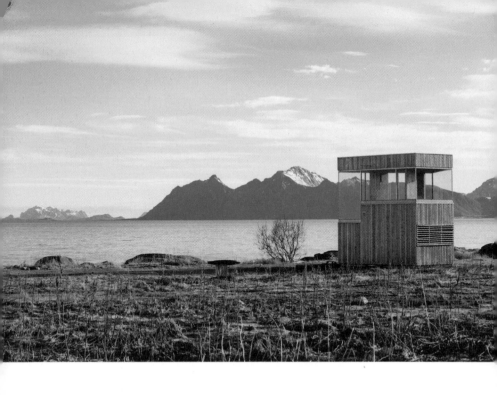

PREVIOUS Waldhaus, the House of
the Forest Owls, by Bernd Riegger
Design in Wolfurt, Austria
CONTRIBUTED BY Adolf Bereuter

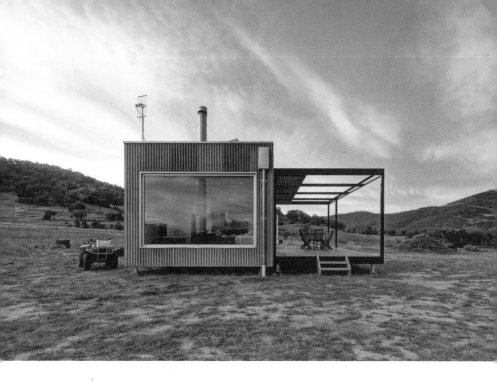

A free shelter for cyclists along the
National Tourist Route in Grunnfør,
Austvågøy, in the Lofoten Islands
CONTRIBUTED BY Pierre Wikberg

Prefabricated cabin with solar panels,
as well as septic and rainwater tanks,
in Tintaldra, Australia
CONTRIBUTED BY Jaime Diaz-Berrio

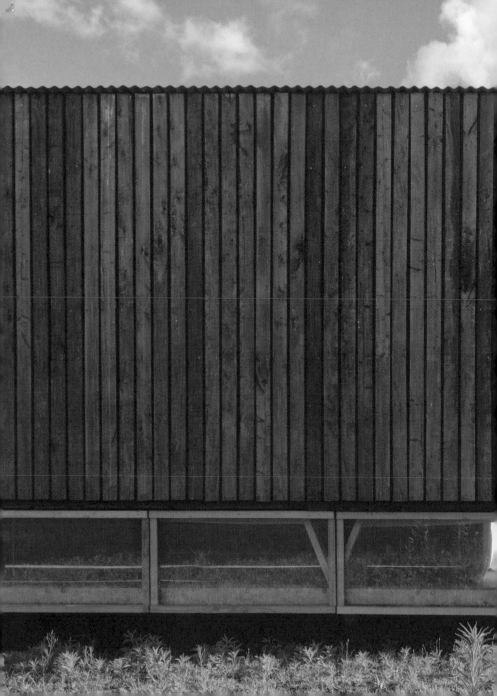

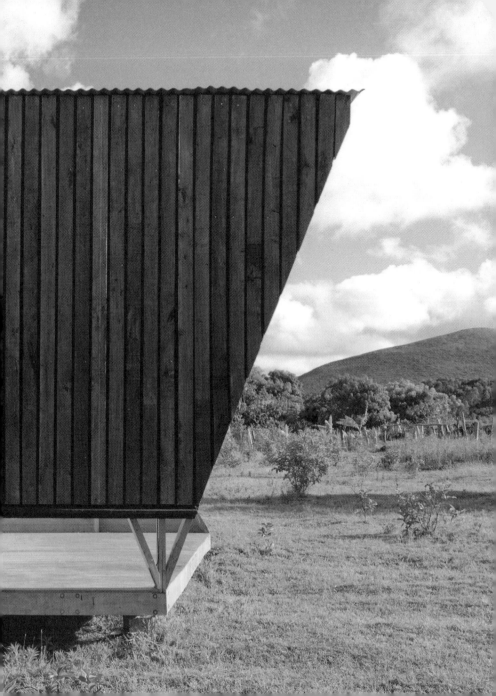

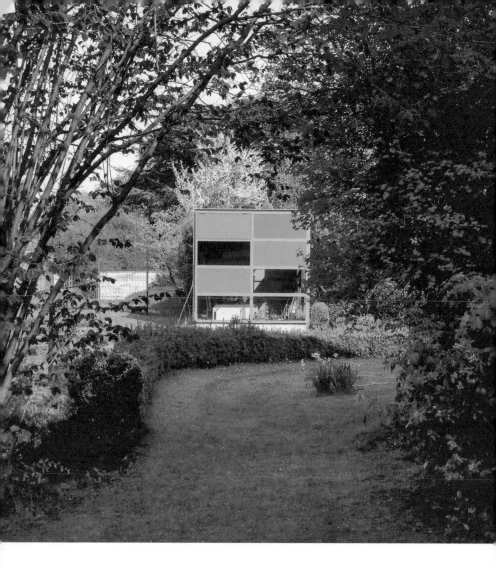

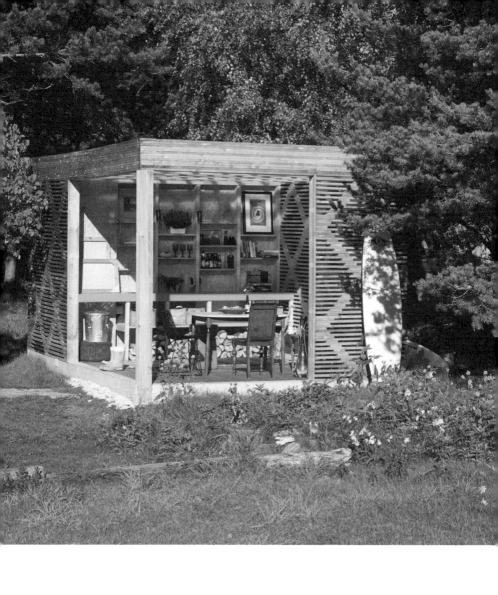

Garden cottage designed by
Vadim Sérandon in Rhone, France
CONTRIBUTED BY Vadim Sérandon

Surfer's shed designed by Tarmo Piirmets
on the island of Hiiumaa, Kalana, in Estonia
CONTRIBUTED BY Virge Viertek

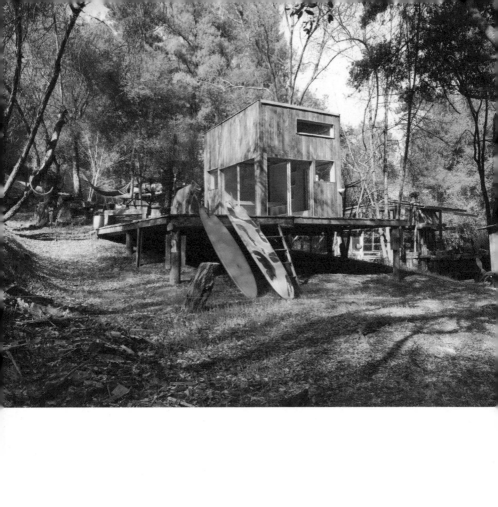

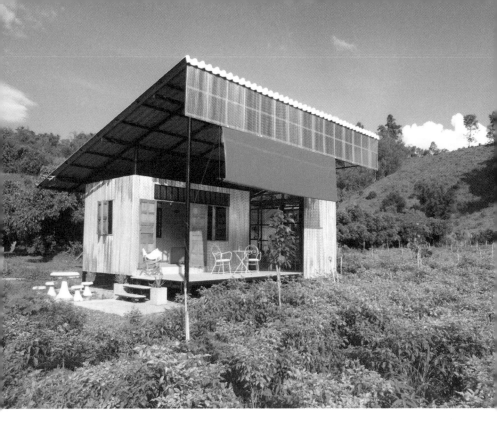

Handmade home in Topanga, California
CONTRIBUTED BY Mason St. Peter

Chiang Dao, Chiang Mai, Thailand
CONTRIBUTED BY Clyde Fowle

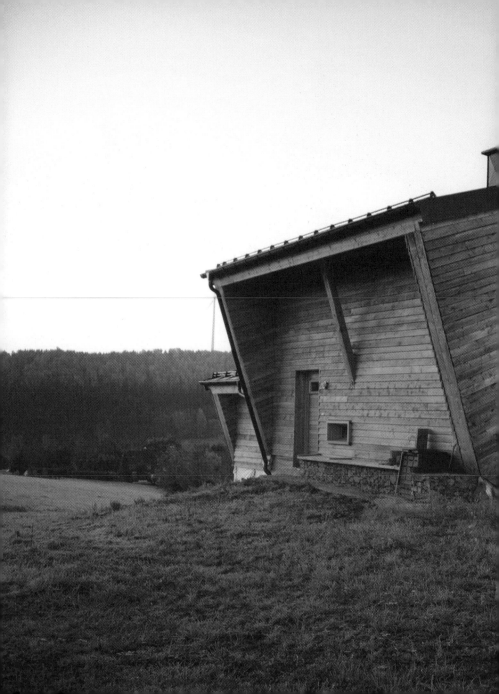

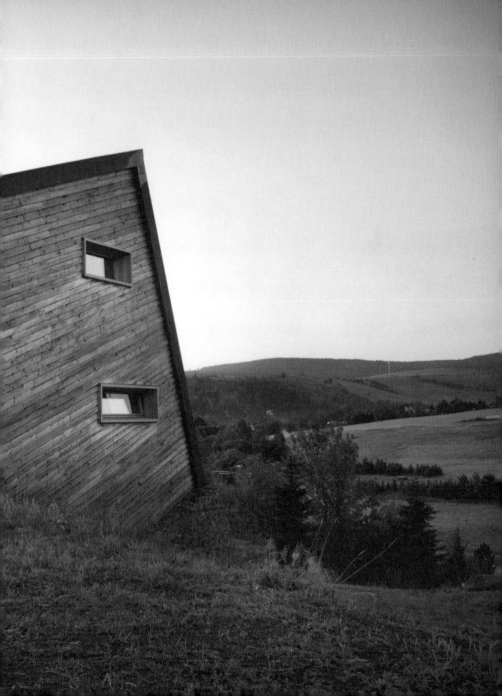

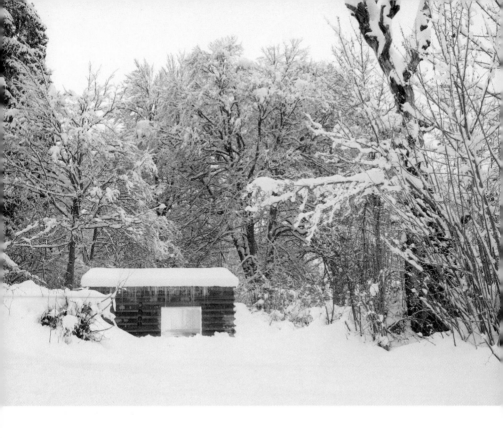

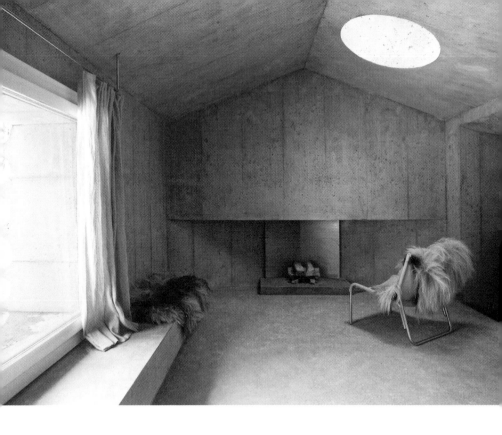

The Refugi Lieptgas in Flims, Switzerland, designed by Nickisch
Sano Walder Architekten. A historic log barn was used as the
external form for pouring a new concrete structure in its place.
CONTRIBUTED BY Gaudenz Danuser

EARTHEN

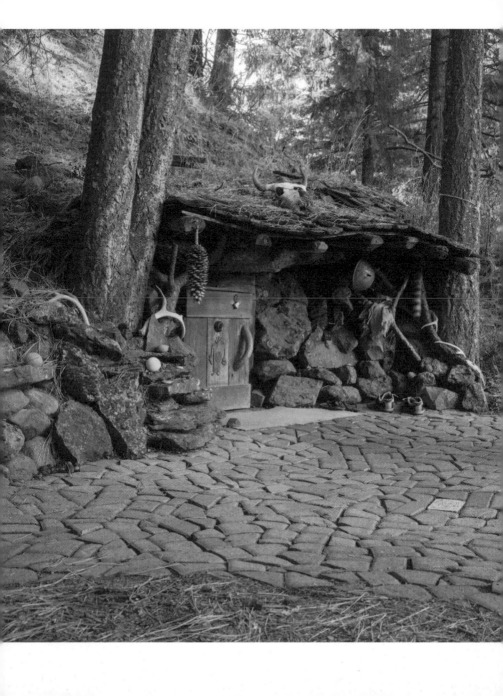

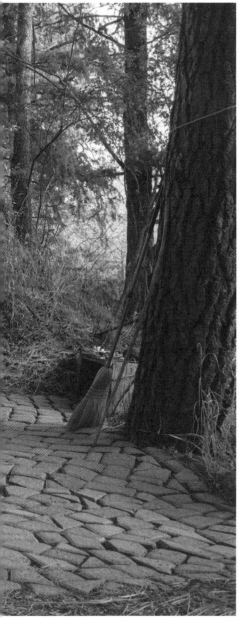

The hut is dug into a hillside, 6-feet deep and supported by a wooden frame.

An artist carves his
own place into a hillside.

How to Live Underground

**Joseph,
Oregon**

Before he reached his shack, Dan Price could tell something was wrong. The front door was hanging off its hinges. Someone had broken into his home. Dan stepped through the doorway and looked around. His laptop, outdoor gear, a bunch of clothes, and three cameras were missing, including the weatherworn Leica M42 he'd spent more than a decade using as a photojournalist. Dan was angry and devastated. Still, he felt this had to have happened for a reason. Dude, he assured himself. The universe is telling you you've got too much shit. Get rid of it.

Dan immediately began deconstructing his cedar-shingled shack board by board. Two years earlier, in 1996, he'd spent two weeks building the 6-by-10-foot structure on a hillside overlooking a meadow in Joseph, Oregon. A tiny town in the northeastern part of the state, Joseph is the last town on a two-lane highway that ascends and ends in the Wallowa Mountains. Known as the Oregon Alps, the snow-peaked Wallowas stretch roughly 40 miles across a region with dozens of alpine lakes, glacial valleys, and assorted wildlife, including black bears, bald eagles, and bighorn sheep. When thirty-three-year-old Dan moved to Joseph in 1990, he was burned out on working and seeking a quiet place to write and draw. Inspired, in part, by Harlan Hubbard's book *Payne Hollow,* about living a simpler life in a hand-built home, he believed that stripping away modern comforts and living more simply in nature would lead to a more spiritually and creatively fulfilling life. He'd originally wanted to find and fix up an old cabin in the woods. Instead, he stumbled on an empty horse pasture near town and convinced the owners to let him rent their two acres for $100 a year; in exchange, he'd repair their fence, fell trees, and maintain the property.

Situated 100 feet below a dead-end road, nestled along the tree-lined Wallowa River, the land was a blank canvas. Dan didn't want to construct anything permanent. "You really gotta spend time somewhere before you start throwing down concrete," he says. He was ready to experiment. Back then he was already beginning to downsize his possessions. In town, he rented a hotel room as an office, where he published a small photo magazine and stored everything work-related. In the meadow, he put up a tepee. He called it the cloth cathedral. At night, he'd look up through the opening made by the smoke flaps and watch the stars. During a couple summers, his ex-wife and two kids stayed with him and later moved to a town nearby. Eventually, he upgraded to a 16-foot tepee with a wooden floor and electricity, which allowed him finally to ditch the hotel office. In time, he built various small domed sweat lodges and a 4-by-4-foot out-house. He dug out two small ponds for water, planted a garden, and continued beautifying the meadow.

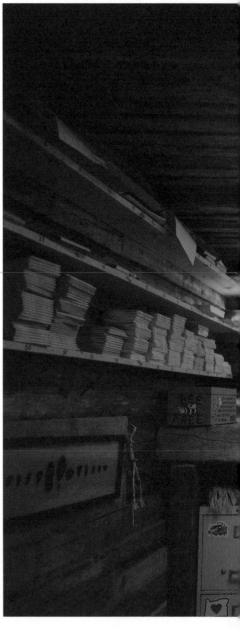

Dan Price has built two dugouts on the same property. The larger one houses his art studio and office.

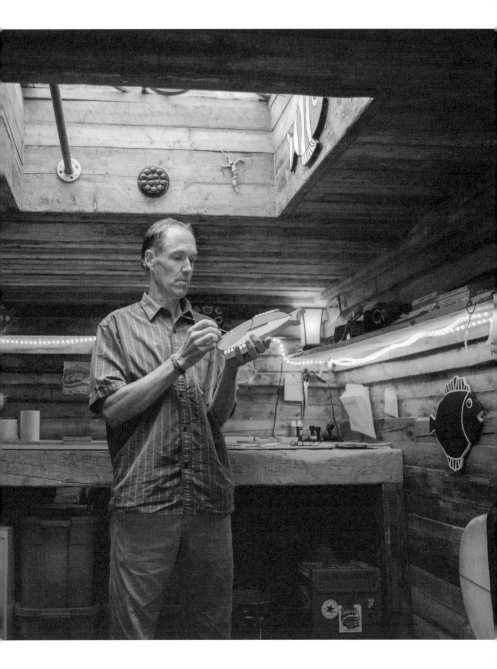

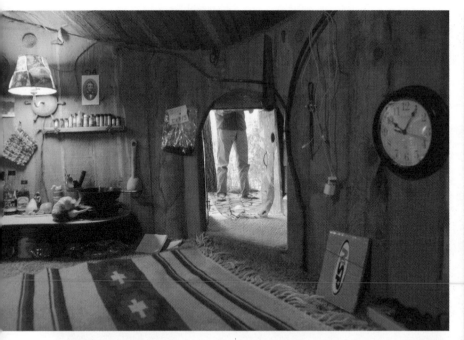

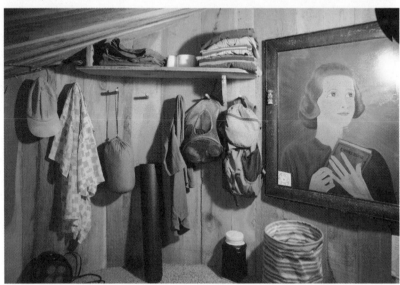

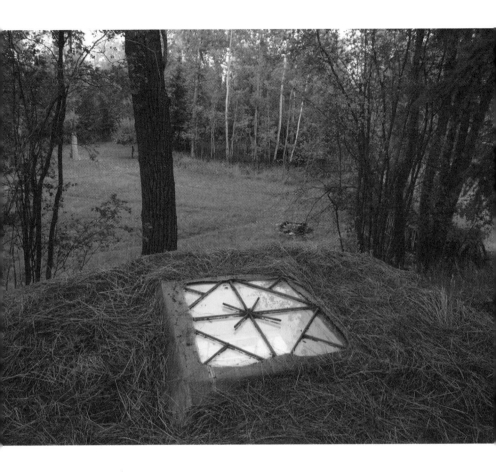

The art studio's skylight was fashioned with Rebar.

OPPOSITE TOP The main hut is a bedroom and kitchen stocked with a hot plate.

After a couple of winters, Dan grew tired of digging his teepee out of the snow and decided it required too much maintenance. So he built a domed 9-by-12-foot hut made from bent red willow covered in burlap. Because he tends to use either cheap or found recycled materials, he never feels heavily invested, either financially or emotionally, in anything he's built. After attaching a second dome to the hut, dissatisfied with the results, he scrapped the structure altogether. "I don't carry baggage of any kind, so I'm just constantly dumping things off, getting rid of things, editing out things in my life," he says. "If a building is not working, it's just removed."

After the 1998 break-in, Dan was also quick to tear

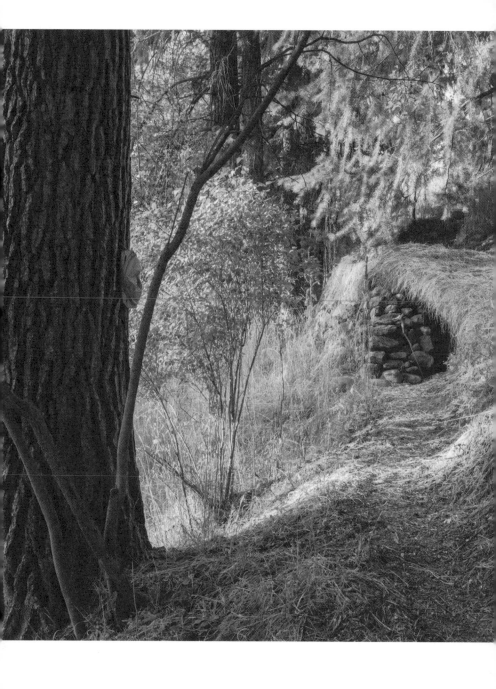

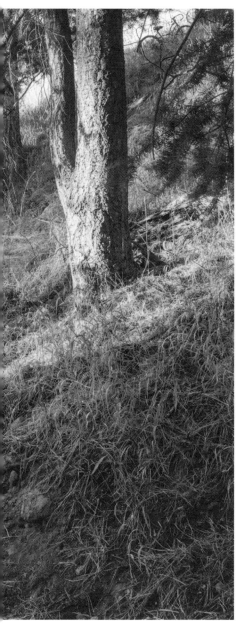

It's easy to miss the art studio's
entrance, which is nestled between
a grassy overhang and stone wall.

down his cedar-shingled shack, because it was difficult to heat in the winter. Besides, after years of living
in circular dwellings, he'd never adjusted to life inside
a rectangle. As the shingles and boards came down,
he kept adding them to a bonfire that burned for three
days with flames 10 feet high. On the third day, the
shack was gone. All that remained was a 2½-foot-wide
tunnel burrowing into the hillside.

One month earlier, Dan had built the tunnel as
part of an addition to his shack. The tunnel led to a
circular underground bedroom 8 feet wide and 3 feet
high. He'd cut a hole in the shack's back left corner
and created a wooden crawl space that connected to
the cavelike enclosure. He was inspired by the ancient
underground kivas found in New Mexico's Chaco
Canyon. To some, Dan's structure is also reminiscent
of a Native American earth lodge. Developed by tribes
on the Great Plains, an earth lodge consists of a post-
and-beam frame covered in a combination of grass,
branches, and sod or mud. It looks like a mound of
earth with a small, low-hanging doorway.

Dan's process was simple. With some help from his
son, he spent three weeks digging into the hill behind
the shack with a pick, a shovel, and their hands. Then
Dan laid down a massive piece of heavy-gauge plastic
sheeting that covered and extended beyond the edges
of the hole. For the walls, he arranged a series of
recycled two-by-sixes perpendicular to the ground and
tacked them together. The frame resembled a wooden
hot tub. For the floor, he laid down used bricks, which
he'd found laying around near town. He covered them
with a layer of plastic, then carpet padding, and finally
shag carpet. For the roof, he stacked two-by-fours all
the way across the top of the circular frame. He cut a
2-by-2-foot hole in the roof for a skylight, then pulled
up the edges of the plastic sheeting and gathered and

stapled the ends together on the roof. He added a few more pieces of plastic on top of the roof before covering it with two or three feet of dirt. The plastic would keep the wood dry. The dirt would keep heat from escaping the bedroom.

With the shack torn down, Dan sat there staring at the entryway to his underground bedroom. What if I just lived in that one round room? he wondered. Getting rid of the table, chair, and chest of drawers from the shack appealed to him. He could redistribute whatever belongings he absolutely couldn't part with—like hand tools—to the outhouse and a small shower shed he'd built down by the river. "This lifestyle is super-clean. It works like a Swiss watch," he says. "Everything I own can fit in a pickup."

Beyond downsizing, there was also something magical about disappearing into the hillside. Integrating into the landscape rather than plopping another structure on top of it felt right to Dan. He spent a few days shortening the tunnel, building a front door using two-by-eights (and two padlocks), redoing the skylight with thicker Plexiglas, and laying down bricks for the patio.

A few years later, the first *Lord of the Rings* film hit theaters. Back when he was twelve years old, Dan had fallen in love with the Tolkien book *The Hobbit* and had even tried building himself an underground fort—a hole covered with a piece of plywood. Now, decades later, the film made him appreciate that he was finally living in a hobbit house. He found a fallen pine tree by the river. Years of flowing water had gently twisted one of its bigger limbs. Dan laid the branch across the front of his home to help create an overhang. Using logs and leftover shingles from a friend, he cobbled together a roof. For the final touch, he assembled a majestic façade by arranging dozens

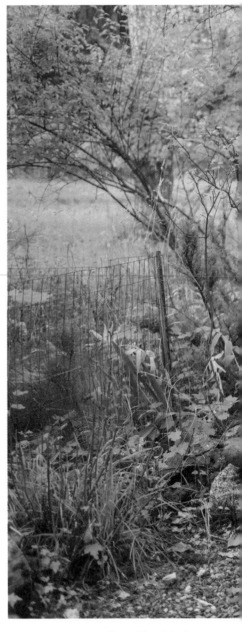

The sweat lodge was built using scrap roof shingles and 2-by-6 boards from a fence torn down by a neighbor.

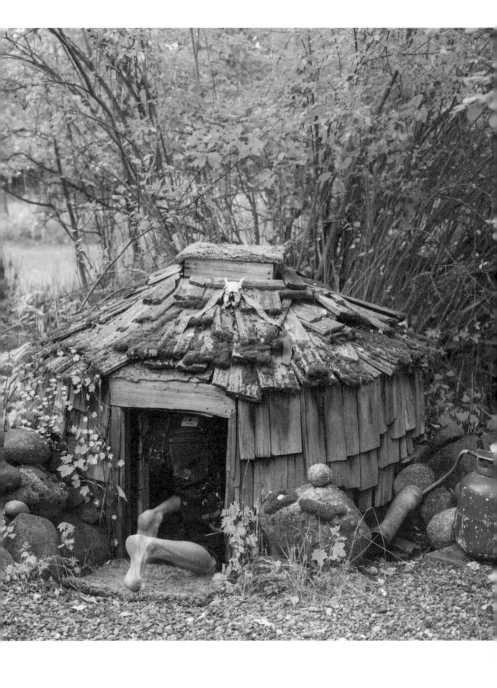

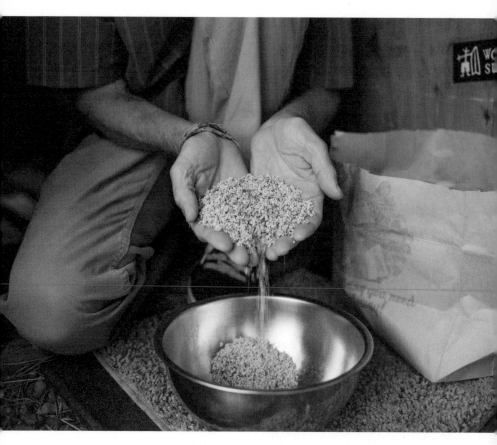

Dan Price harvests local plants for food, including dried elderberry, amaranth, clover, oxeye daisy, plantain, and spearmint.

OPPOSITE TOP A bathhouse and workshop by the river.

OPPOSITE Dan Price has journaled his travels and building projects in *Moonlight Chronicles*.

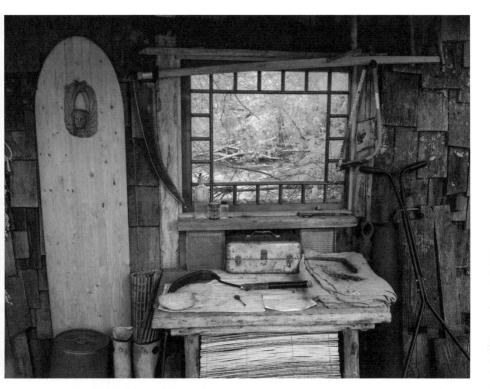

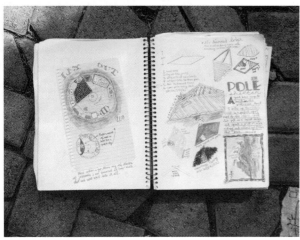

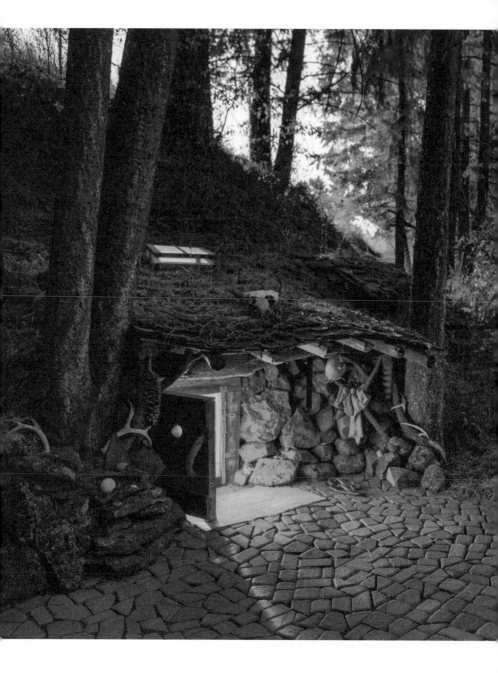

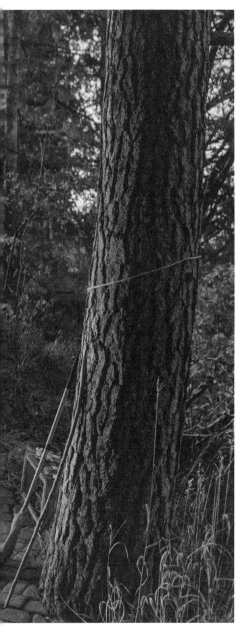

of lichen-covered stones he'd collected by the carload from a canyon cut by the nearby Imnaha River.

"Using old materials makes it feel like it's been here for twenty-nine years," Dan says. "I'm a pretty rough carpenter. I don't like to do a lot of finishing work. I don't use squares or levels. I'll have a pile of random wood and a tape measure and just get going grabbing stuff and then it comes time to put in the last piece and it just fits perfectly. It's Zen. You're just flowing in the moment."

In that sense, his attitude about building mirrors his life philosophy. For years, Dan has traversed the country, just flowing in the moment. He's hopped trains, biked across interstate highways, hiked long distances, and car-camped all over the United States. He spent years documenting his adventures in a hand-drawn zine called *Moonlight Chronicles,* which he produced out of an earthen studio he eventually constructed in 2006 just down the path from his hobbit home. The more he's traveled, the more he's appreciated coming home to his tiny subterranean home, where he wakes up regularly to the sound of deer scampering across his roof.

For the last few years, he's been spending his winters in Hawaii, surfing every day. Every time, before leaving the meadow in Joseph, he locks up and places a small maroon figurine of the Buddha by his front door. "I just sit him there to see if anyone steals him," he says. "No one ever does."

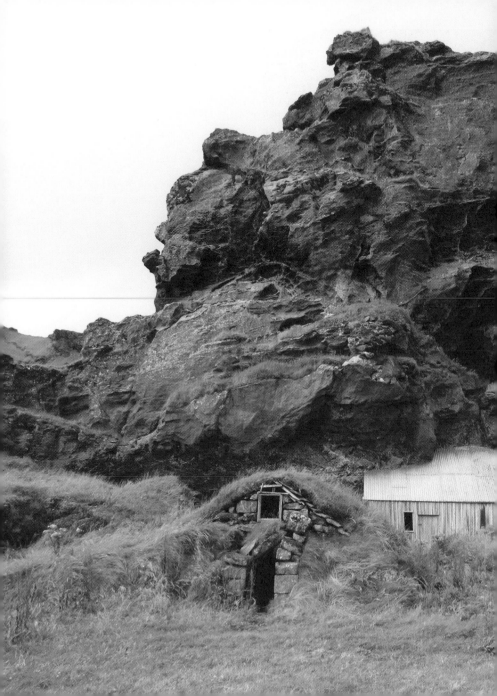

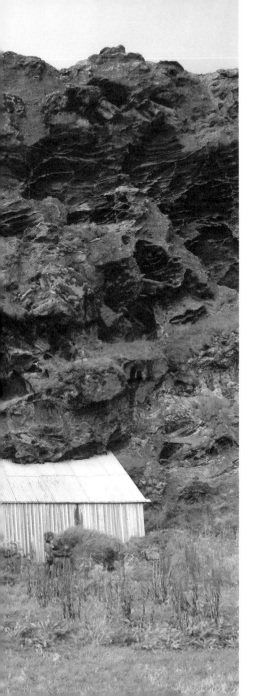

EARTHEN

ARCHIVE

Near Skógarfoss in southern Iceland
CONTRIBUTED BY Kate Stokes

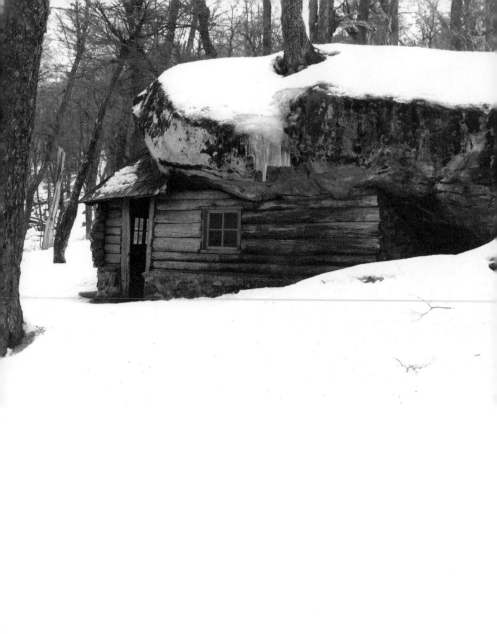

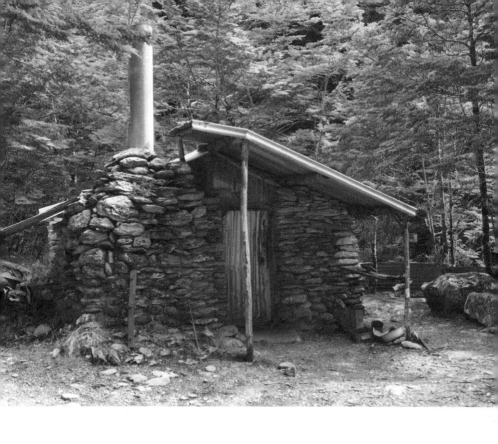

Built into the side of a boulder in San Carlos
de Bariloche, Argentina, el refugio Petricek
contains an old wood-burning stove.
CONTRIBUTED BY Andrew Koester

Sam Summer's Cabin, South Island, New Zealand
CONTRIBUTED BY Chris Menig

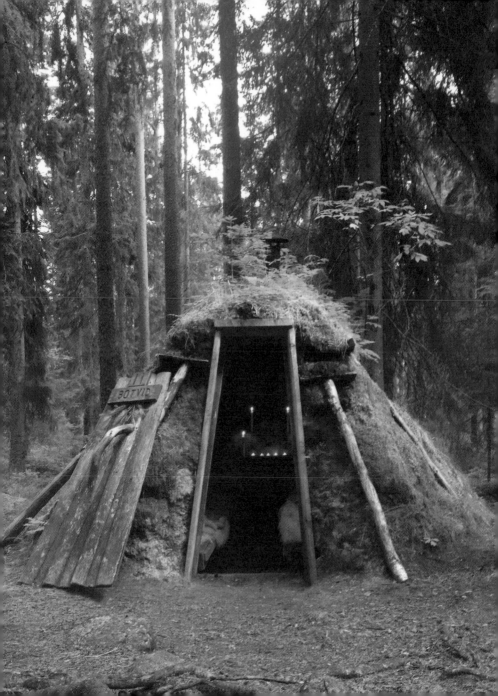

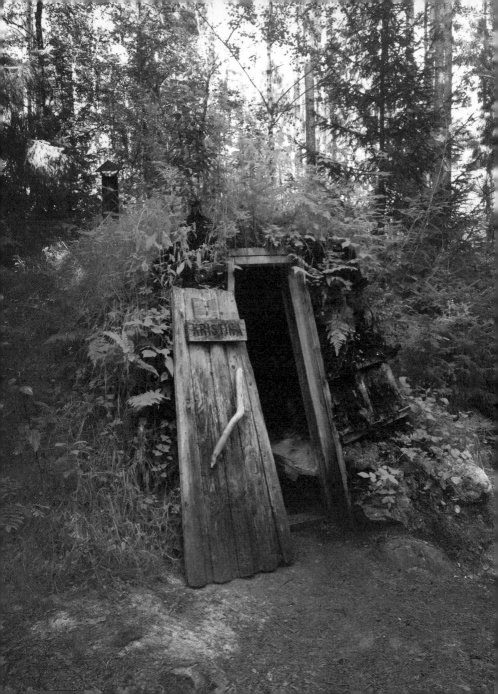

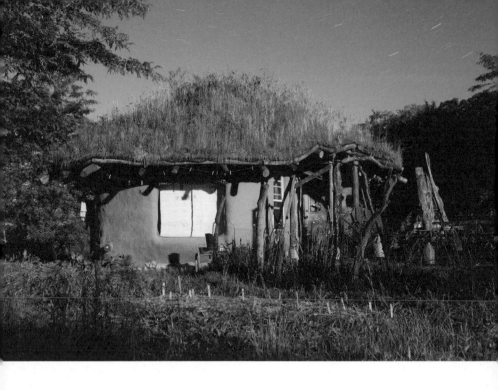

PREVIOUS The Botvid and Kristina forest huts at
Kolarbyn Eco Lodge near Skinnskatteberg, Sweden
CONTRIBUTED BY Sofija Torebo Strindlund

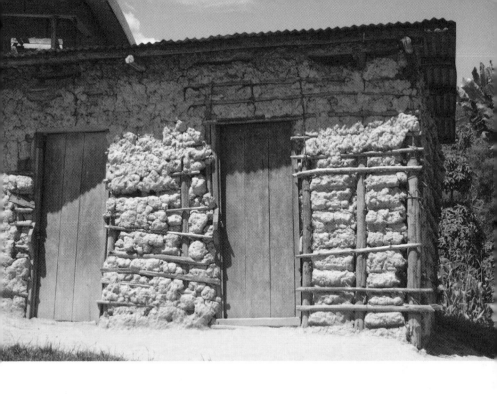

Gobcobatron, a cob house built by Brian "Ziggy" Liloia at the Dancing Rabbit Ecovillage in Rutledge, Missouri
CONTRIBUTED BY Stephen Shapiro

A stick frame structure with clay walls, this retail shop opened in 2013 in the village of Kanyamahene in the Bwindi Impenetrable Forest, Uganda.
CONTRIBUTED BY Hosanna Aughtry

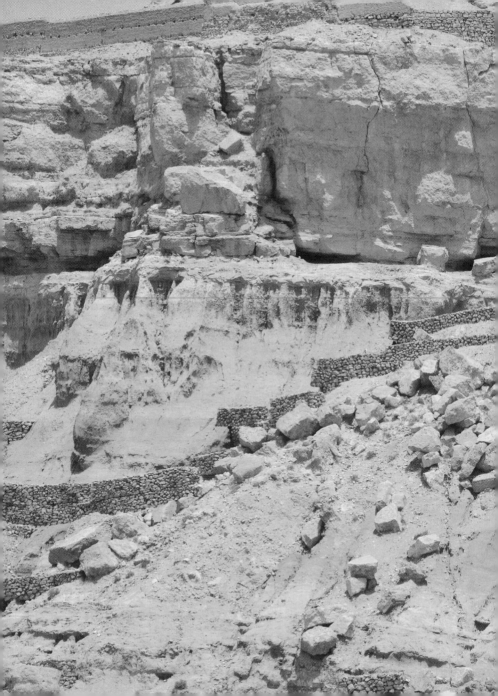

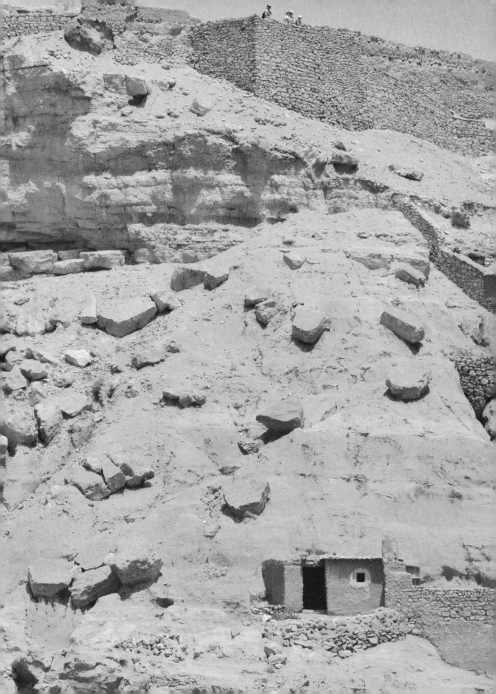

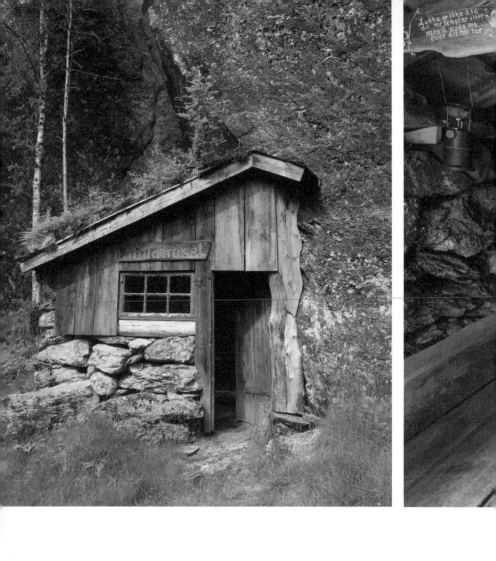

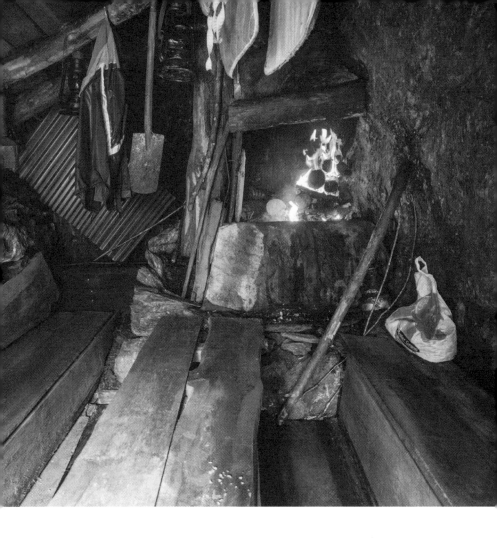

Moldhuset, aka "the earth/soil house." Built by
Ole Fatland in the mountains of Vikedal, Norway.
CONTRIBUTED BY Johannes Grødem (Ole's grandson)

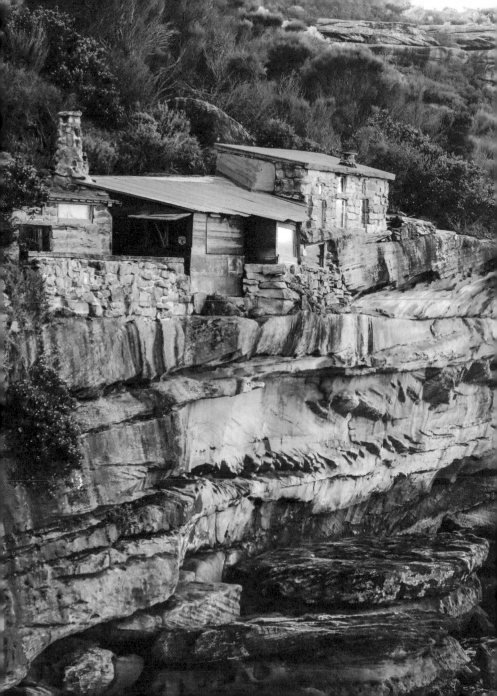

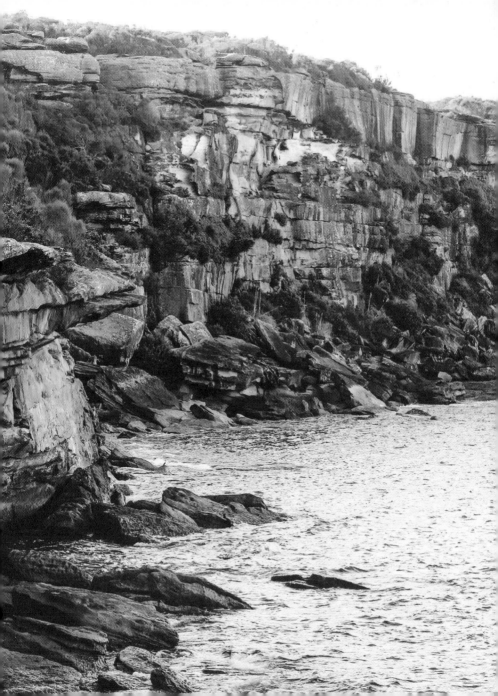

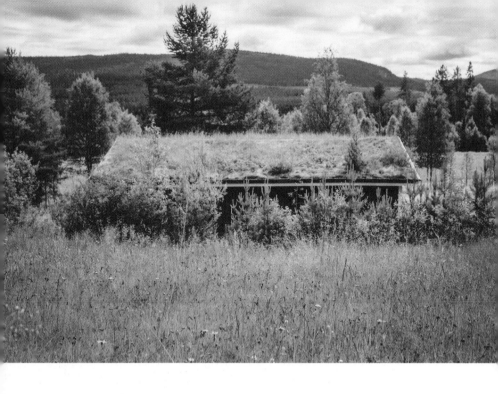

PREVIOUS Crater Cove fisherman huts,
Sydney, New South Wales, Australia
CONTRIBUTED BY Chloe Snaith

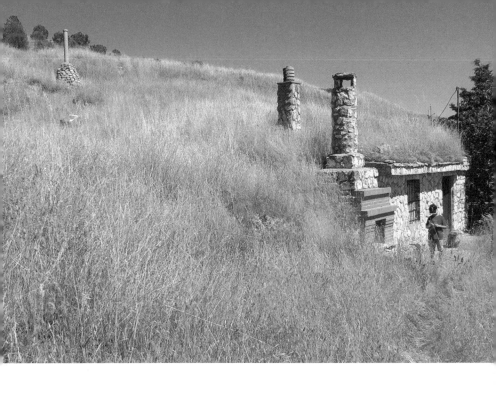

Dalsvallen, Härjedalen, Sweden
CONTRIBUTED BY Kristoffer Marchi

Härjedalen, Sweden
CONTRIBUTED BY Edu Lartzanguren

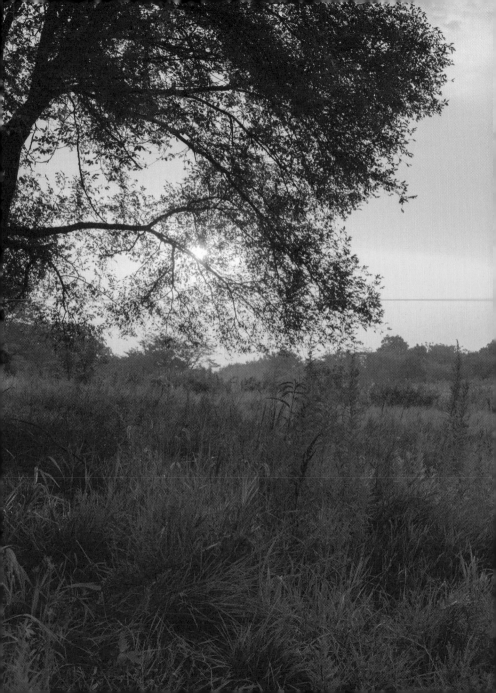

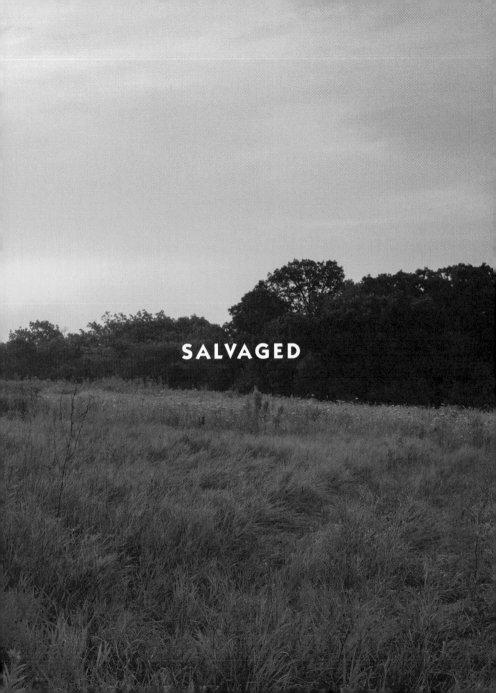

SALVAGED

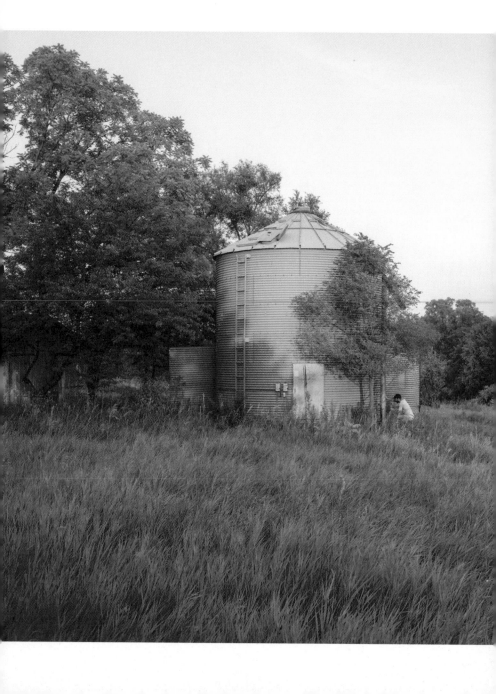

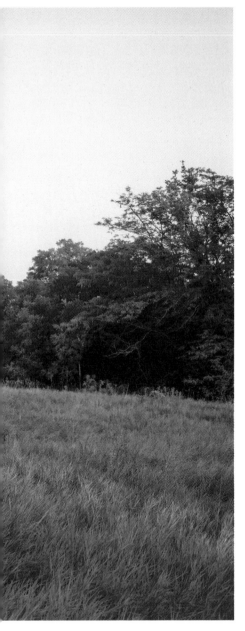

8

SALVAGED

Two brothers and a
hands-on designer give new life
to an abandoned structure.

How to Convert
a Grain Silo

**Grant City,
Missouri**

Kyle Davis climbed the metal ladder bolted to the side
of the silo and pulled open the hatch. A gust of hot
air rushed out, blowing bits of straw and hundreds
of ladybugs out into the wind. The empty corrugated-
steel grain storage silo, which hadn't been used in
years, was baking in the afternoon heat in a field on
the outskirts of Grant City, Missouri, a farm town near
the border of Iowa with a population of 859. It was
spring 2011, and the air was already beginning to
feel muggy. As sunbeams streamed through the hatch
down into the dark, Kyle studied the interior. There
was a 20-foot metal auger extending from the roof to
the floor. Shaped like a big hockey stick, the auger
was attached to an old motor that hadn't churned
grain in decades. "All right," said Kyle with a relaxed
Midwestern twang. "Let's just take that out right now."

Standing outside the silo, 20 feet below, were
brothers Taimoor and Rehan Nana. For a couple years,
the brothers had been talking about putting up some
type of cabin on their family's land. Purchased by their

great-great-uncle around 1910, the plot consists of 307 acres of prairie that over the years had been parceled up and rented out. In 1985, the family committed 207 acres to a conservation reserve program, meaning that portion would no longer be plowed for agriculture or developed with new construction.

As kids, the brothers drove up from Kansas City to explore the overgrown forests and seek out turtles and frogs. In time, they began hunting birds on the land with their father, who had moved from Pakistan to Kansas City in the 1970s, and their great-uncle, a farmer from Sheridan, Missouri. They would come up from the city on weekends and camp in tents inside one of the old barns. Scattered around the property between thickets of walnut, locust, and elm trees are various abandoned and boarded-up buildings in all states of disrepair, including a post-and-beam barn from the 1800s, a schoolhouse from the early 1900s, and a farmhouse built in the 1950s.

By 2008, when Taimoor was thirty and Rehan was twenty-four, the brothers decided they wanted a more permanent structure where they could sleep, cook, and shower. Refurbishing one of the ramshackle structures would be costly. It might also contradict the family's philosophy of preservation. Taimoor had researched shipping containers. He loved the idea of appropriating something industrial and modern. But a shipping container would look out of place in the middle of the prairie.

Taimoor started eyeing the old grain bin by the barn where they usually camped. Adapting the silo made a lot of sense. On the drive north from Kansas City to Grant City, there are silos everywhere. In the last fifty years, the industrialization of farming has increased the scale and pace at which farms operate. Smaller silos are no longer in demand, so they sit

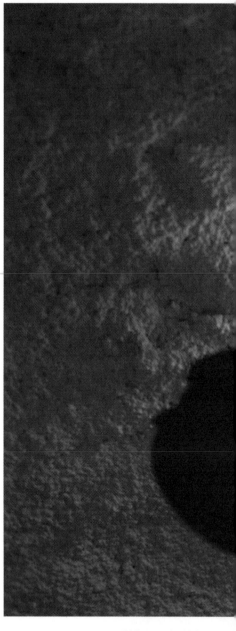

Kyle Davis peers down into the interior of the grain silo, which he insulated with spray foam.

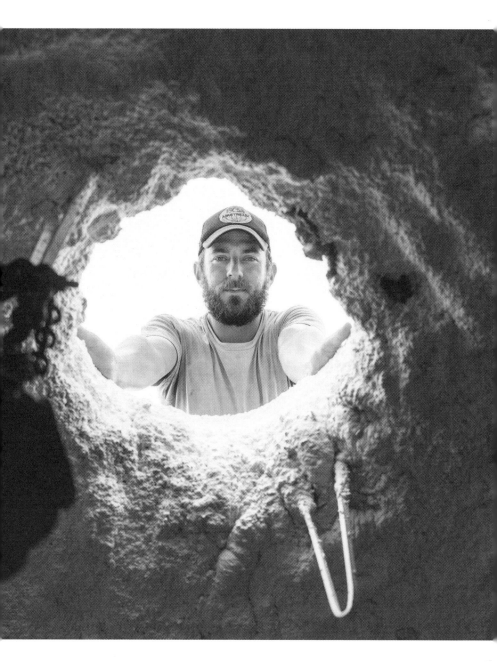

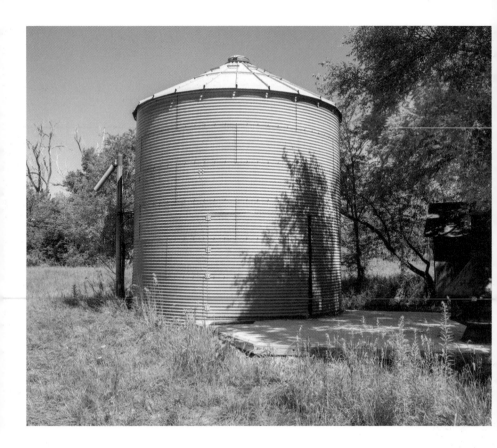

vacant, gathering rust. Some are sold online for as little as $250. Many landowners are happy to give away silos to anyone willing to disassemble and move them off a property. Taimoor and Rehan already had a bin. They just had no experience with construction or carpentry. They needed to find someone who could not only build out their bin, but would include them in the process. They wanted to have a hand in crafting their shelter.

Taimoor's childhood friend Loren Schieber introduced them to Kyle, a friend he'd met playing Ultimate Frisbee at the University of Kansas in Lawrence. An Eagle Scout who'd worked summer construction jobs in high school, he helped build the first LEED platinum home in Kansas City. (LEED, or Leadership in Energy

and Environmental Design, is a green building-certification program.) After college, he'd eventually settled in Manhattan, Kansas, and founded his own design and construction firm. In the spring of 2009 when Taimoor and Rehan showed Kyle the grain silo, he didn't hesitate to begin the project. Minutes after poking his head down the hatch, Kyle grabbed a rope, tied it to the motor, and labored with the others to lower the auger and wrestle it out through the silo's tiny lower back door. Once the auger was removed, it was easier to see how much potential there was inside the silo's hollow shell. Taimoor and Kyle started sketching ideas. Simply erecting a cabin with four walls inside the bin wasn't satisfying. They didn't want to camouflage the circular interior. They wanted to showcase it.

In September 2011, Kyle packed up his tools, hired

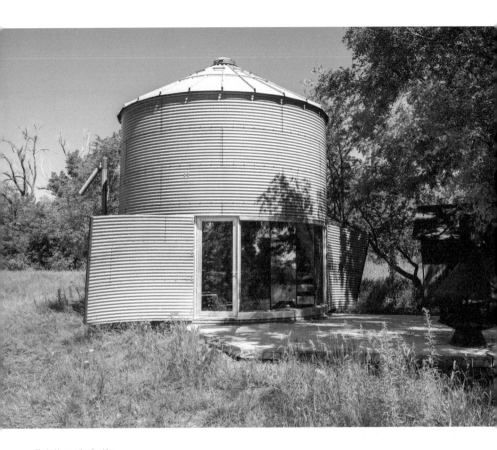

The builders cut the silo with a
circular saw, and reinforced the
doors with a new frame filled with
standard patio door glass panes.

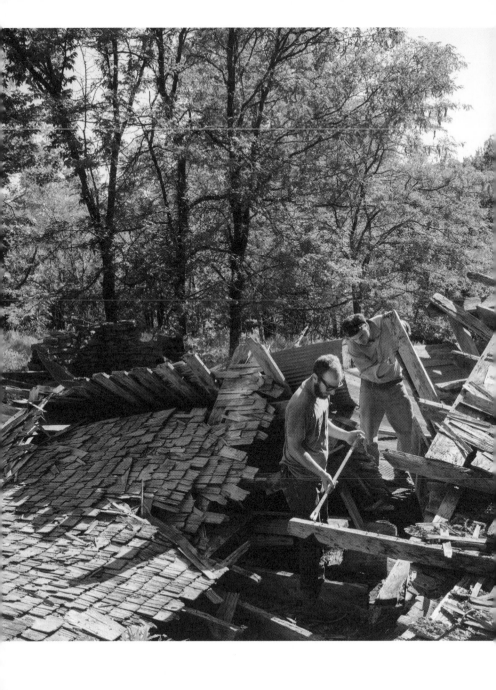

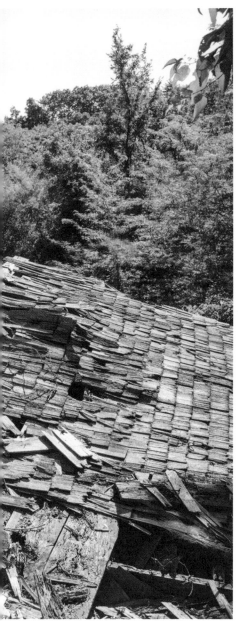

Kyle Davis and Rehan Nana salvage
materials from a dilapidated barn
from the 1800s.

two other friends, and met Taimoor, Rehan, and
Loren at the site. They set up a woodworking shop
with a gas-powered generator by the nearby barn
and began combing the property for materials.
Seven years before, a tornado had destroyed a barn
a five-minute drive from the silo. Built in the late
1800s, the 60-by-40-foot post-and-beam structure had
devolved into a massive pile of debris. The top layer,
which was mostly unusable, had preserved many of
the boards and beams beneath. Kyle and his team
carefully removed bits and pieces and brought them
back to the woodshop. The men also investigated the
barn hayloft above the space. Underneath a 2-foot
layer of straw and dust, they found a series of pine
boards and picked out ones that hadn't succumbed to
dry rot. Then Kyle taught the brothers how to use an
electric planer. The task itself was noisy and monot-
onous, but stripping away the weathered outer layer
and reexposing the wood grain proved rewarding.

As the brothers continued feeding boards through
the planer, Kyle went to work on the bin. The plan
was to cut out a large chunk of the silo and install
a long panel of windows. The cut metal would be
reattached to function as an enclosure that would
protect the glass when the silo wasn't in use. Rather
than doing a custom window order, Kyle chose to use
patio door blanks, because they're relatively inexpen-
sive and come in a standard size. The southern side
of the silo was chosen for the window, because that
location would maximize warm direct sunlight in the
winter and minimize the heat of the setting sun during
the summer. Also, from the nearby dirt road, no one
would be able to see the opening. To casual passersby,
it would still look like an old forsaken silo sitting in an
overgrown field.

Kyle had his doubts about cutting into the silo. By

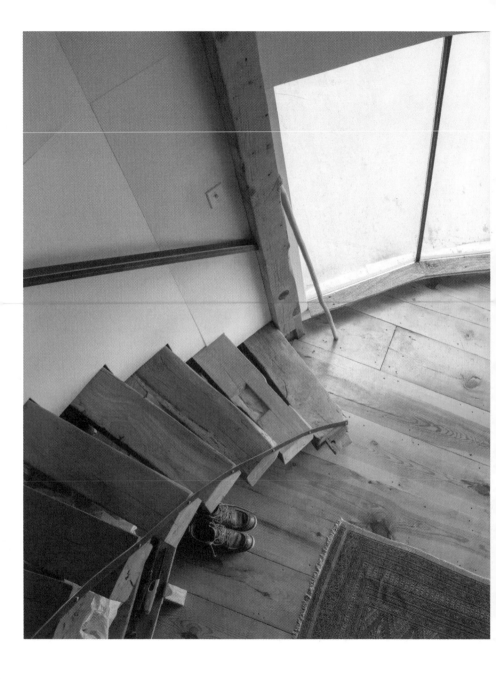

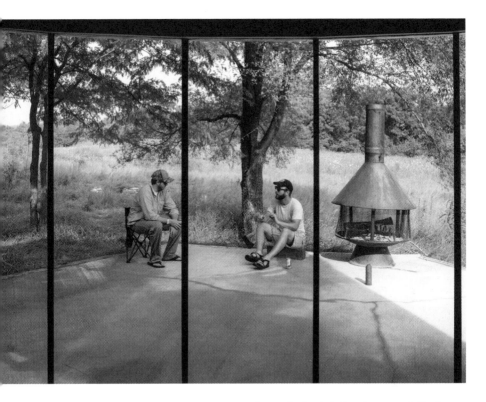

removing a 7-by-14-foot section, they'd compromise the structural integrity. When Kyle pressed the circular saw down into the metal, sparks flew. Everyone should have been wearing earplugs. "Inside, it was just deafening," Kyle recalls. "The silo was just a huge reverberation chamber. You could just not think in here, it was so loud." The first two cuts were made vertically from top to bottom, marking the opposite ends of the space where the window would go. Kyle bolted hinges to each end. He wanted to ensure that the hardware was in place before each door was fully cut. Otherwise, they'd have to try and hold up each piece manually as they attached the hinges.

As soon as Kyle made the final two horizontal cuts— across the width of the silo—the building sagged outward a half inch. They quickly grabbed a long piece of angle iron and wedged the metal bar between the ground and the silo. They kept the temporary support in place as they continued to work on other elements of the bin.

Eventually, they bolted two beams vertically along either side of the window frame to provide permanent support for the bin.

From there, the project was a matter of basic framing. For the next two weeks, the crew continued planing boards, sanding down beams, and assembling the interior. Every morning, they'd wake up, grab bacon-sausage-ham breakfast sandwiches at the local truck stop, and drive to the bin to pull fifteen-hour days on-site. The floor joists, the support beams for the loft, and all of the steps for the floating stairwell were installed in one day. They created a substrate insulated floor by putting down a layer of pink Styrofoam insulation, then unfinished barn boards as a middle layer, and finally finished floorboards, which were bolted directly into the unfinished boards. The stairs were cut from two large support beams that were salvaged from the barn and sanded down. Each step was

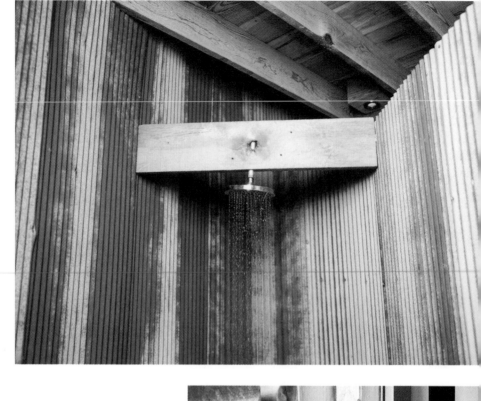

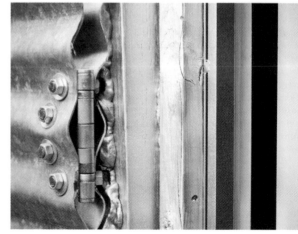

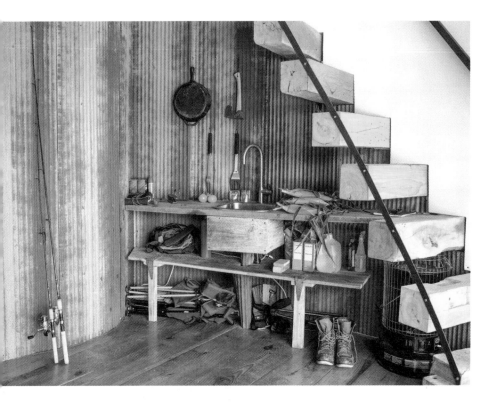

affixed to the silo wall using four 10-inch bolts. Although each floating step felt secure, Kyle bolted in a strip of steel connecting them all for added support. He also added a handrail, a long section of thick tube steel running up along the side of the silo. To get the straight piece to curve, he propped up one end on a log and jumped up and down on the middle. At the time, the others were skeptical. But Kyle understood they didn't have any other options. "We're in the middle of nowhere. So it's just like, Well, let's figure it out," he says. "It gets a little bit tight in one spot where you can barely slide your hand behind the rail. But for jumping on a log, I mean, it's pretty damn good."

By the time they framed out the window using two-by-fours and caulked all five windows in place and installed a custom glass door, the silo had been transformed. Since there had once been power lines running to the silo's motor, all they had to do was reroute the electrical system and get the power turned back on. During the

Each of the steps was bolted into the side of the silo. A strip of steel provides added support.

OPPOSITE TOP Walls for a private shower were constructed using corrugated metal found on the property.

OPPOSITE Hinges allow the owners to close and lock up the silo's two large doors.

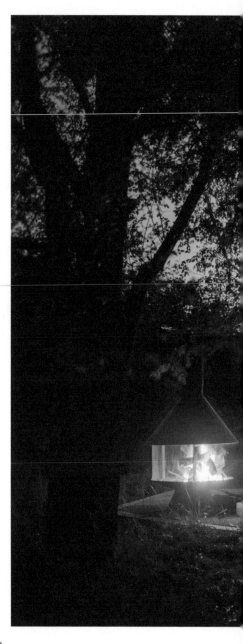

frigid winters, the brothers plug in a small electric
heater. During hot, humid summers, they run an
air-conditioner.

Mostly the brothers visit the land during the fall
and spring when the weather is more agreeable and
conducive to planting. In 2013, they began converting
the 207 conserved acres back into rough prairie. After
removing invasive brome and fescue grasses, they set
up 14 acres' worth of pollinator plots throughout the
property. Stocked with seeds of native grasses and
flowers, these areas help attract and support regional
insect and bird populations, especially pheasant
and quail, which nest in the grass. The brothers also
planted sorghum and millet to help attract and feed
larger wildlife, such as whitetail deer. They hope the
land will one day look the way it did 500 years ago.
In time, the unused buildings will be swallowed up by
the landscape. "There's all these little markers of the
people who lived here before. The silo is our genera-
tion's mark on this land," Rehan says. "My brother's got
kids. I'm hoping to have kids. I'd love for them to be
out here and take care of this place."

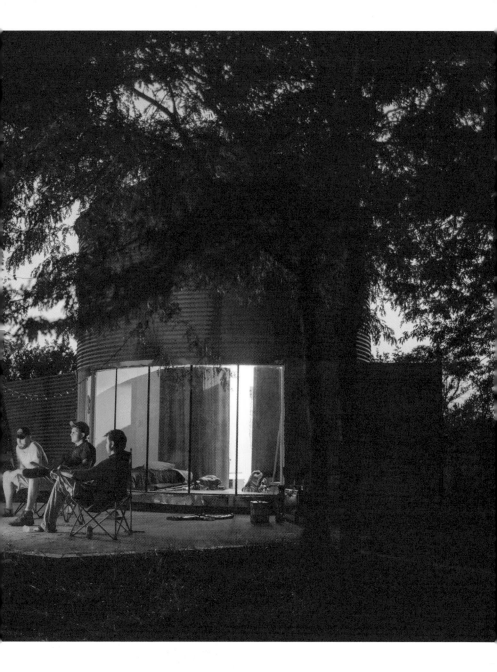

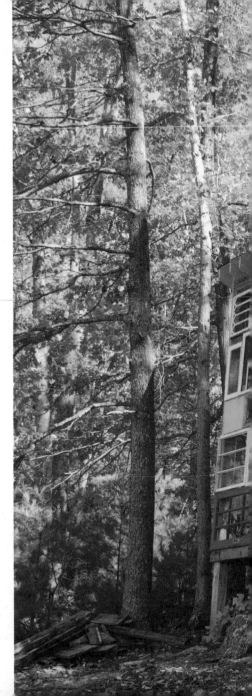

SALVAGED

ARCHIVE

The Sunset House in West Virginia was built by Lilah and
Nick using windows reclaimed from junkyards. The lumber,
which was repurposed from a barn on the property, had been
cut and milled many years earlier by the former landowner.
CONTRIBUTED BY Lilah Horwitz & Nick Olson

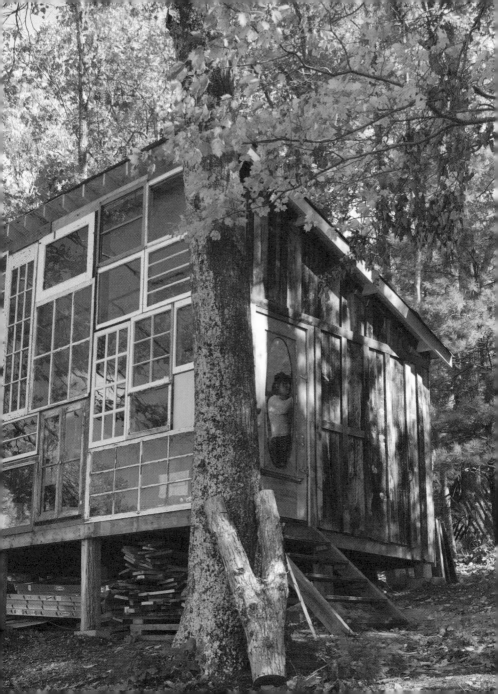

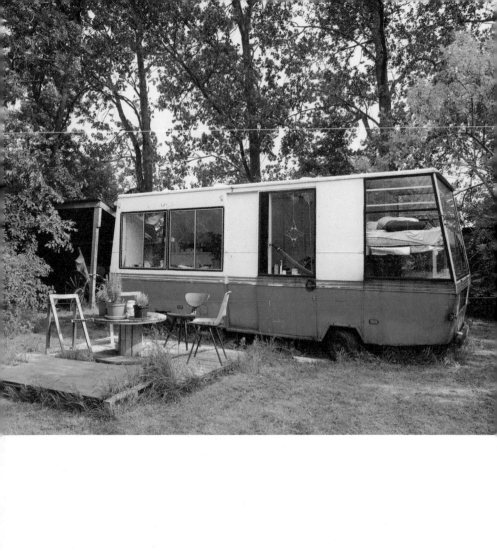

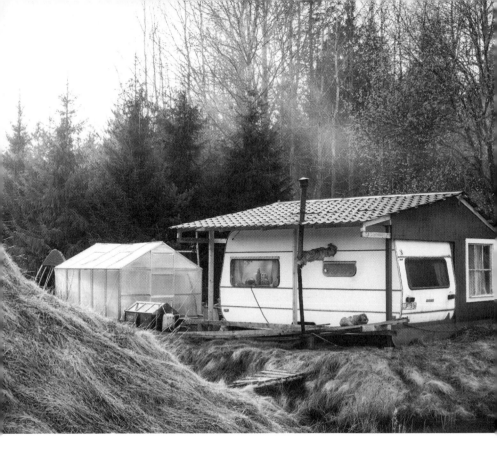

A moving grocery shop, now a bedroom
for a teenager, Groningen, Netherlands
CONTRIBUTED BY Marieke Kijk in de Vegte

Trailer cabin in Sweden
CONTRIBUTED BY Reidar Pritzel

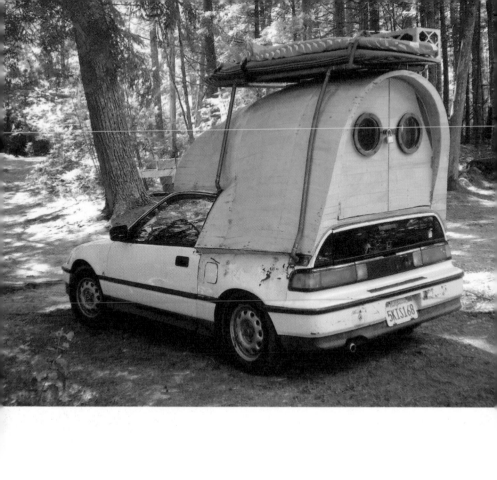

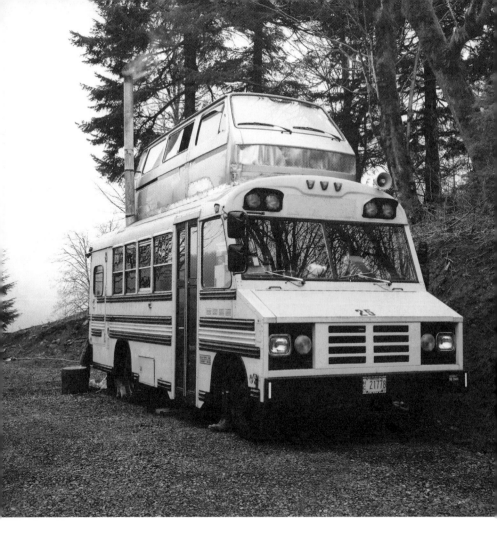

Honda Civic camper
CONTRIBUTED BY Jay Nelson

Bluebird school bus with a Vanagon on top
CONTRIBUTED BY Foster Huntington

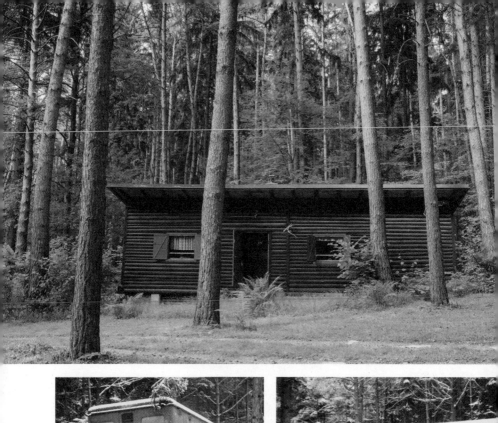

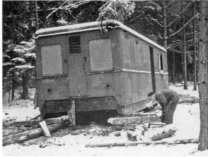

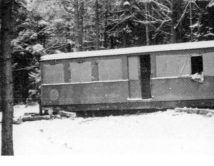

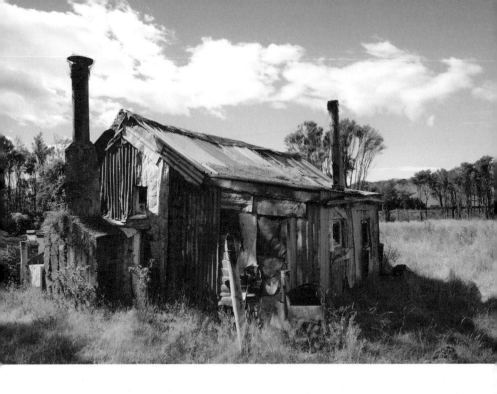

Converted train car
in Prievidza, Slovakia
CONTRIBUTED BY Katarina Dubcova

Shack at an old sheep-herding camp in a
remote area of Fiordland in New Zealand
CONTRIBUTED BY Chris Menig

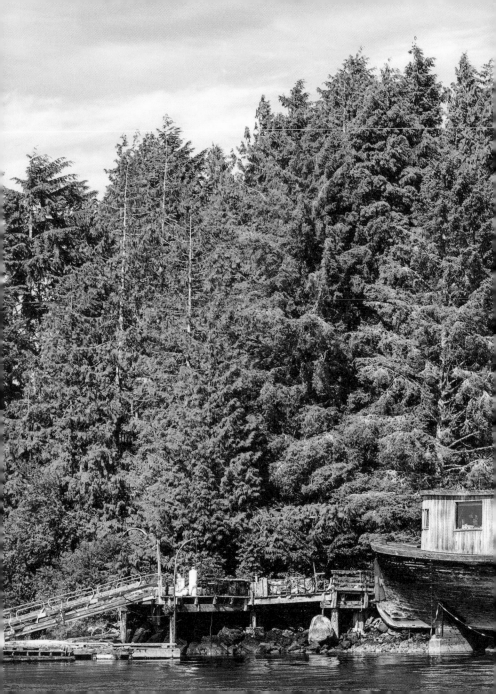

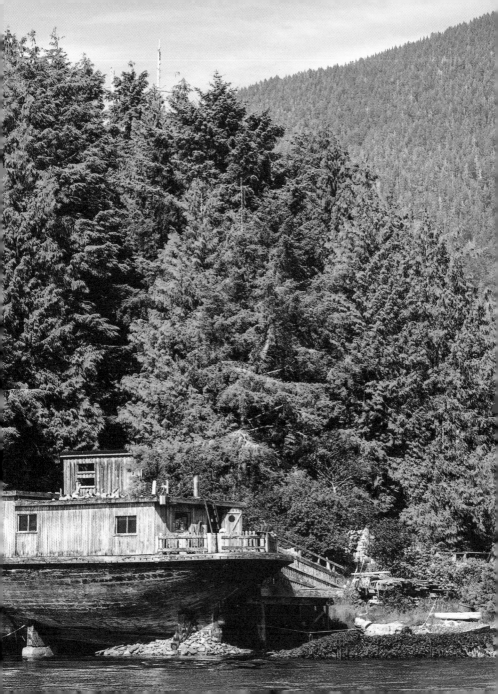

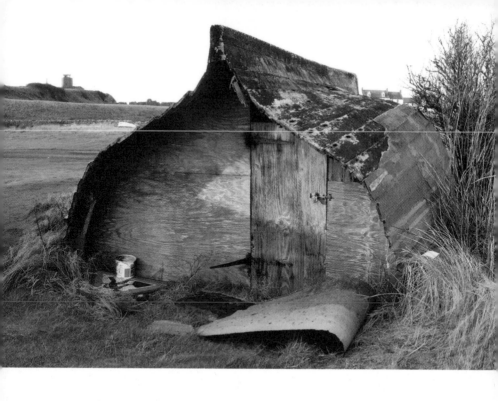

PREVIOUS Eight children were born and raised in this
ship cabin on the coast of British Columbia, Canada.
CONTRIBUTED BY Mark McInnis

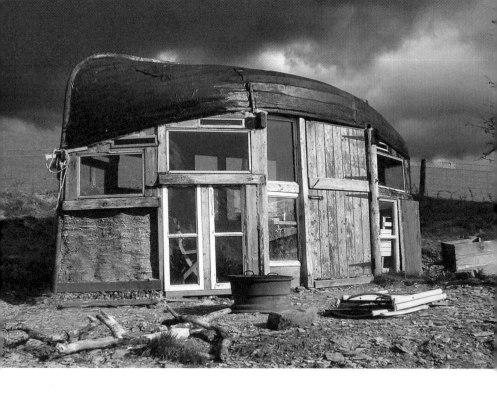

Lindisfarne, an island off the coast
of Northumberland, England
CONTRIBUTED BY Lynn Patrick

Machynlleth, Wales, UK
CONTRIBUTED BY Alex Holland

279 SALVAGED

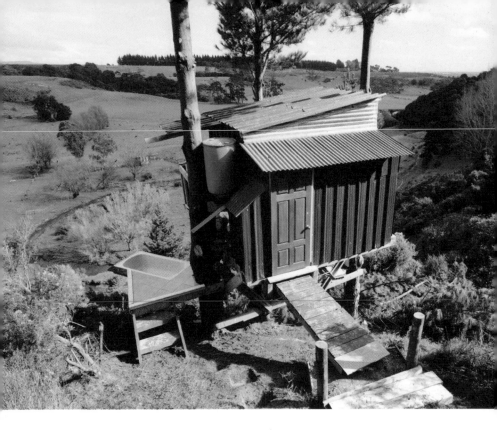

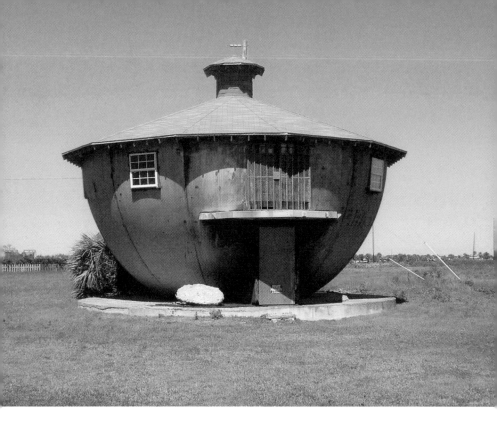

Built in Manawatu-Wanganui, New Zealand, for less than
$1,500, using mostly scavenged or donated materials, the
Best Hut includes solar panels, rainwater collection, a gas-
fired outdoor bathtub, and a radio-controlled drawbridge.
CONTRIBUTED BY Jono Williams

Teakettle house in Galveston, Texas
CONTRIBUTED BY Ryder W. Pierce

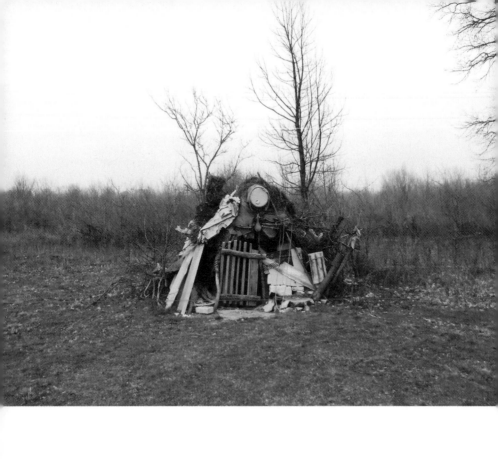

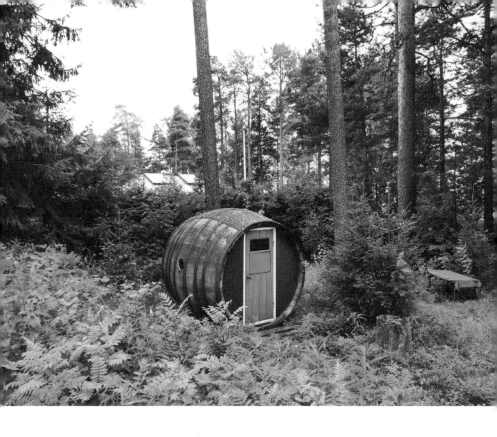

Belgrade, Serbia
CONTRIBUTED BY Francois Lombarts

Made from a barrel once used to carry wine on a ship, the cabin was coopered near Luleå, Sweden.
CONTRIBUTED BY Kim Walker

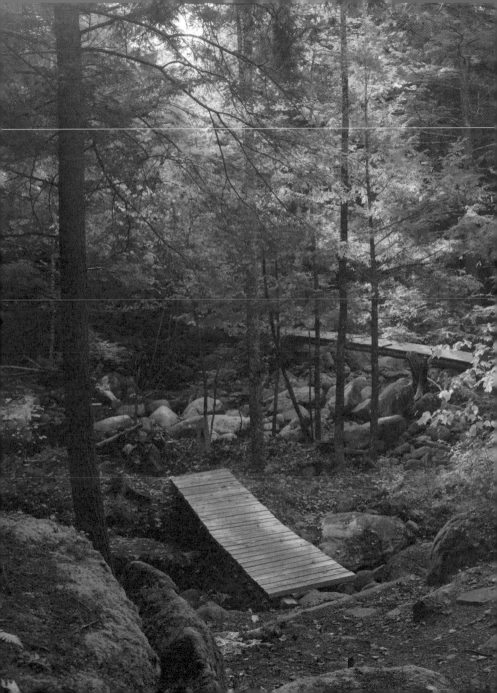

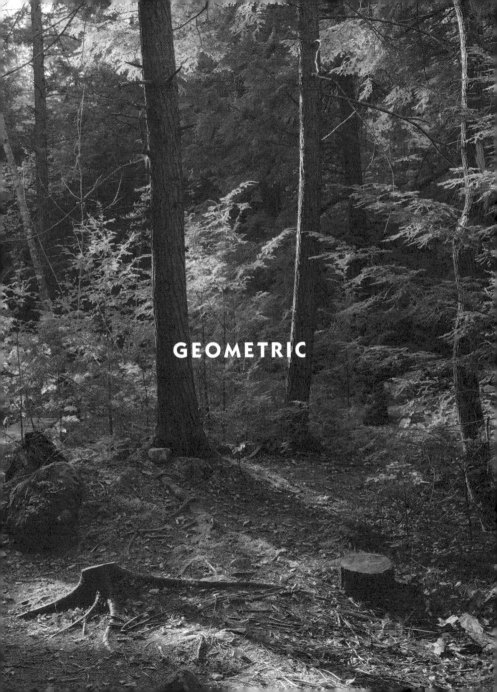

GEOMETRIC

9

GEOMETRIC

Two sons put their stamp
on their family's off-grid retreat.

How to
Build a Yurt

Keene,
New York

In the spring of 2002, Nick Farrell told his father he
wanted to build another yurt. It was a warm afternoon,
and they were standing beside the 320-square-foot
wooden yurt Nick's parents, Greg and Cathy, had
constructed in 1976 on their 90-acre property in Keene,
New York. Nick's father had discovered the tiny village
in the northeastern Adirondack Mountains in 1956
when he worked as a counselor at Camp Dudley, a
nearby summer camp that's been in operation since
1885. Leading canoe trips and hikes through the region's
lush forests of pine, hemlock, spruce, and beech trees
had a profound impact on Greg. Over the years, he continued to frequent the northern Adirondacks to camp,
hike, and fish. When he met Cathy in 1965, their second
date was a trek on Mount Marcy, a forested 5,344-foot
peak that is the tallest mountain in New York.

By 1973, the married couple was living in a Manhattan loft, daydreaming about finding their own land
up north. That year, during one of their trips to Keene,
a local real estate agent showed them 100 acres of
dense forest that abuts abandoned logging trails. Greg

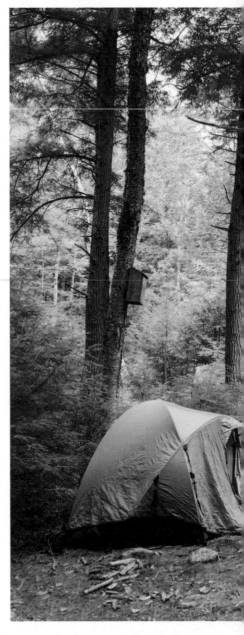

The first, and smaller, of two
hand-built yurts on the property.

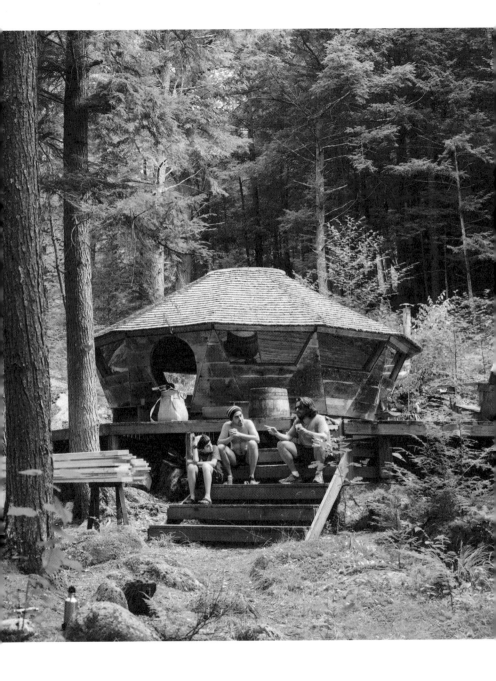

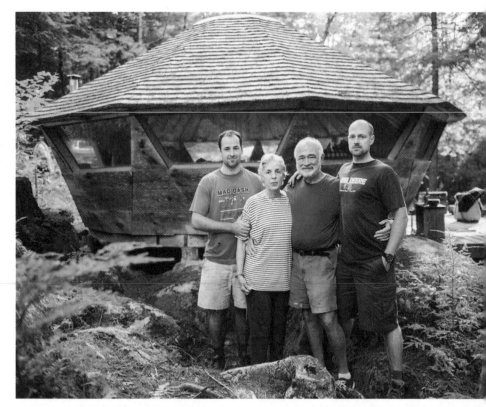

was especially fond of the brook cutting through the middle. Throughout the year, the sound of running water drowns the forest in white noise. To get to the stream, visitors hike a quarter mile from the road through the woods. There is no path wide enough for a truck, which means all gear and supplies must be packed in to the off-grid site. After a few years of camping in tents, Greg and Cathy decided it was time for a permanent rustic shelter by the stream bank. They wanted to build it themselves. But Greg had limited carpentry experience—he'd never assembled anything more complicated than a birdhouse. Also, the couple had only two weeks of vacation from their jobs in the city, so they understood that their architectural options were limited. A friend suggested they consider a circular dwelling called a yurt. He recommended Greg contact a man named Bill Coperthwaite.

At the time, Coperthwaite was developing a reputation for designing simple do-it-yourself yurts that were popular among back-to-the-landers across North America. Used by Central Asian nomads for thousands of years, traditional yurts are tentlike structures with collapsible wooden frames covered in fabric and held together by rope. Bill, a shaggy-haired former math teacher who died in 2013, pioneered a way of building a modernized, more robust version of a yurt. In 1968, while earning a PhD in education at Harvard University, he constructed and lived in a small red-roofed yurt on campus; he built the structure in two days using $600 worth of materials. By 1973, he was living alone on 500 acres in the woods of Machiasport, Maine, where he wound up constructing no fewer than six yurts—including a hulking three-tiered yurt topped by a cupola. He relied mostly on hand tools. His compound had no phone or electricity. To contact Bill, aspiring yurt builders

Nick, Cathy, Greg, and
Andrew Farrell.

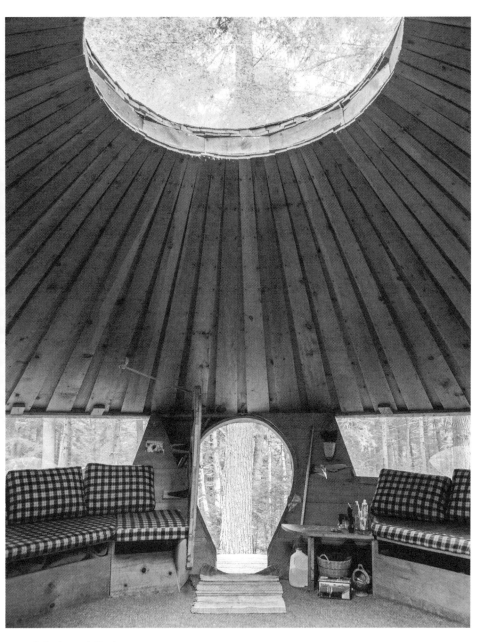

Pine boards were soaked in water
then bent to create the doorway
for the original yurt.

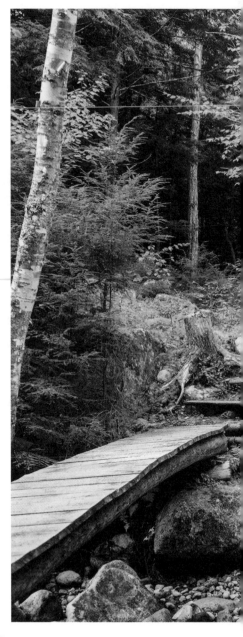

wrote snail mail. If interested, he would reply with a hand-drawn map showing the way to his home.

In 1976, Greg and Cathy hiked the 1½-mile trail lined with thick brush to visit Bill. When they asked him to help them create a yurt in Keene, he agreed. "There was explicitly no talk of money," Greg recalls. "We talked about an exchange of energy." Soon after, in August 1976, Greg and Cathy welcomed Bill to their land. With a rotating crew of fifty friends, parents, coworkers, and locals, they erected a modest yurt perched beside the stream. It took nine days to finish everything but the door and windows. The build required no power tools except for a chain saw, which was used to prep the foundation's four immense hemlock posts. The process wasn't easy, but it was pleasurable. For the yurt's curved, hobbit-style doorway, Bill instructed Greg to soak ¼-by-4-inch pine boards, then slowly bend them into place. Greg took the first board and did as he was told, but as he tried bending it into the keyhole-shaped doorway, the wood cracked and splintered. So he soaked another board and tried again. And again. Finally, on the fifth try, he bent his fifth presoaked board into place. Then he repeated the process with four or five more boards to create a strong, multilayered frame. Finishing the structure did more than simply provide Greg and Cathy with shelter. The yurt made them feel anchored to the land. People from town would visit the Farrells just to admire their unusual round structure.

Prior to building the yurt, the couple had constructed a bridge to an island in the middle of the river. There they built a pantry, a picnic table, and a brick fireplace where they could cook trout fished from the brook. "Pantry Island" was the first of many projects. Using felled trees—mostly hemlock—the family has installed and replaced eight simple bridges

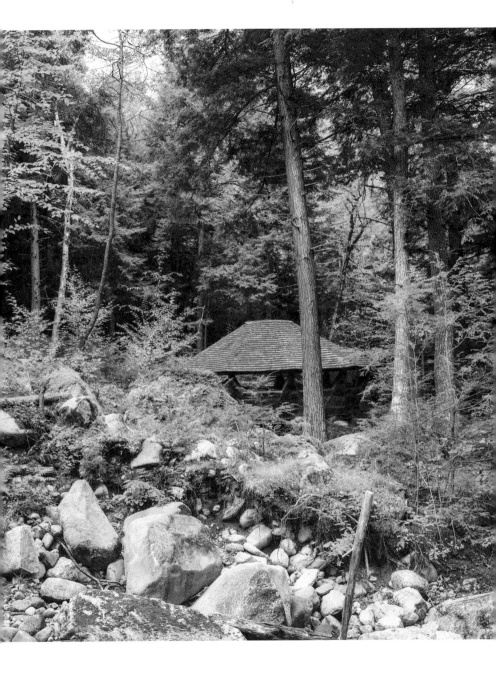

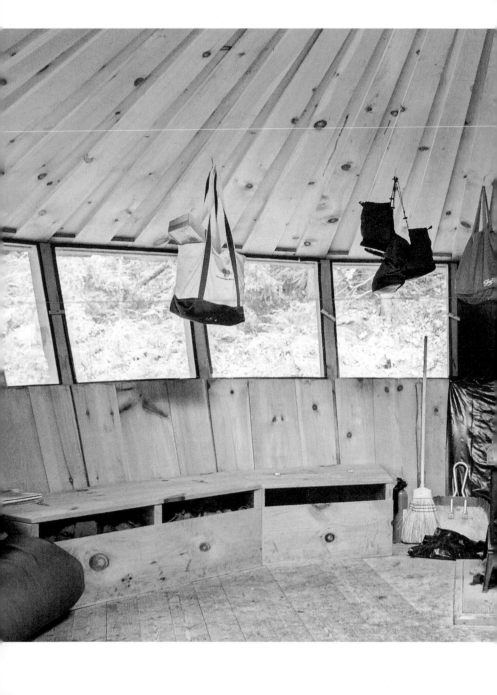

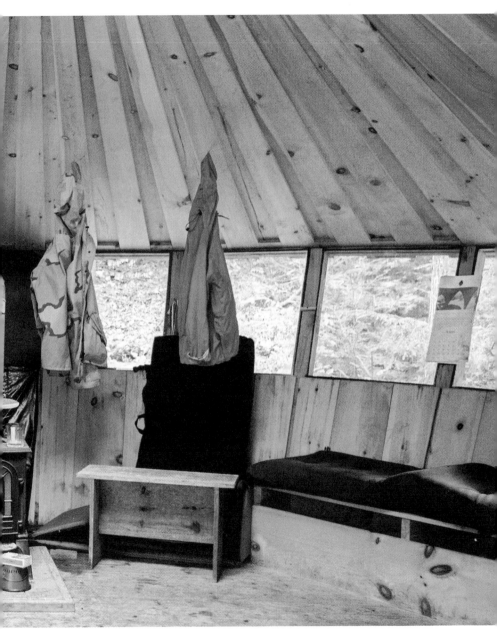

The newer, larger yurt's bench
seating also provides storage.

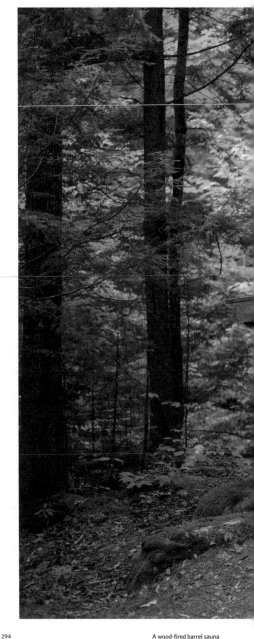

across various jags along the river. In the 1980s, when Nick and his brother, Andrew, were young, the family installed a barrel sauna. Next came a hot tub with a wood-burning Snorkel stove. By 1990, a teepee downstream from the yurt was replaced with a lean-to, a robust three-sided log structure popular in the Adirondacks. "There was no plan. One thing just led to another," Greg says. "And it came out beautifully."

Their family camp has endured as a Neverland-like getaway from the city. All four Farrells spent years camping together in the yurt. Greg and Cathy would read to the boys by candlelight. In time, the brothers learned to catch fish, climb trees, chop firewood for the yurt's wood-burning stove, and camp by themselves in the lean-to. They raced birch-bark rafts down the brook and played "chuck-rock" by casting rocks into the stream. In recent years, they installed a zip line running down the center of the stream.

By the spring of 2002, when Nick was twenty, he was thinking that someday he and his brother would both likely get married and have children. Eventually, the family would need another structure to accommodate everyone. "That sounds like impeccable logic," Greg replied. Another yurt seemed only fitting, Nick told his father. So Greg mailed a letter to his friend Bill. In the spring of 2003, the brothers and their father traveled to Machiasport to discuss the build with Bill. "He was not a hugger," Nick recalls. "He had kind of a gruff demeanor." When the brothers suggested they build a two-story yurt, not unlike Bill's multilevel yurts, Bill shot down that idea. He had something big but less complicated and time-consuming in mind. He supplied Nick and Andrew with a lumber list.

The brothers spent the summer prepping and carrying in all the tools to the stream bank. They chose a site upstream from the original yurt, a spot overgrown

A wood-fired barrel sauna
sits near the original yurt.

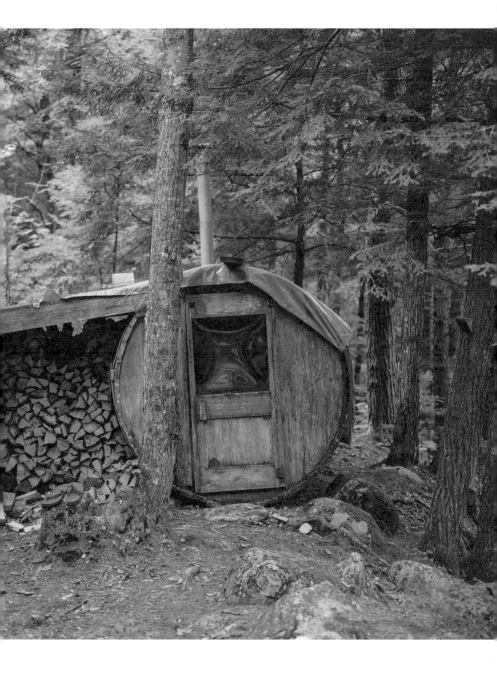

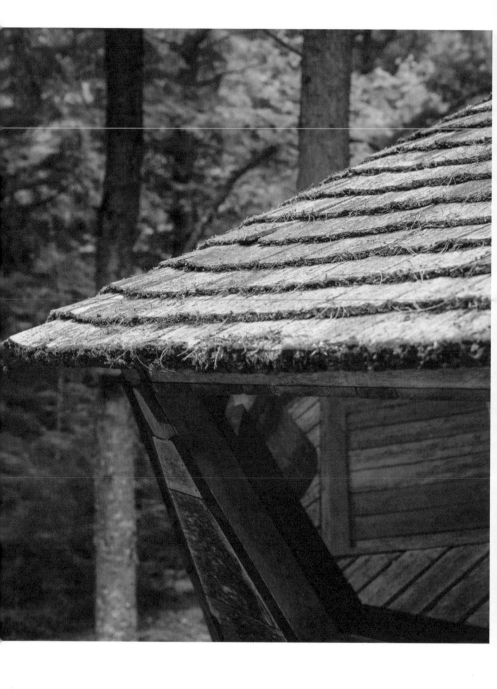

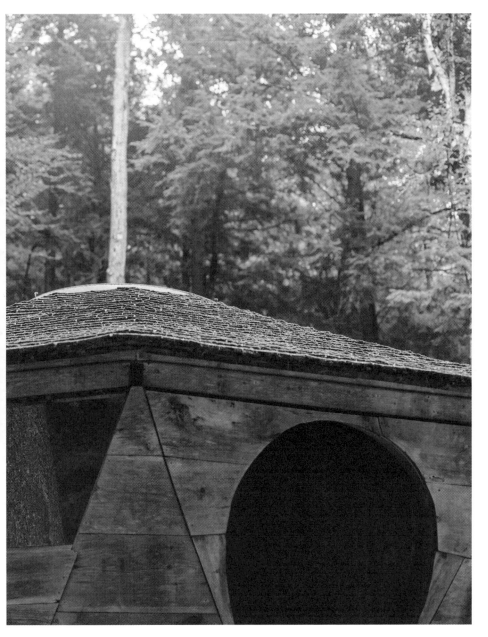

with hemlock saplings. At nights and on weekends—
between working odd jobs that included reroofing
a friend's geodesic dome—the brothers spent hours
clear-cutting. They dug 3½-foot-deep holes for the posts
and poured concrete for the foundation. They invited
their friends to help with the yurt build. So did Greg
and Cathy. Ultimately, another rotating crew of nearly
fifty workers—some of whom had helped with the first
yurt in 1976—agreed to pitch in.

Every evening, the brothers and their friends would
stay up drinking whiskey and Saranac Pale Ale by
the campfire until 1 a.m. They'd wake for breakfast at
6:30 a.m. and get working by 7:00, Bill's preferred start
time. The hardest task for Nick involved cutting several
wooden blocks for the skylight. Bill used a bevel to
mark precise angles that couldn't be cut with a hand-
saw. Nick, who had never used a table saw, spent hours
working with one of his neighbor's power tools. When he
returned with the finished pieces, Bill seemed pleased.

In two weeks, the upper yurt was finished. Every
summer since 2006, the family has hosted a long
weekend during which thirty to forty friends and family
camp on the property, cook out, play guitar and drums,
and crash in the yurts. They've dubbed their annual
event YurtFest. In 2014, the brothers organized a build
project on Pantry Island. Beforehand, Greg offered Nick
one piece of advice: "Relax and accept the mistakes
your friends make." They collaborated with friends to
build a bigger pantry where they can store more food
and supplies to support their growing community.
Often, the brothers invite a few more friends to join
them at YurtFest. "It's a triumph of fatherhood," Greg
says. "I shouldn't get too much credit. I didn't have a
strong commanding intention that Nick and Andy carry
it on. I'm always kind of surprised and delighted by how
much they love it."

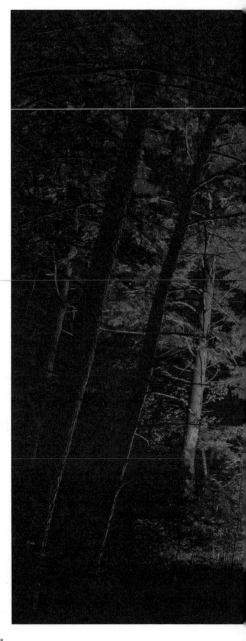

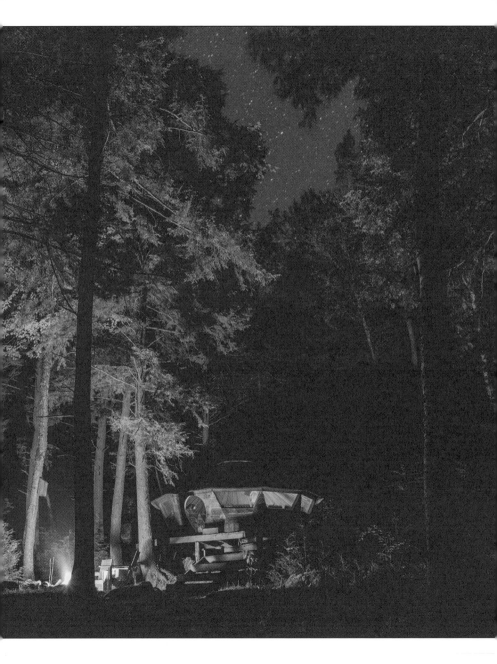

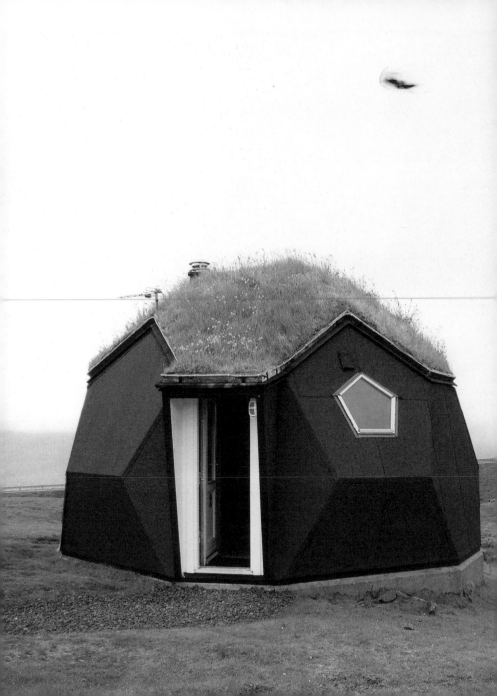

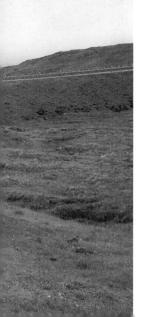

GEOMETRIC

ARCHIVE

Geodesic igloo in Kivik on the Faroe Islands
CONTRIBUTED BY Sara Mattei

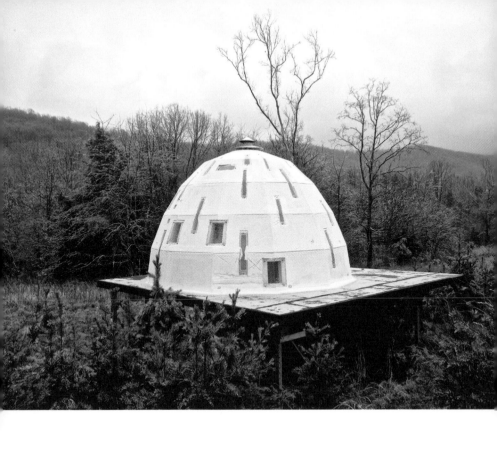

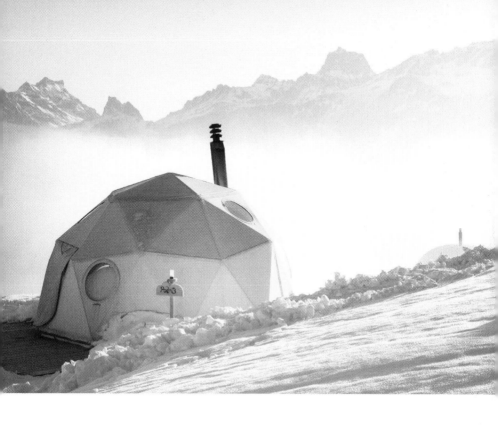

Foam Dome Home in Batesville, Virginia
CONTRIBUTED BY Seth Denizen

Whitepod in Les Cerniers, Switzerland
CONTRIBUTED BY Sofija Torebo Strindlund

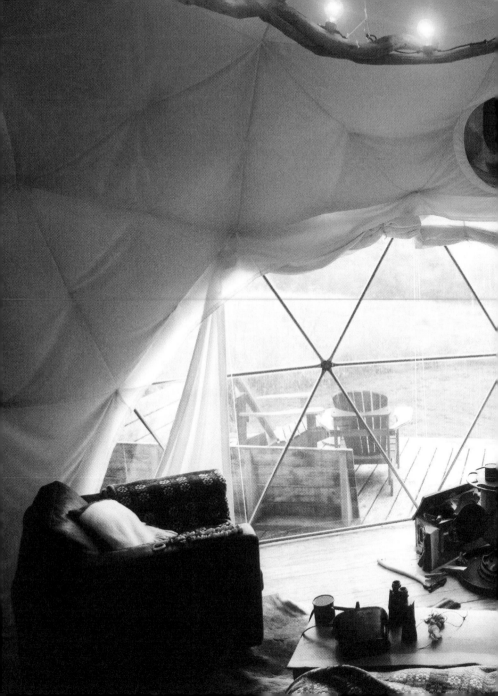

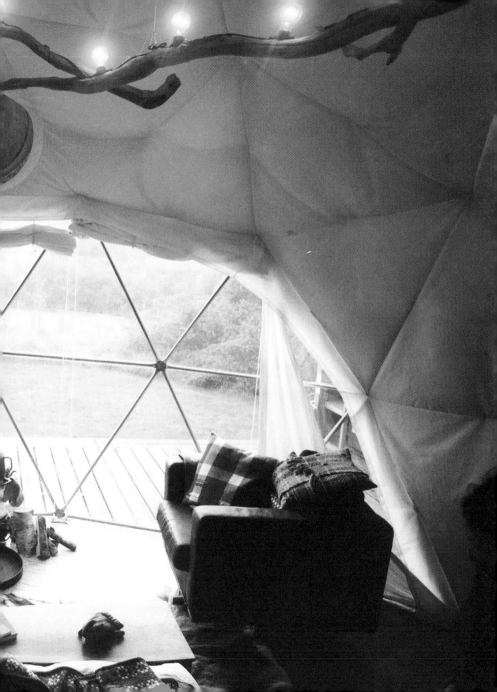

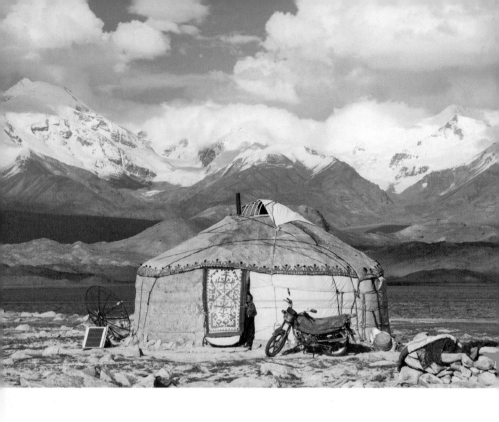

PREVIOUS fforest Camp near Cardigan, Wales
CONTRIBUTED BY Jackson Tucker Lynch

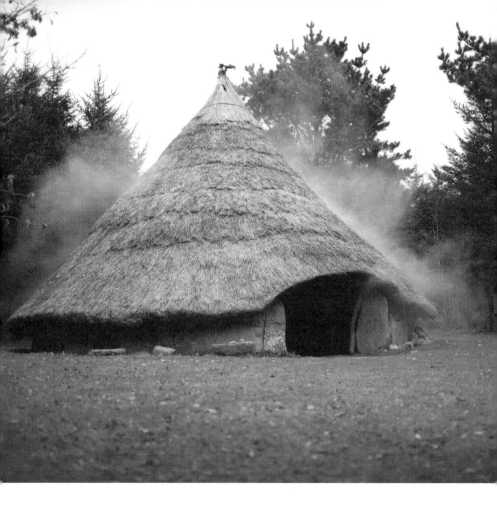

Yurt along the Silk Road, China.
CONTRIBUTED BY Amelia Anderson

Bodrifty Roundhouse
in West Cornwall, UK.
CONTRIBUTED BY Ian Kingsnorth

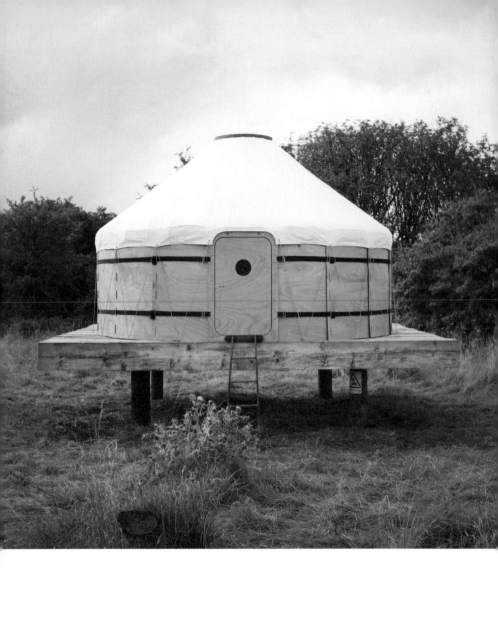

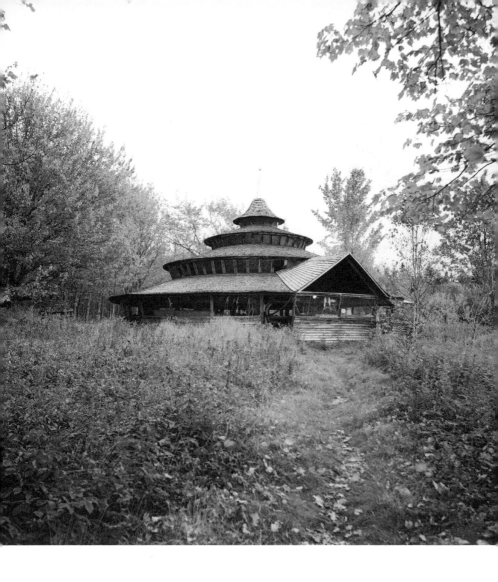

Contemporary yurt built by Alec Farmer and
Uula Jero in Dumfries and Galloway, Scotland
CONTRIBUTED BY Niall M. Walker

The concentric yurt home of William
Coperthwaite near Machiasport, Maine
CONTRIBUTED BY Andrew William Frederick

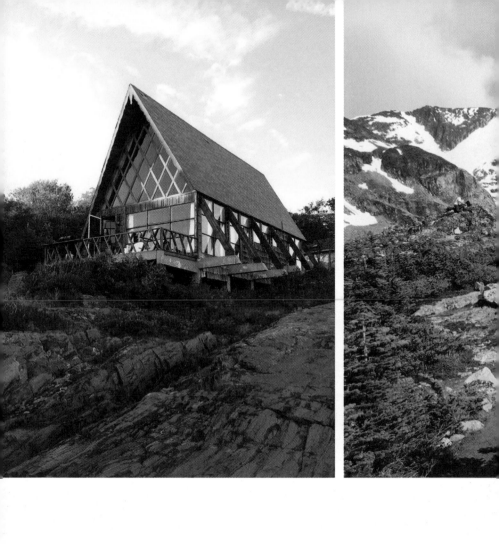

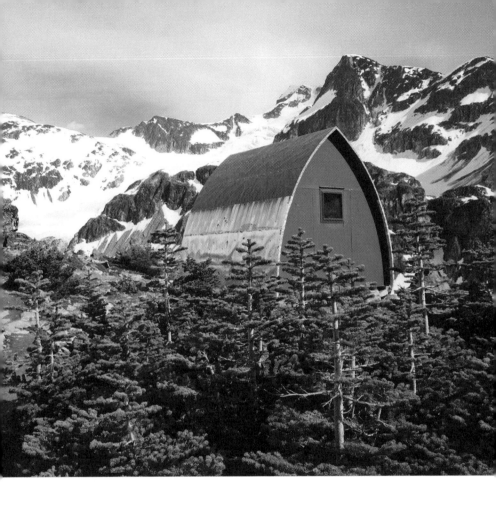

Indian Point in Georgetown, Maine
CONTRIBUTED BY Thomas Moses

The Wedgemount Lake Hut in Garibaldi
Provincial Park, British Columbia, Canada
CONTRIBUTED BY Ethan Welty

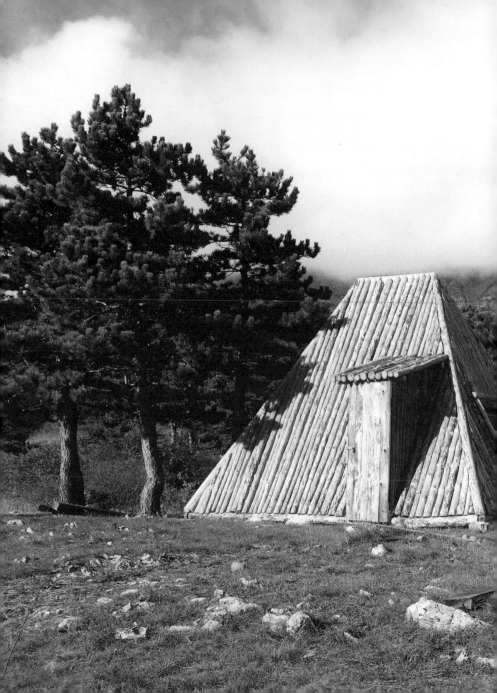

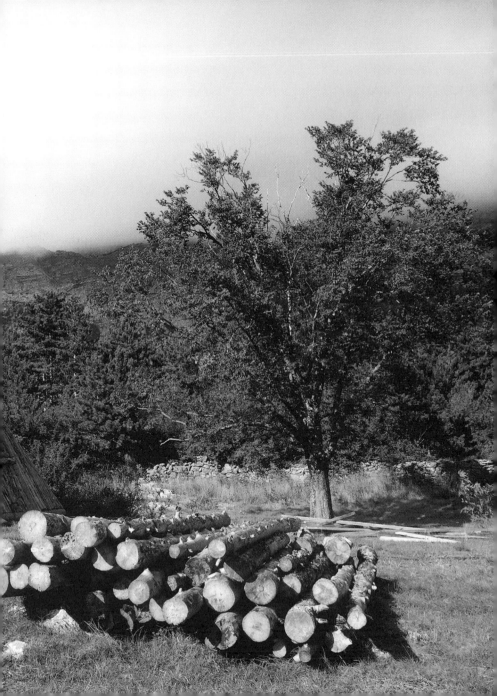

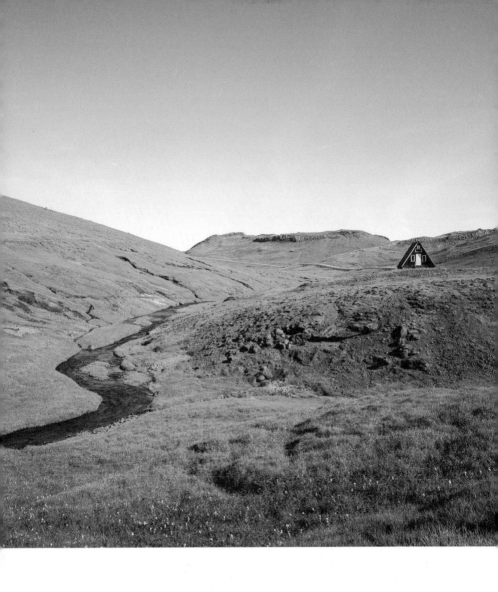

PREVIOUS Shelter in the Veliko
Rujno Valley, Velebit, Croatia
CONTRIBUTED BY Matea Sjauš

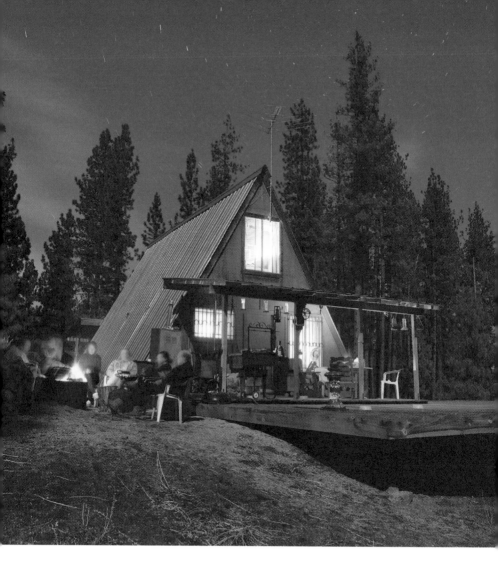

A-frame near Stykkishólmur, Iceland
CONTRIBUTED BY Peter Baker

A-frame in Claraville, California,
near Sequoia National Forest
CONTRIBUTED BY Aaron Chervenak

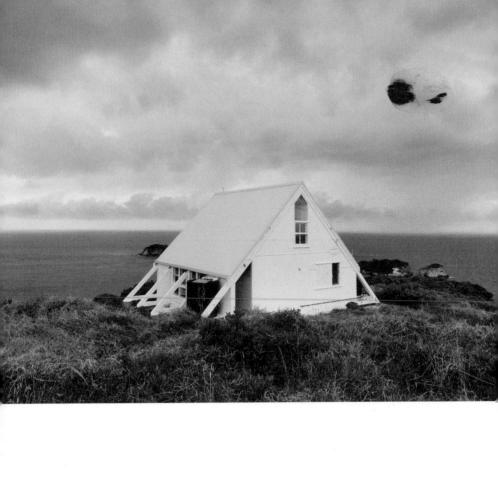

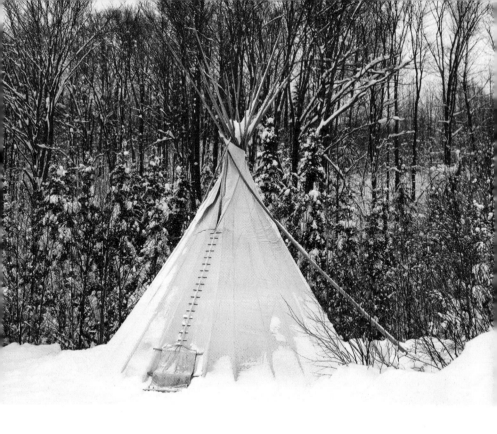

Lighthouse keeper's house in the
Mokohinau Islands, New Zealand
CONTRIBUTED BY Tim Dolamore

Teeppee in Kanatha Aki, Canada
CONTRIBUTED BY Mina Seville

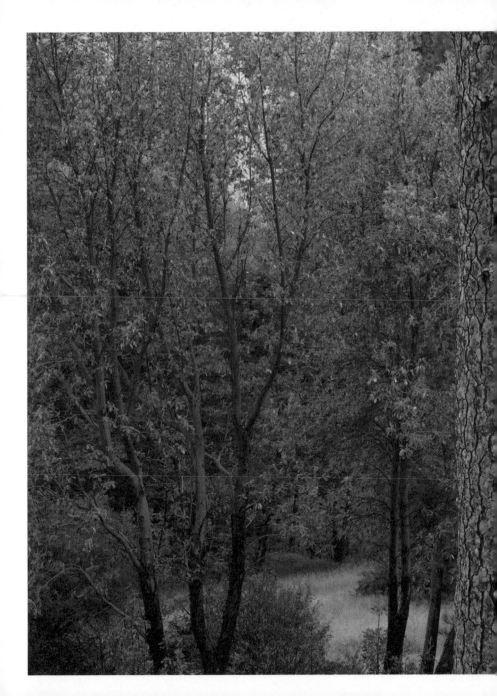

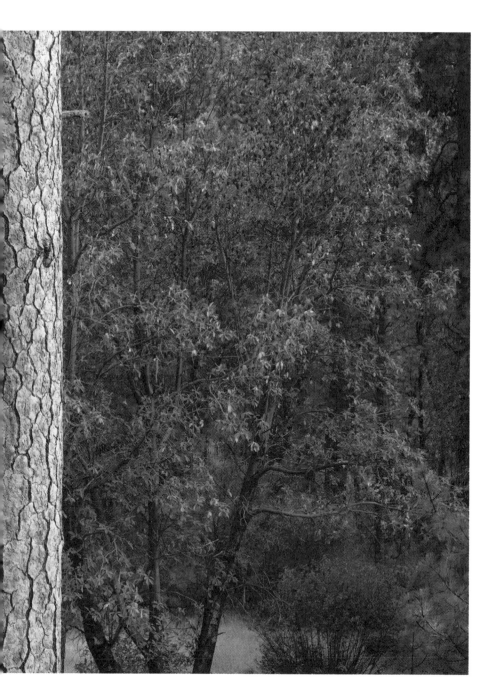

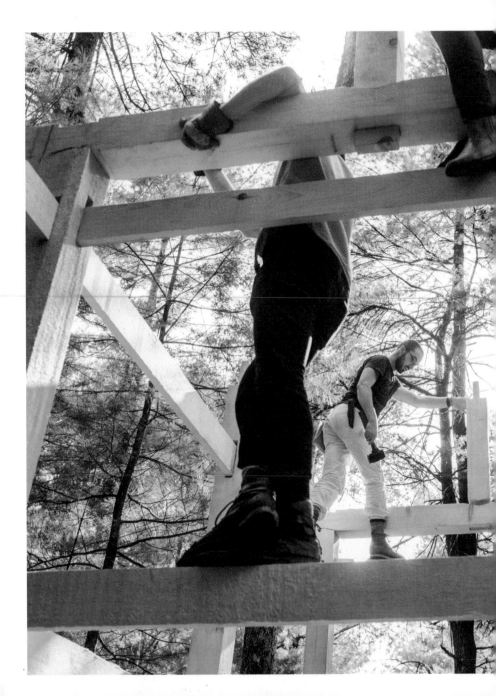

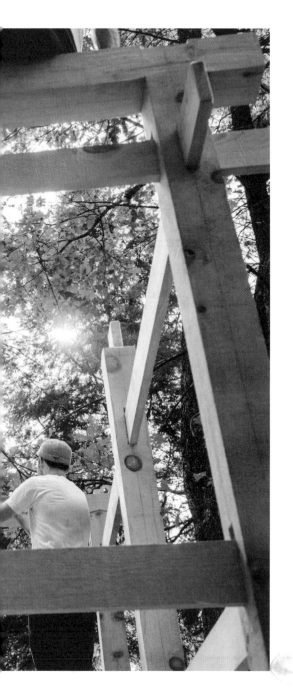

LAYOUT & DESIGN
Matt Cassity

PHOTO EDITOR
Kristen Fortier

ILLUSTRATIONS
Daren Rabinovitch

PHOTO POST-PRODUCTION
Zach Vitale

RESEARCH
Timothy Lesle

BEAVER BROOK RESIDENTS

Tom Bonamici	Nell Klein
Christina Cohen	Zach Klein
Ellie Cohen	Derek Lasher
Idan Cohen	Matt Lehrer
Jace Cooke	Cassie Marketos
Jason Fried	Mirza Nagji
Brian Jacobs	Irene Polnyi
Noah Kalina	Jamie Wilkinson
Grace Kapin	Paloma "Poppy" Wilkinson
Courtney Klein	Armin Zomorodi

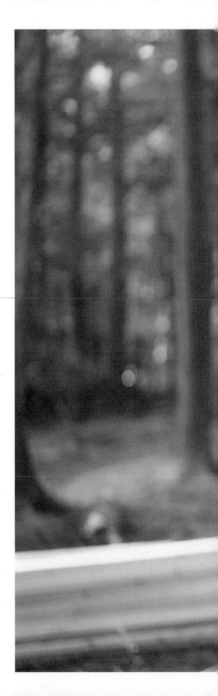

Many Thanks to Our Gracious Hosts

Dennis & Crystal English,
Lisa Sitko & Douglas Armour,
Dennis Carter & Anneli Carter-Sundqvist,
Sam & Ruben Caldwell, Dave Cummings,
Ethan Schlussler & Julie McCallan,
Dave Frazee, Victor Sidy & Indira Berndtson,
Dan Price, Kyle Davis, Taimoor & Rehan Nana,
Loren Schieber, The Farrell Family

Special Thanks

Richard Pine, Garrett McGrath, Scott Newkirk

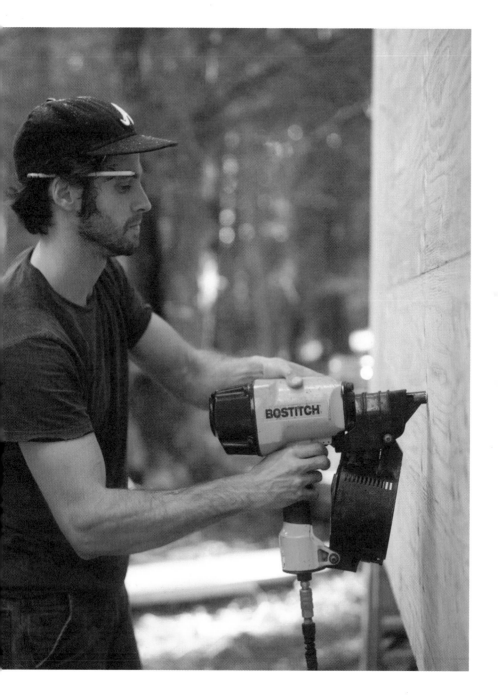

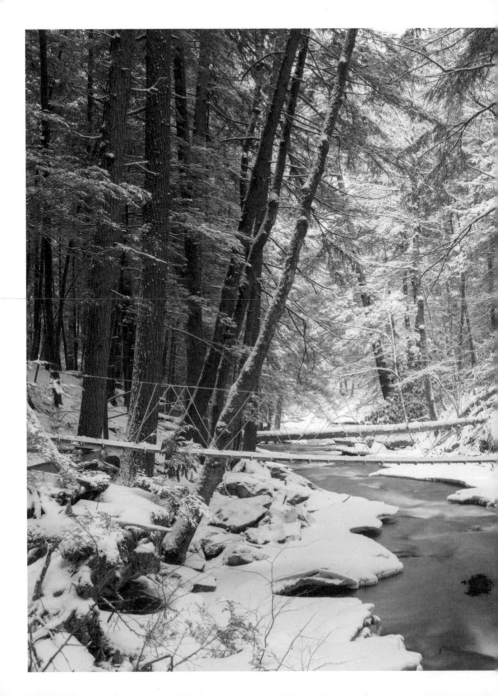

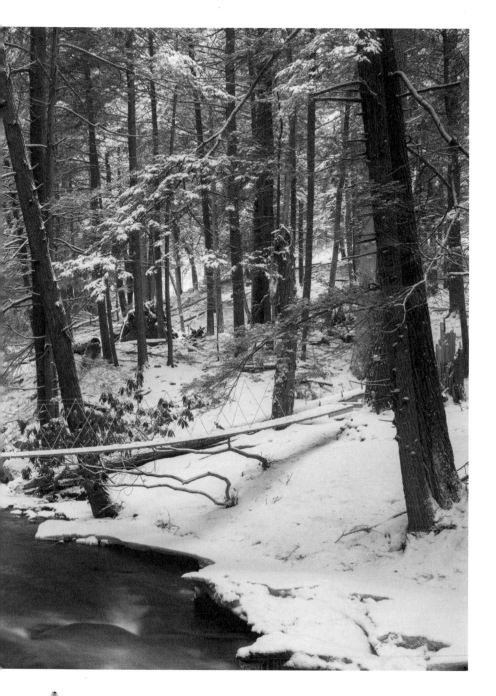

Visit
cabinporn.com/submit
to share your cabin with
the community.

Contributors

Connor Charles

Anka Lamprecht & Lukas Wezel

Henrik Bonnevier

Dr. Julius Christopher Barsi

Taylor L. Applewhite

Peter Turner

Tyler Austin Bradley

Haukur Sigurdsson

Tom Powell

Inge Wegge & Jørn Nyseth Ranum

Jonas Loiske

James Bowden

Joshua Langlais

John T. Foster

Maria Polyakova

Rustan Karlsson

J. L. Kane

Stefan Guzy

Kate Stokes

Ruedi Walti

Patrick Joust

Vincent Menu

Brice Portolano

Randel Plowman

Stephanie Schuster

Mina Seville
sending-postcards.com

Kristoffer Marchi

Kate Barrett

Scott Meivogel

Brittany Cole Bush

Marieke Kijk in de Vegte

Nicolas Schoof

Donna Irvine

Jenn & Willie Witte

Kyle Johnson

Casey Greene

Joonas Mikola

Jonathan Cherry
jonathancherry.net

Ethan Welty
hutmap.com

Jason Vaughn
jasonvaughnart.com

Stu J. Beesley
stujbeesley.co.uk

Jaharn Giles
misterweekender.com

Peter McLaren

Foster Huntington

Francesco Mattuzzi

Dean Azim

Kursten Bracchi

Linda Aldredge

Alec Miller

YestermorrowDesign/Build School

Erik A. Jensen

Katy Anderson

Matt Beckemeyer
@nycviaco

Andrew Ranville
andrewranville.com

Joel Allen

Rok Pezdirc

Peter Lundström
WDO

Penny Clay

Adolf Bereuter

Pierre Wikberg

Jaime Diaz-Berrio

Sebastián Cerda Pé
AATA Arquitectos

Vadim Sérandon

Virge Viertek

Mason St. Peter

Clyde Fowle

Sebastian Heise
batah.de

Gaudenz Danuser
gaudenzdanuser.com

Andrew Koester

Chris Menig

Sofija Torebo Strindlund

Stephen Shapiro

Hosanna Aughtry

Olivia & Eve Macfarlane

Johannes Grødem

Chloe Snaith

Edu Lartzanguren

Lilah Horwitz & Nick Olson

Reidar Pritzel

Jay Nelson

Katarina Dubcova
katarinadubcova.tumblr.com

Mark McInnis

Lynn Patrick

Alex Holland

Jono Williams

Ryder W. Pierce

Francois Lombarts

Kim Walker

Sara Mattei

Seth Denizen

Jackson Tucker Lynch

Amelia Anderson

Ian Kingsnorth
hiddenhideaways.co.uk

Niall M. Walker

Andrew William Frederick

Thomas Moses

Matea Sjauš

Peter Baker

Aaron Chervenak

Tim Dolamore